# SECRET AVENGERS

## MISSION TO MARS

WRITER
**ED BRUBAKER**

ARTIST, ISSUES #1-4
**MIKE DEODATO**
WITH **WILL CONRAD** (ISSUE #2)

COLOR ARTIST, ISSUES #1-4
**RAIN BEREDO**

ARTISTS, ISSUE #5
**DAVID AJA, MICHAEL LARK**
& **STEFANO GAUDIANO**

COLOR ARTIST, ISSUE #5
**JOSE VILLARRUBIA**

LETTERER
**DAVE LANPHEAR**

COVER ART
**MARKO DJURDJEVIC**

ASSOCIATE EDITOR
**LAUREN SANKOVITCH**

EDITOR
**TOM BREVOORT**

Collection Editor: JENNIFER GRÜNWALD • Editorial Assistants: JAMES EMMETT & JOE HOCHSTEIN
Assistant Editors: ALEX STARBUCK & NELSON RIBEIRO • Editor, Special Projects: MARK D. BEAZLEY
Senior Editor, Special Projects: JEFF YOUNGQUIST • Senior Vice President of Sales: DAVID GABRIEL
Book Design: JEFF POWELL

Editor in Chief: JOE QUESADA • Publisher: DAN BUCKLEY • Executive Producer: ALAN FINE

**SECRET AVENGERS VOL. 1: MISSION TO MARS.** Contains material originally published in magazine form as SECRET AVENGERS #1-5. First printing 2011. ISBN# 978-0-7851-4599-8. Published by MARVEL WORLDWIDE, INC., a subsidiary of MARVEL ENTERTAINMENT, LLC. OFFICE OF PUBLICATION: 135 West 50th Street, New York, NY 10020.  $24.99 per copy in the U.S. and $27.99 in Canada (GST #R127032852); Canadian Agreement #40668537.  **Printed in the U.S.A.** ALAN FINE, EVP - Office of the President, Marvel Worldwide, Inc. and EVP & CMO Marvel Characters B.V.; DAN BUCKLEY, Chief Executive Officer and Publisher - Print, Animation & Digital Media; JIM SOKOLOWSKI, Chief Operating Officer; DAVID GABRIEL, SVP of Publishing Sales & Circulation; DAVID BOGART, SVP of Business Affairs & Talent Management; MICHAEL PASCIULLO, VP Merchandising & Communications; JIM O'KEEFE, VP of Operations & Logistics; DAN CARR, Executive Director of Publishing Technology; JUSTIN F. GABRIE, Director of Publishing & Editorial Operations; SUSAN CRESPI, Editorial Operations Manager; ALEX MORALES, Publishing Operations Manager; STAN LEE, Chairman Emeritus. For information regarding advertising in Marvel Comics or on Marvel.com, please contact Ron Stern, VP of Business Development, at rstern@marvel.com. For Marvel subscription inquiries, please call 800-217-9158. **Manufactured between 12/6/10 and 1/5/11 by R.R. DONNELLEY, INC., SALEM, VA, USA.**

10 9 8 7 6 5 4 3 2 1

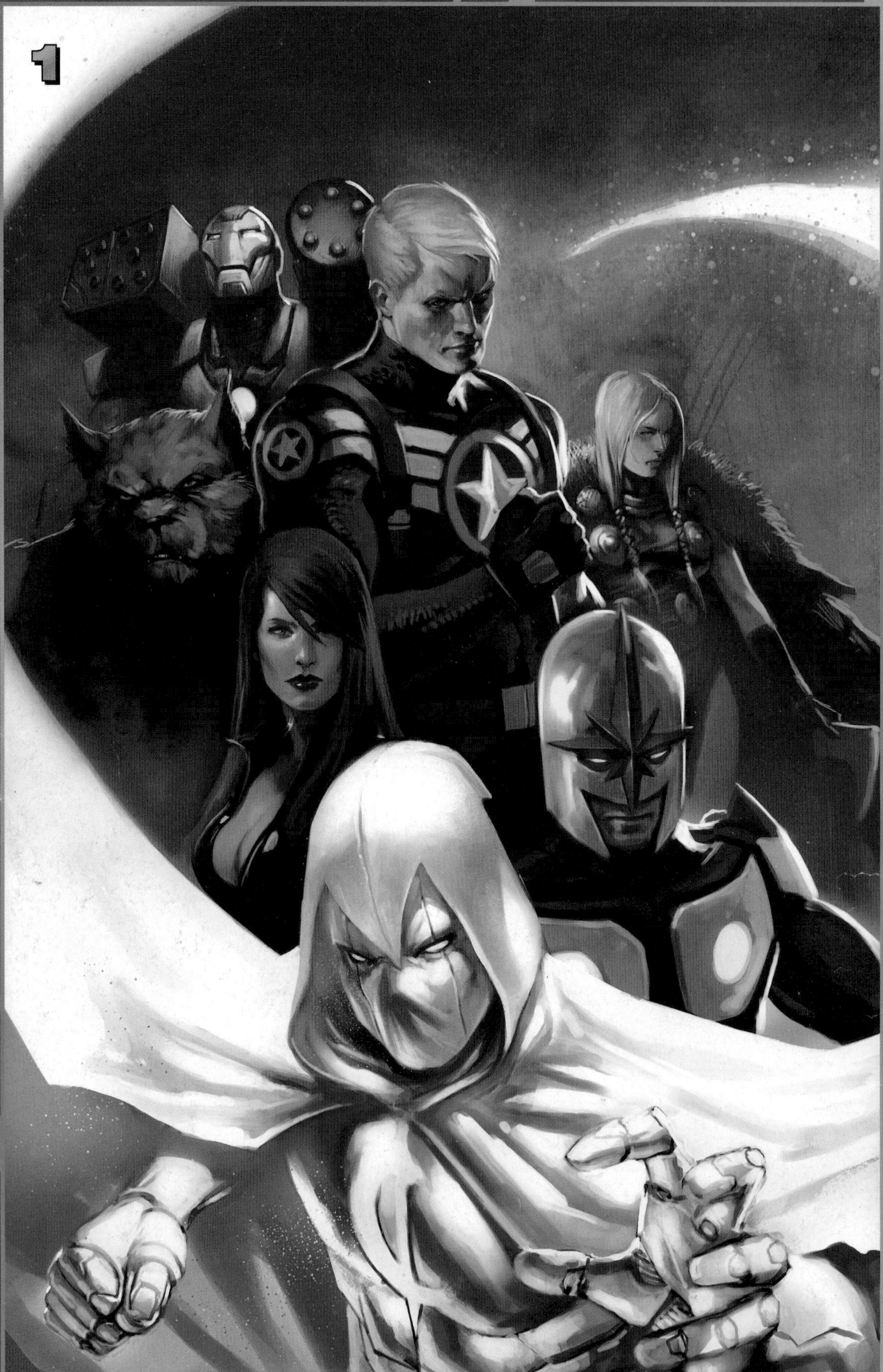
1

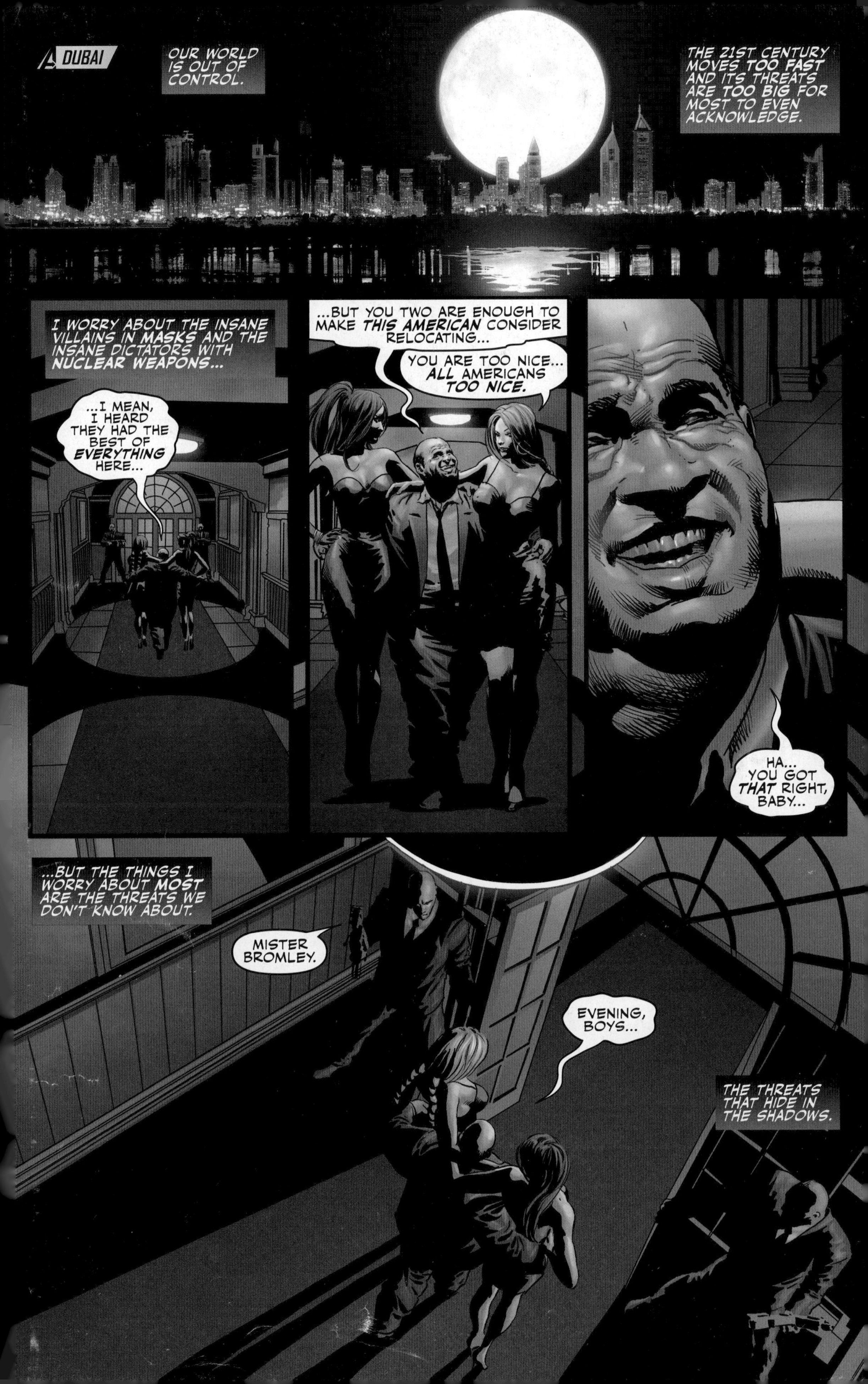
DUBAI
OUR WORLD IS OUT OF CONTROL.
THE 21ST CENTURY MOVES TOO FAST AND ITS THREATS ARE TOO BIG FOR MOST TO EVEN ACKNOWLEDGE.
I WORRY ABOUT THE INSANE VILLAINS IN MASKS AND THE INSANE DICTATORS WITH NUCLEAR WEAPONS...
...I MEAN, I HEARD THEY HAD THE BEST OF EVERYTHING HERE...
...BUT YOU TWO ARE ENOUGH TO MAKE THIS AMERICAN CONSIDER RELOCATING...
YOU ARE TOO NICE... ALL AMERICANS TOO NICE.
HA... YOU GOT THAT RIGHT, BABY...
...BUT THE THINGS I WORRY ABOUT MOST ARE THE THREATS WE DON'T KNOW ABOUT.
MISTER BROMLEY.
EVENING, BOYS...
THE THREATS THAT HIDE IN THE SHADOWS.

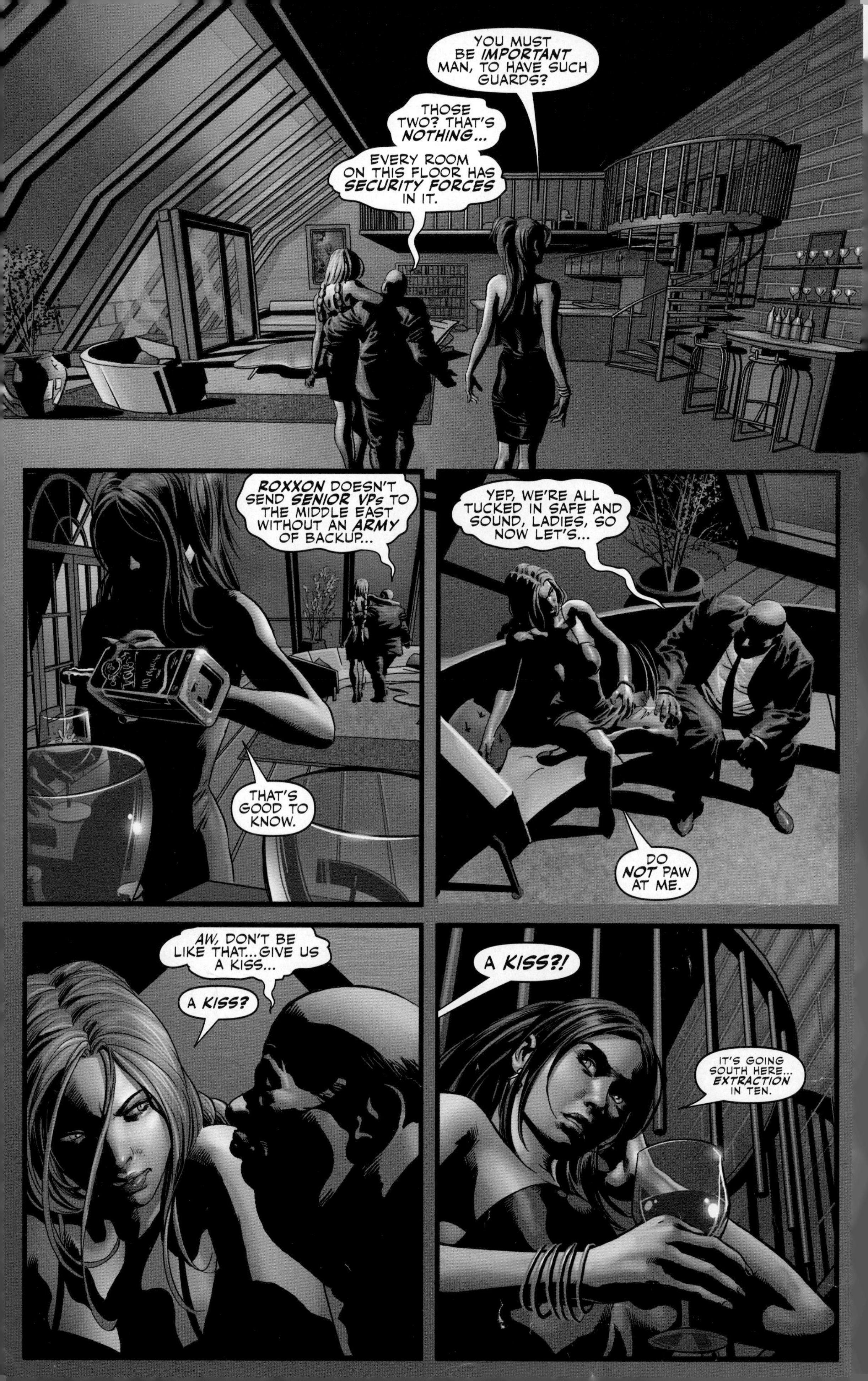

YOU MUST BE IMPORTANT MAN, TO HAVE SUCH GUARDS?
THOSE TWO? THAT'S NOTHING...
EVERY ROOM ON THIS FLOOR HAS SECURITY FORCES IN IT.
ROXXON DOESN'T SEND SENIOR VPs TO THE MIDDLE EAST WITHOUT AN ARMY OF BACKUP...
THAT'S GOOD TO KNOW.
YEP, WE'RE ALL TUCKED IN SAFE AND SOUND, LADIES, SO NOW LET'S...
DO NOT PAW AT ME.
AW, DON'T BE LIKE THAT...GIVE US A KISS...
A KISS?
A KISS?!
IT'S GOING SOUTH HERE... EXTRACTION IN TEN.

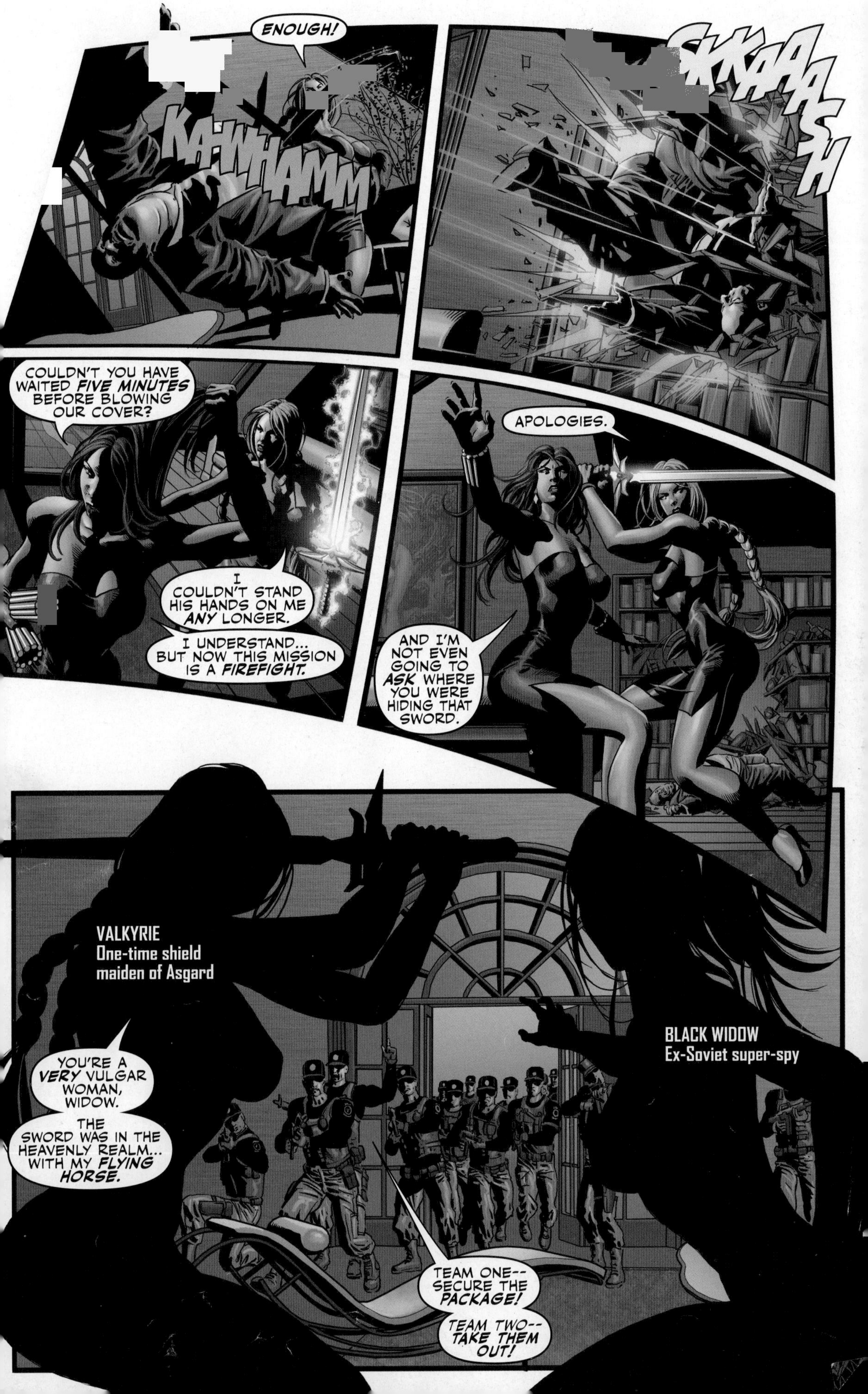
ENOUGH!
KAWHAMM
SKKAAAASH
COULDN'T YOU HAVE WAITED FIVE MINUTES BEFORE BLOWING OUR COVER?
I COULDN'T STAND HIS HANDS ON ME ANY LONGER.
I UNDERSTAND... BUT NOW THIS MISSION IS A FIREFIGHT.
APOLOGIES.
AND I'M NOT EVEN GOING TO ASK WHERE YOU WERE HIDING THAT SWORD.
VALKYRIE
One-time shield maiden of Asgard
BLACK WIDOW
Ex-Soviet super-spy
YOU'RE A VERY VULGAR WOMAN, WIDOW.
THE SWORD WAS IN THE HEAVENLY REALM... WITH MY FLYING HORSE.
TEAM ONE-- SECURE THE PACKAGE!
TEAM TWO-- TAKE THEM OUT!

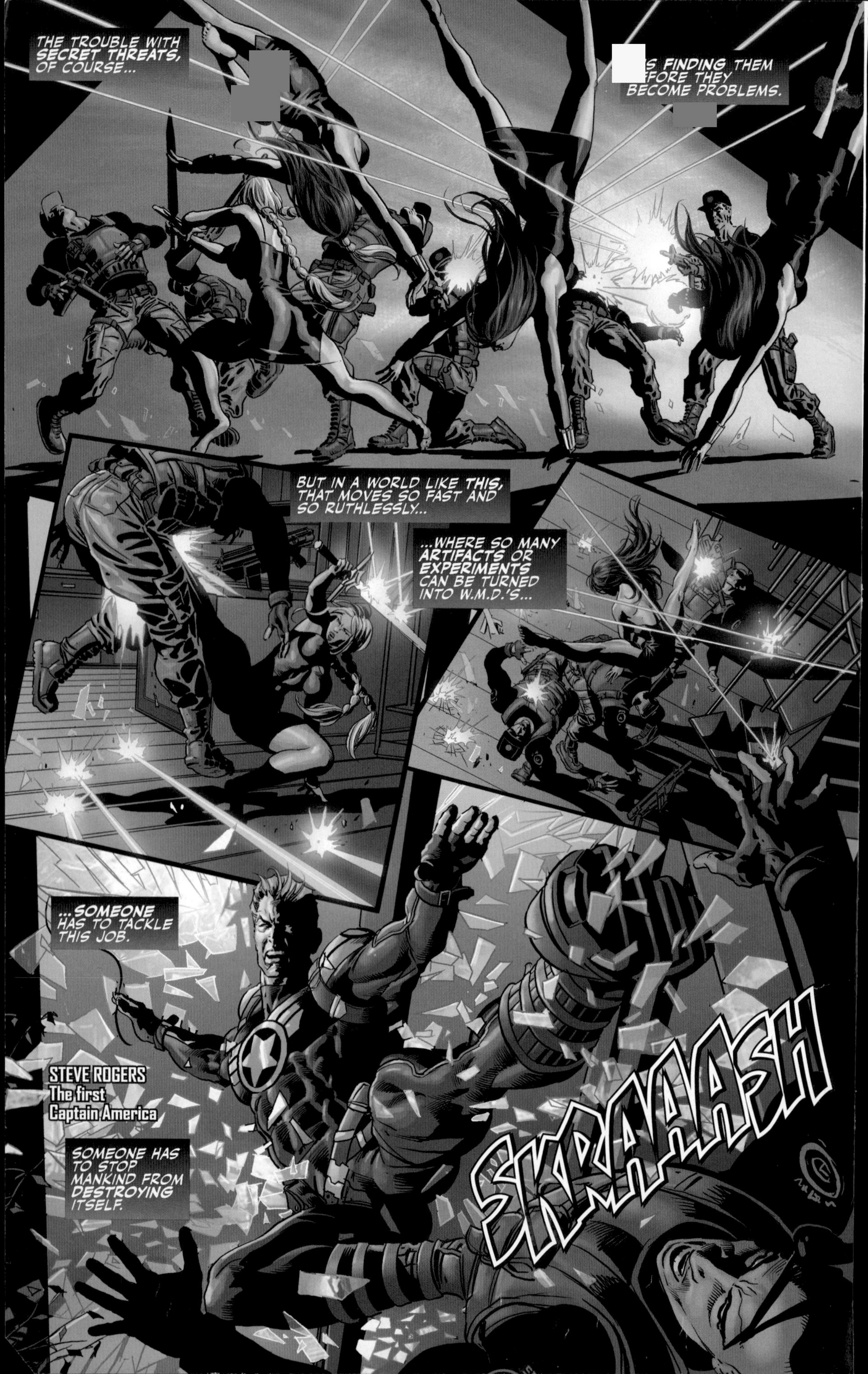
THE TROUBLE WITH SECRET THREATS, OF COURSE...
S FINDING THEM EFORE THEY BECOME PROBLEMS.
BUT IN A WORLD LIKE THIS, THAT MOVES SO FAST AND SO RUTHLESSLY...
...WHERE SO MANY ARTIFACTS OR EXPERIMENTS CAN BE TURNED INTO W.M.D.'S...
...SOMEONE HAS TO TACKLE THIS JOB.
STEVE ROGERS
The first Captain America
SOMEONE HAS TO STOP MANKIND FROM DESTROYING ITSELF.
SKRAAASH

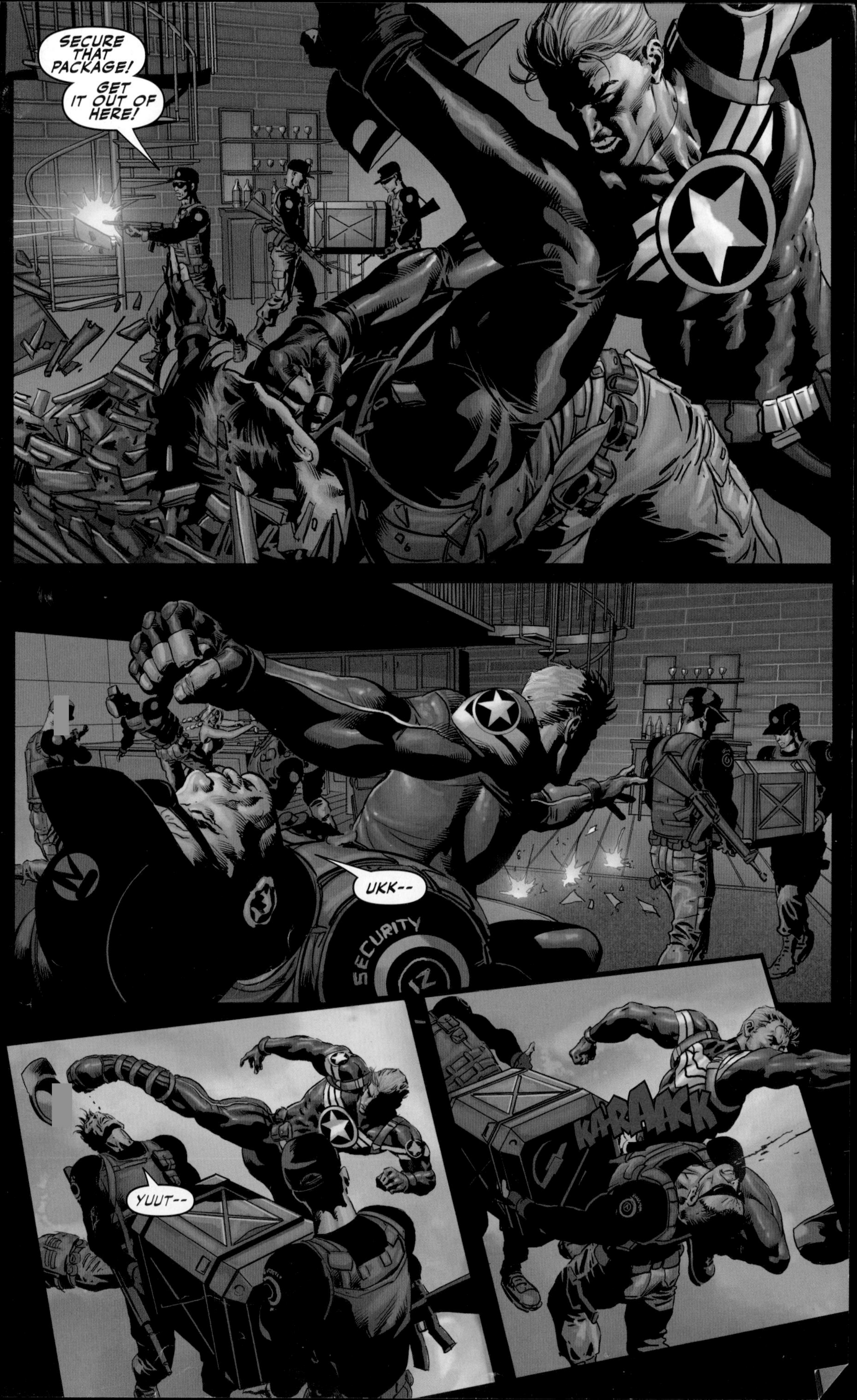
SECURE THAT PACKAGE!
GET IT OUT OF HERE!
UKK--
SECURITY 12
YUUT--
KARAAKK

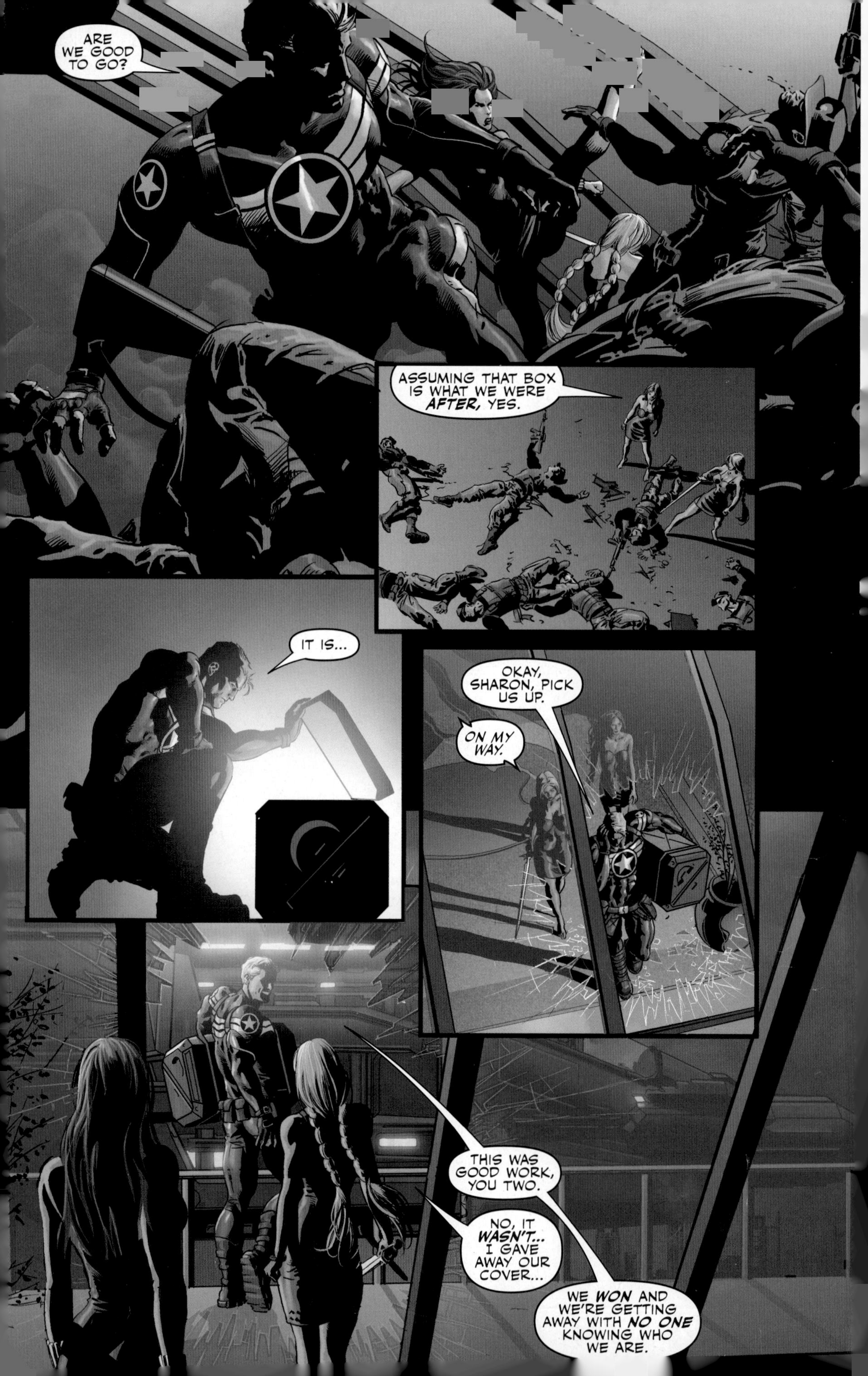
ARE WE GOOD TO GO?
ASSUMING THAT BOX IS WHAT WE WERE AFTER, YES.
IT IS...
OKAY, SHARON, PICK US UP.
ON MY WAY.
THIS WAS GOOD WORK, YOU TWO.
NO, IT WASN'T... I GAVE AWAY OUR COVER...
WE WON AND WE'RE GETTING AWAY WITH NO ONE KNOWING WHO WE ARE.

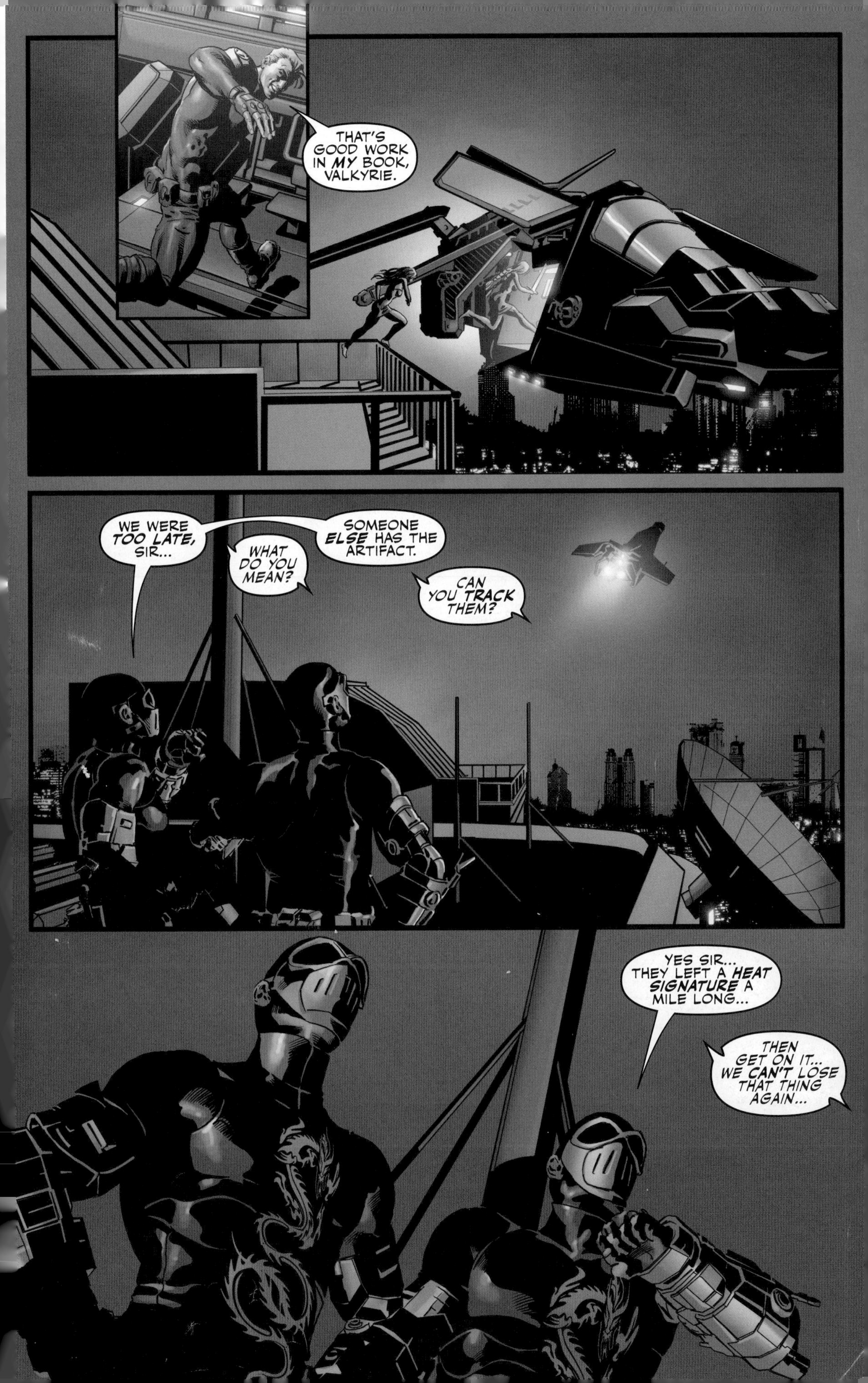
THAT'S GOOD WORK IN MY BOOK, VALKYRIE.
WE WERE TOO LATE, SIR...
WHAT DO YOU MEAN?
SOMEONE ELSE HAS THE ARTIFACT.
CAN YOU TRACK THEM?
YES SIR... THEY LEFT A HEAT SIGNATURE A MILE LONG...
THEN GET ON IT... WE CAN'T LOSE THAT THING AGAIN...

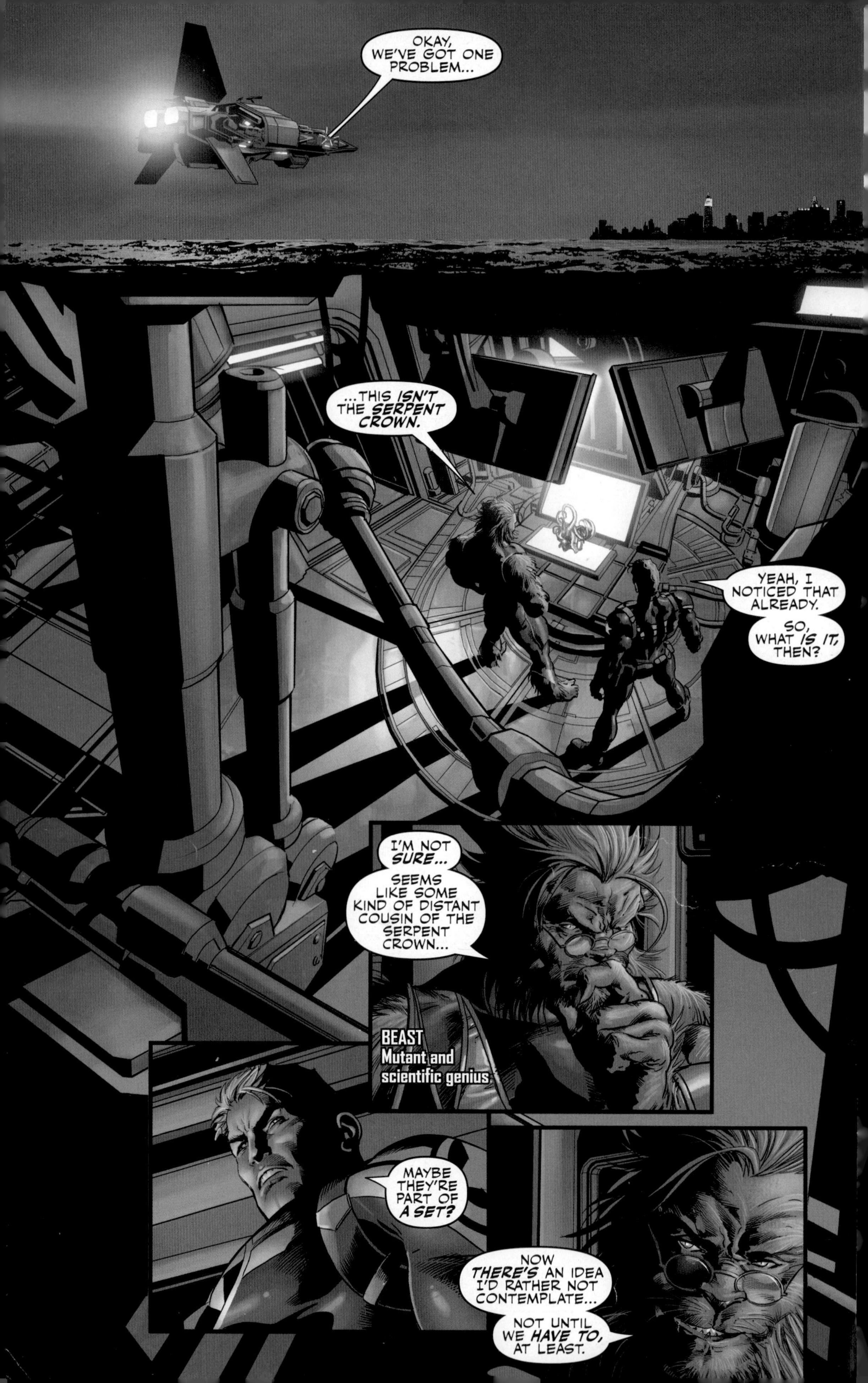

OKAY, WE'VE GOT ONE PROBLEM...
...THIS ISN'T THE SERPENT CROWN.
YEAH, I NOTICED THAT ALREADY.
SO, WHAT IS IT, THEN?
I'M NOT SURE...
SEEMS LIKE SOME KIND OF DISTANT COUSIN OF THE SERPENT CROWN...
BEAST Mutant and scientific genius
MAYBE THEY'RE PART OF A SET?
NOW THERE'S AN IDEA I'D RATHER NOT CONTEMPLATE...
NOT UNTIL WE HAVE TO, AT LEAST.

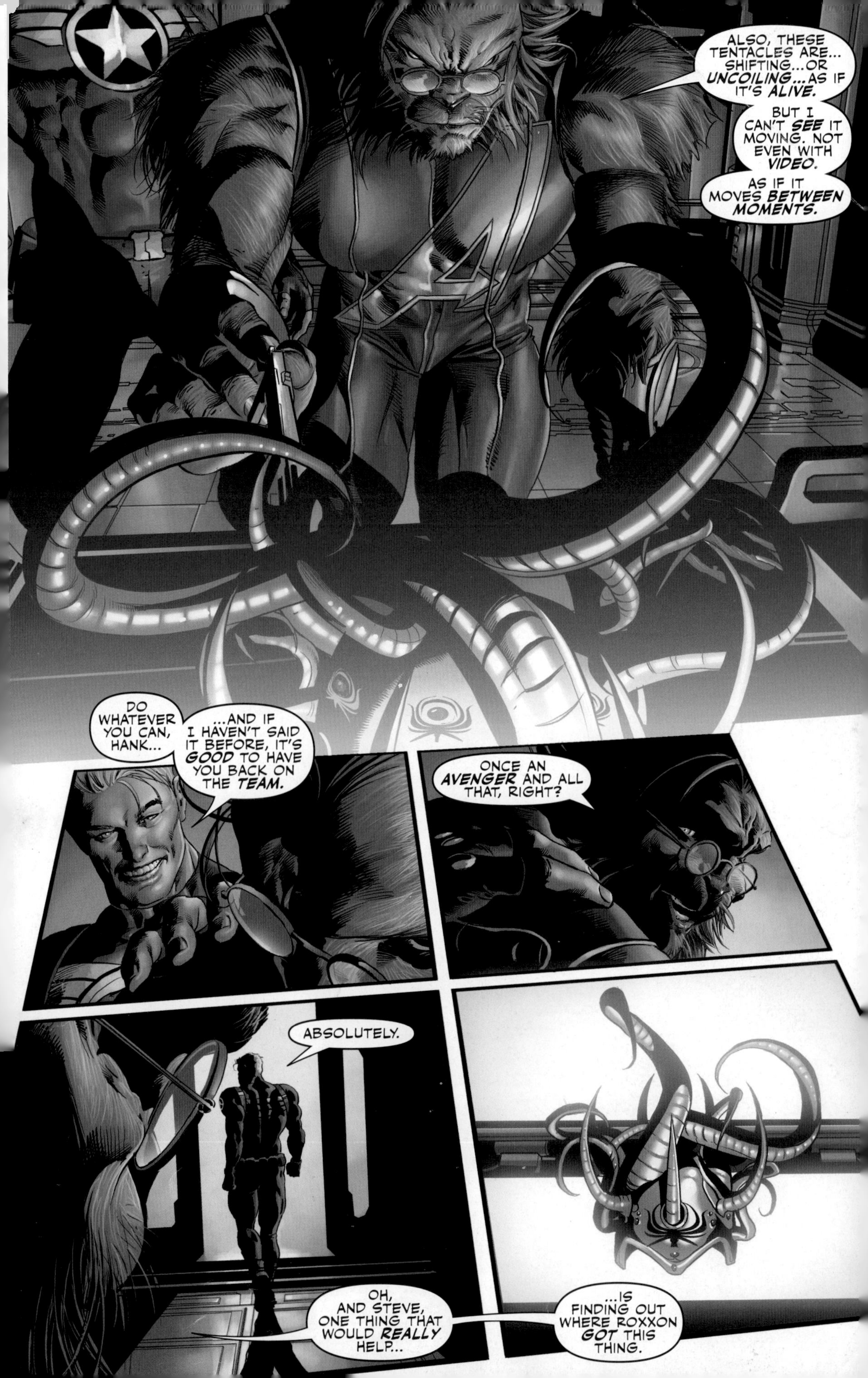
ALSO, THESE TENTACLES ARE... SHIFTING...OR UNCOILING...AS IF IT'S ALIVE.
BUT I CAN'T SEE IT MOVING. NOT EVEN WITH VIDEO.
AS IF IT MOVES BETWEEN MOMENTS.
DO WHATEVER YOU CAN, HANK...
...AND IF I HAVEN'T SAID IT BEFORE, IT'S GOOD TO HAVE YOU BACK ON THE TEAM.
ONCE AN AVENGER AND ALL THAT, RIGHT?
ABSOLUTELY.
OH, AND STEVE, ONE THING THAT WOULD REALLY HELP...
...IS FINDING OUT WHERE ROXXON GOT THIS THING.

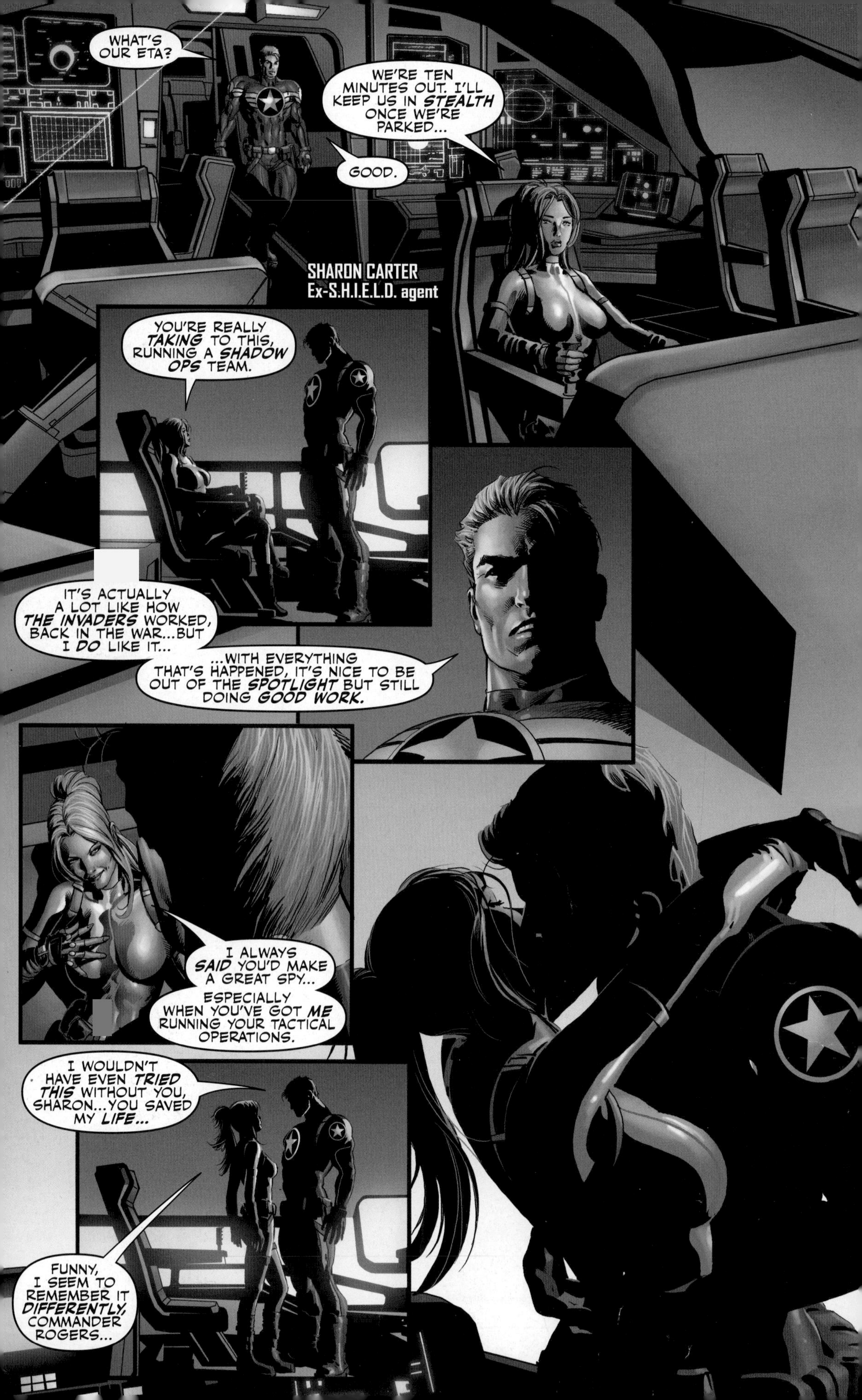
WHAT'S OUR ETA?
WE'RE TEN MINUTES OUT. I'LL KEEP US IN STEALTH ONCE WE'RE PARKED...
GOOD.
SHARON CARTER
Ex-S.H.I.E.L.D. agent
YOU'RE REALLY TAKING TO THIS, RUNNING A SHADOW OPS TEAM.
IT'S ACTUALLY A LOT LIKE HOW THE INVADERS WORKED, BACK IN THE WAR...BUT I DO LIKE IT...
...WITH EVERYTHING THAT'S HAPPENED, IT'S NICE TO BE OUT OF THE SPOTLIGHT BUT STILL DOING GOOD WORK.
I ALWAYS SAID YOU'D MAKE A GREAT SPY... ESPECIALLY WHEN YOU'VE GOT ME RUNNING YOUR TACTICAL OPERATIONS.
I WOULDN'T HAVE EVEN TRIED THIS WITHOUT YOU, SHARON...YOU SAVED MY LIFE...
FUNNY, I SEEM TO REMEMBER IT DIFFERENTLY, COMMANDER ROGERS...

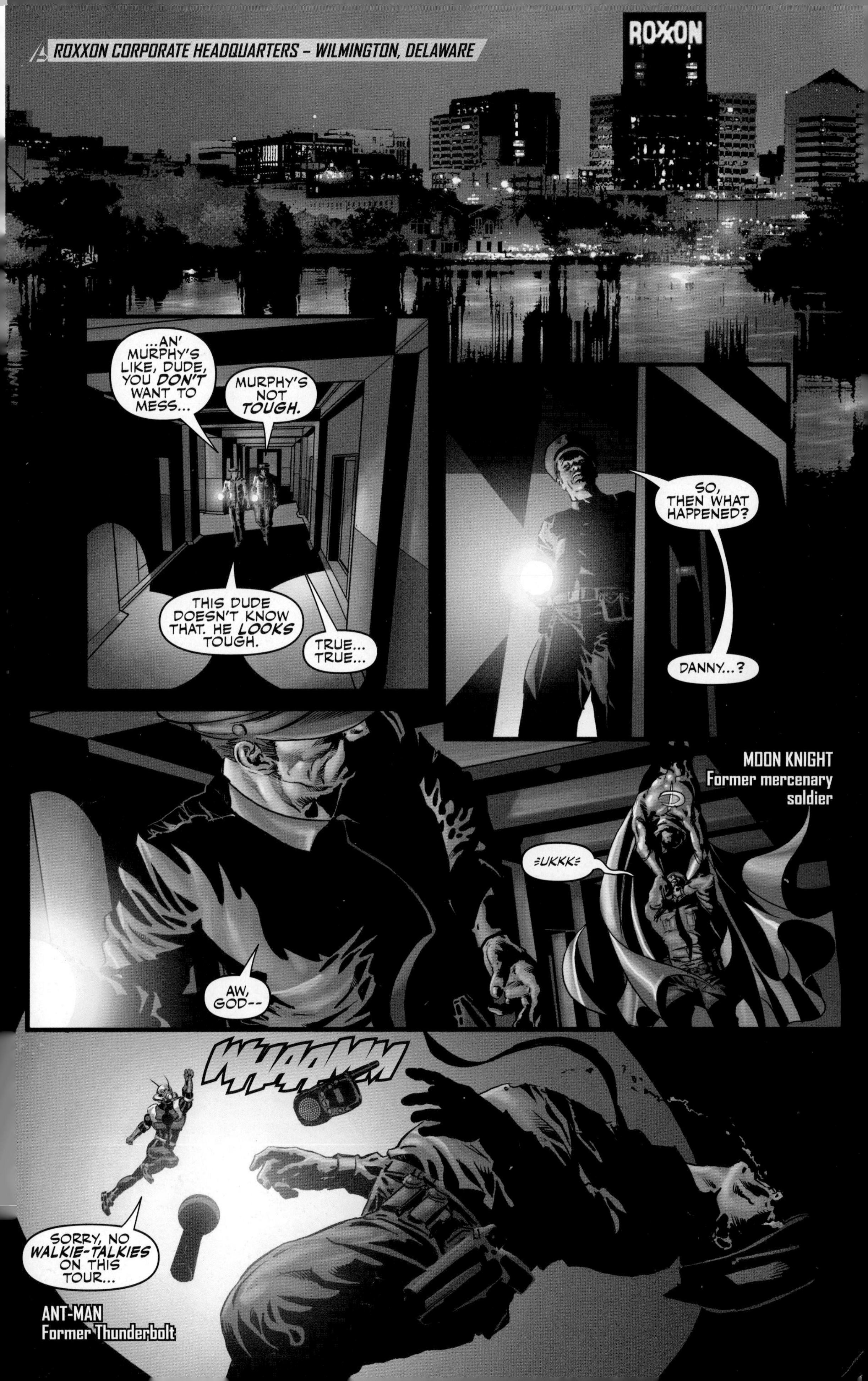
ROXXON CORPORATE HEADQUARTERS – WILMINGTON, DELAWARE
ROXXON
...AN' MURPHY'S LIKE, DUDE, YOU DON'T WANT TO MESS...
MURPHY'S NOT TOUGH.
THIS DUDE DOESN'T KNOW THAT. HE LOOKS TOUGH.
TRUE... TRUE...
SO, THEN WHAT HAPPENED?
DANNY...?
MOON KNIGHT
Former mercenary soldier
=UKKK=
AW, GOD--
WHAAMM
SORRY, NO WALKIE-TALKIES ON THIS TOUR...
ANT-MAN
Former Thunderbolt

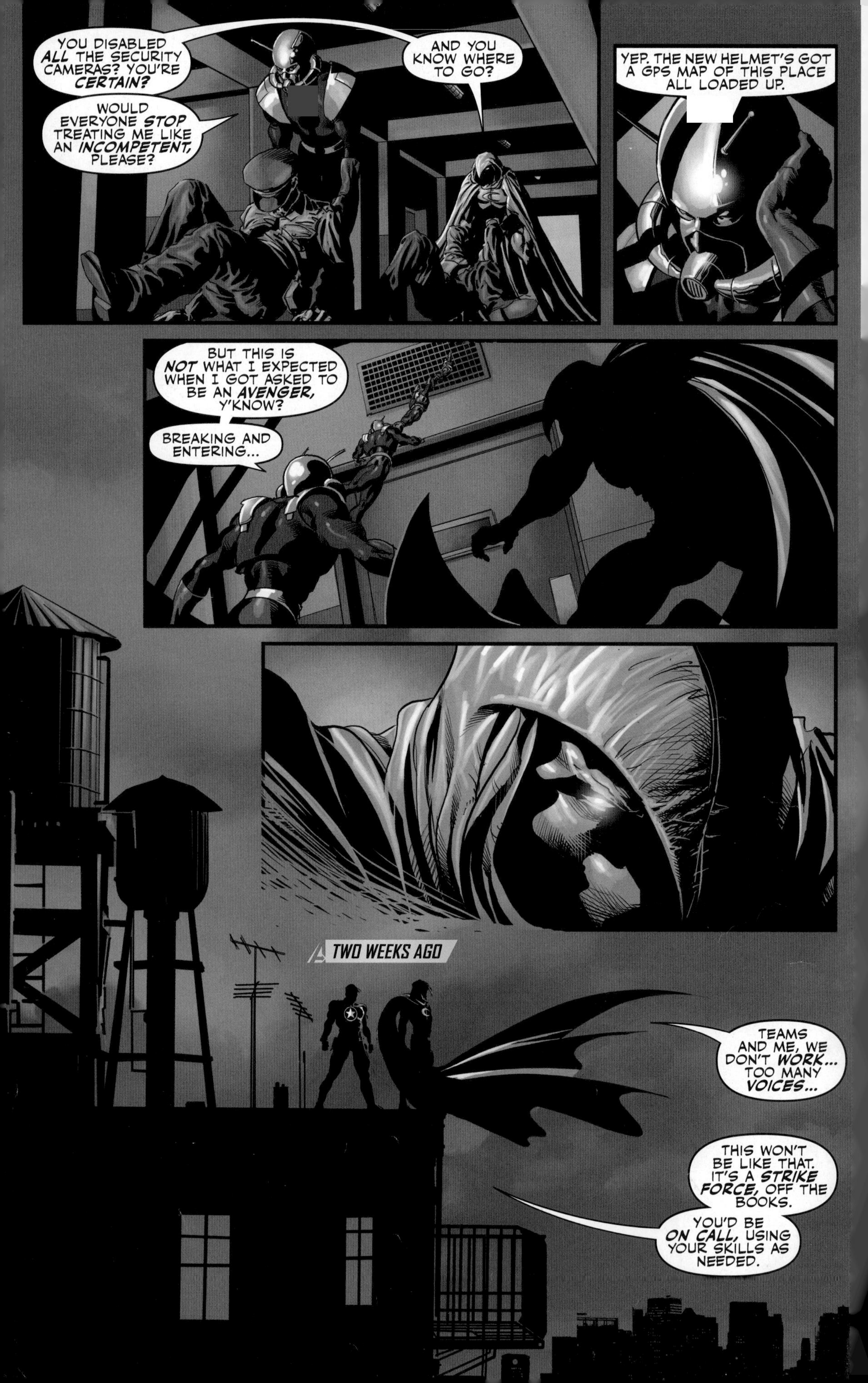
YOU DISABLED ALL THE SECURITY CAMERAS? YOU'RE CERTAIN?
WOULD EVERYONE STOP TREATING ME LIKE AN INCOMPETENT, PLEASE?
AND YOU KNOW WHERE TO GO?
YEP. THE NEW HELMET'S GOT A GPS MAP OF THIS PLACE ALL LOADED UP.
BUT THIS IS NOT WHAT I EXPECTED WHEN I GOT ASKED TO BE AN AVENGER, Y'KNOW?
BREAKING AND ENTERING...
TWO WEEKS AGO
TEAMS AND ME, WE DON'T WORK... TOO MANY VOICES...
THIS WON'T BE LIKE THAT. IT'S A STRIKE FORCE, OFF THE BOOKS.
YOU'D BE ON CALL, USING YOUR SKILLS AS NEEDED.

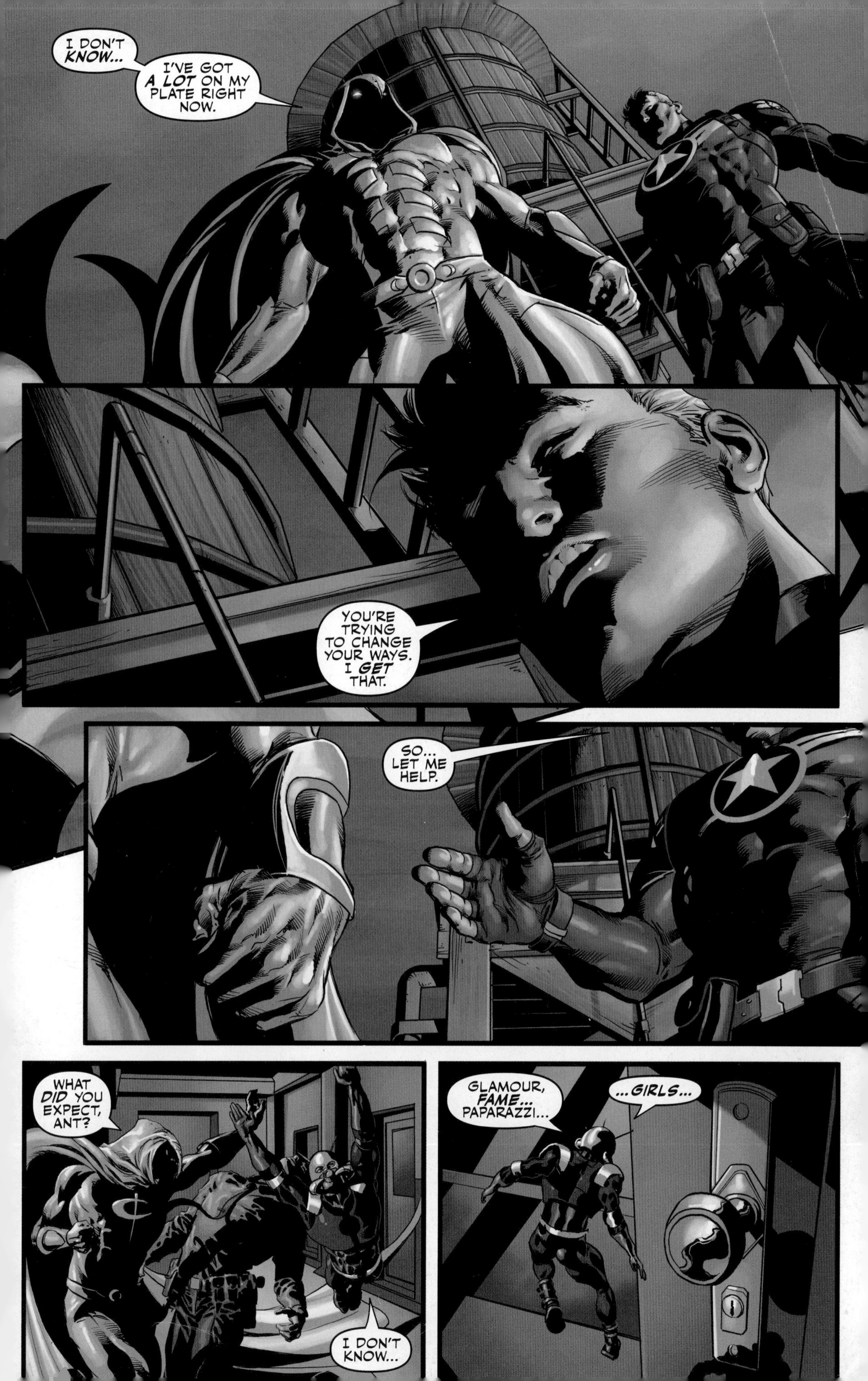
I DON'T KNOW...
I'VE GOT A LOT ON MY PLATE RIGHT NOW.
YOU'RE TRYING TO CHANGE YOUR WAYS. I GET THAT.
SO... LET ME HELP.
WHAT DID YOU EXPECT, ANT?
I DON'T KNOW...
GLAMOUR, FAME... PAPARAZZI...
...GIRLS...

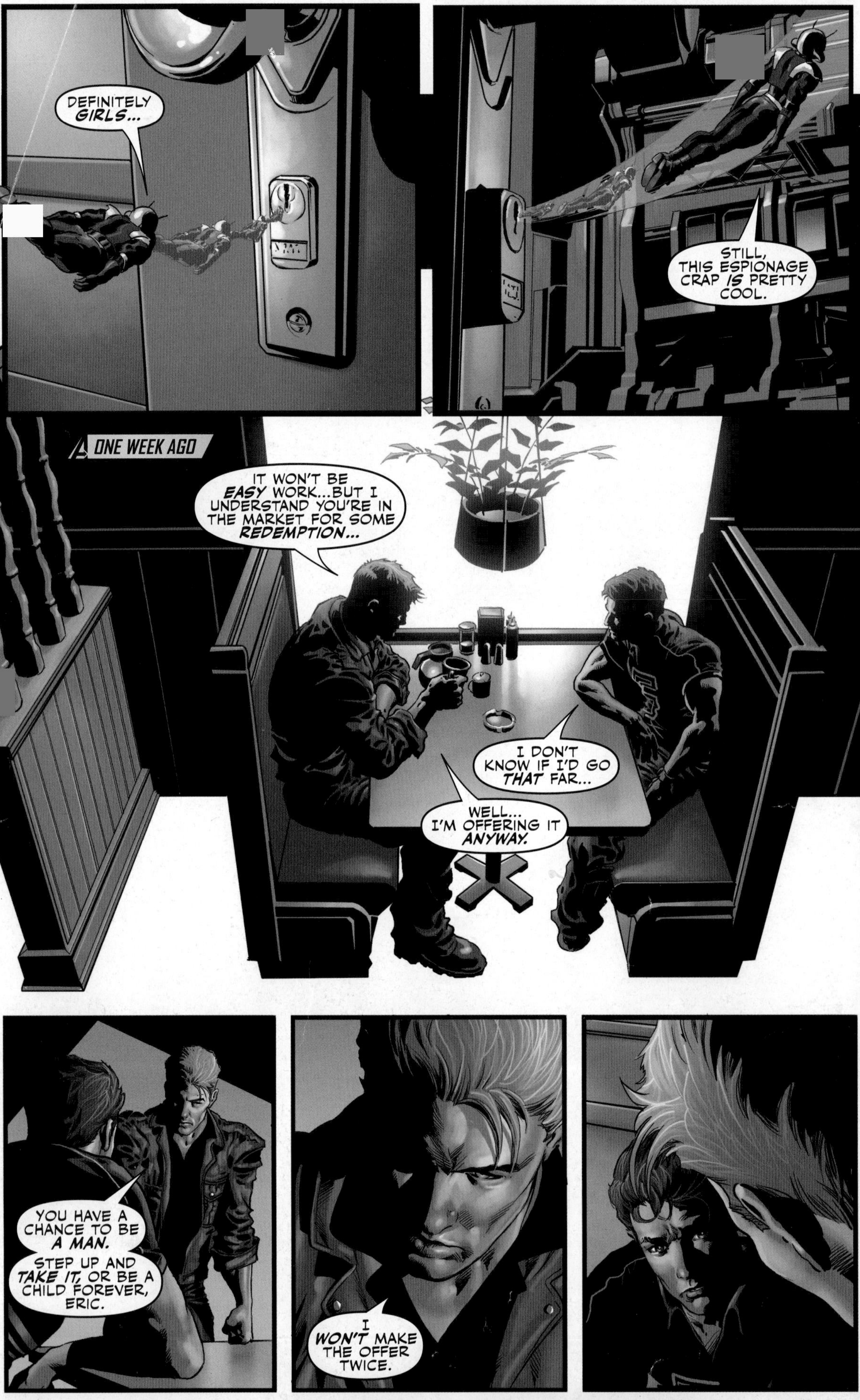
DEFINITELY GIRLS...
STILL, THIS ESPIONAGE CRAP IS PRETTY COOL.
ONE WEEK AGO
IT WON'T BE EASY WORK...BUT I UNDERSTAND YOU'RE IN THE MARKET FOR SOME REDEMPTION...
I DON'T KNOW IF I'D GO THAT FAR...
WELL... I'M OFFERING IT ANYWAY.
YOU HAVE A CHANCE TO BE A MAN.
STEP UP AND TAKE IT, OR BE A CHILD FOREVER, ERIC.
I WON'T MAKE THE OFFER TWICE.

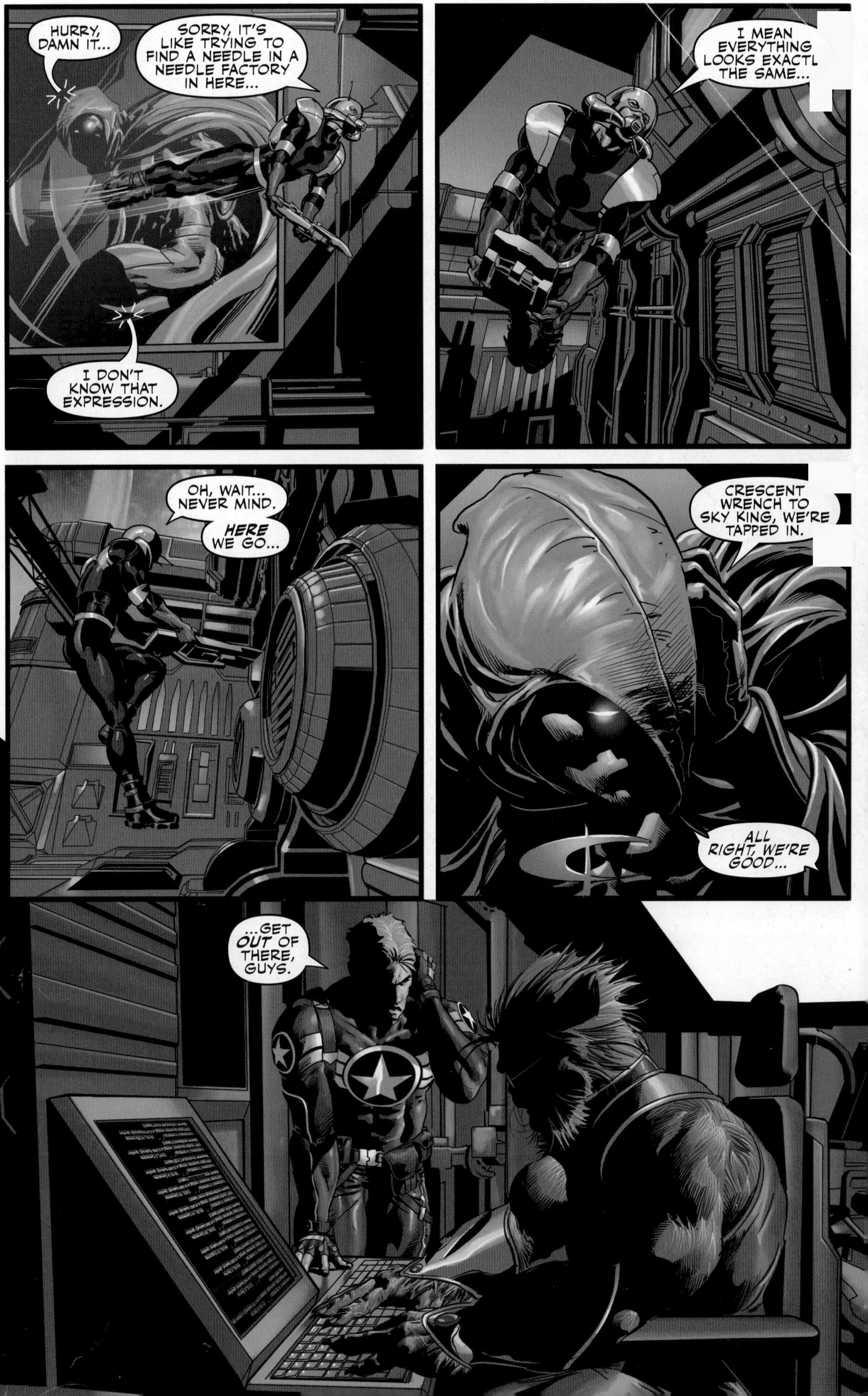
HURRY, DAMN IT...
SORRY, IT'S LIKE TRYING TO FIND A NEEDLE IN A NEEDLE FACTORY IN HERE...
I DON'T KNOW THAT EXPRESSION.
I MEAN EVERYTHING LOOKS EXACTL THE SAME...
OH, WAIT... NEVER MIND.
HERE WE GO...
CRESCENT WRENCH TO SKY KING, WE'RE TAPPED IN.
ALL RIGHT, WE'RE GOOD...
...GET OUT OF THERE, GUYS.

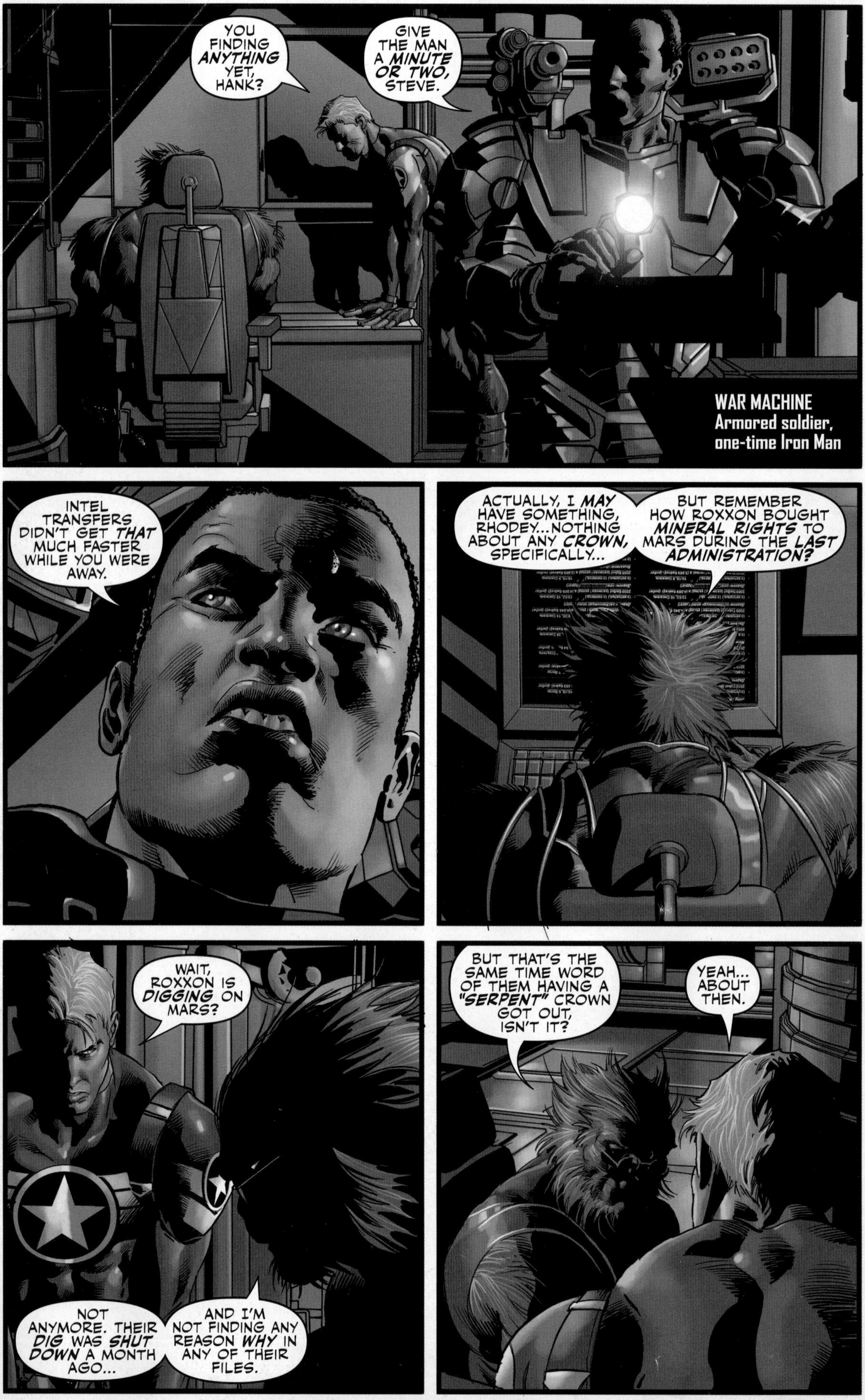
YOU FINDING *ANYTHING* YET, HANK?
GIVE THE MAN A *MINUTE OR TWO,* STEVE.
WAR MACHINE
Armored soldier, one-time Iron Man
INTEL TRANSFERS DIDN'T GET *THAT* MUCH FASTER WHILE YOU WERE AWAY.
ACTUALLY, I *MAY* HAVE SOMETHING, RHODEY...NOTHING ABOUT ANY *CROWN,* SPECIFICALLY...
BUT REMEMBER HOW ROXXON BOUGHT *MINERAL RIGHTS* TO MARS DURING THE *LAST ADMINISTRATION?*
WAIT, ROXXON IS *DIGGING* ON MARS?
NOT ANYMORE. THEIR *DIG* WAS *SHUT DOWN* A MONTH AGO...
AND I'M NOT FINDING ANY REASON *WHY* IN ANY OF THEIR FILES.
BUT THAT'S THE SAME TIME WORD OF THEM HAVING A *"SERPENT"* CROWN GOT OUT, ISN'T IT?
YEAH... ABOUT THEN.

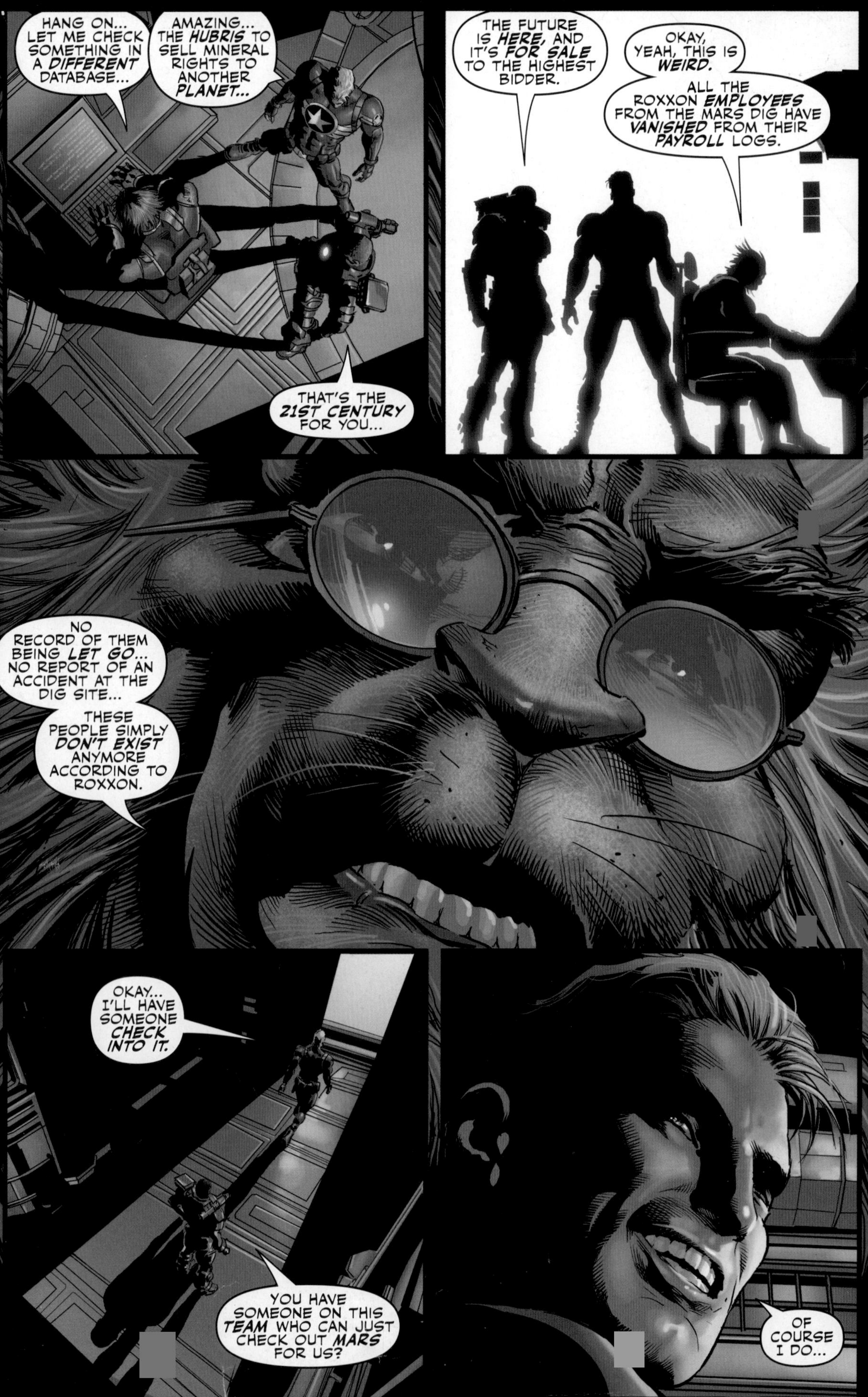
HANG ON... LET ME CHECK SOMETHING IN A DIFFERENT DATABASE...
AMAZING... THE HUBRIS TO SELL MINERAL RIGHTS TO ANOTHER PLANET...
THAT'S THE 21ST CENTURY FOR YOU...
THE FUTURE IS HERE, AND IT'S FOR SALE TO THE HIGHEST BIDDER.
OKAY, YEAH, THIS IS WEIRD.
ALL THE ROXXON EMPLOYEES FROM THE MARS DIG HAVE VANISHED FROM THEIR PAYROLL LOGS.
NO RECORD OF THEM BEING LET GO... NO REPORT OF AN ACCIDENT AT THE DIG SITE...
THESE PEOPLE SIMPLY DON'T EXIST ANYMORE ACCORDING TO ROXXON.
OKAY... I'LL HAVE SOMEONE CHECK INTO IT.
YOU HAVE SOMEONE ON THIS TEAM WHO CAN JUST CHECK OUT MARS FOR US?
OF COURSE I DO...

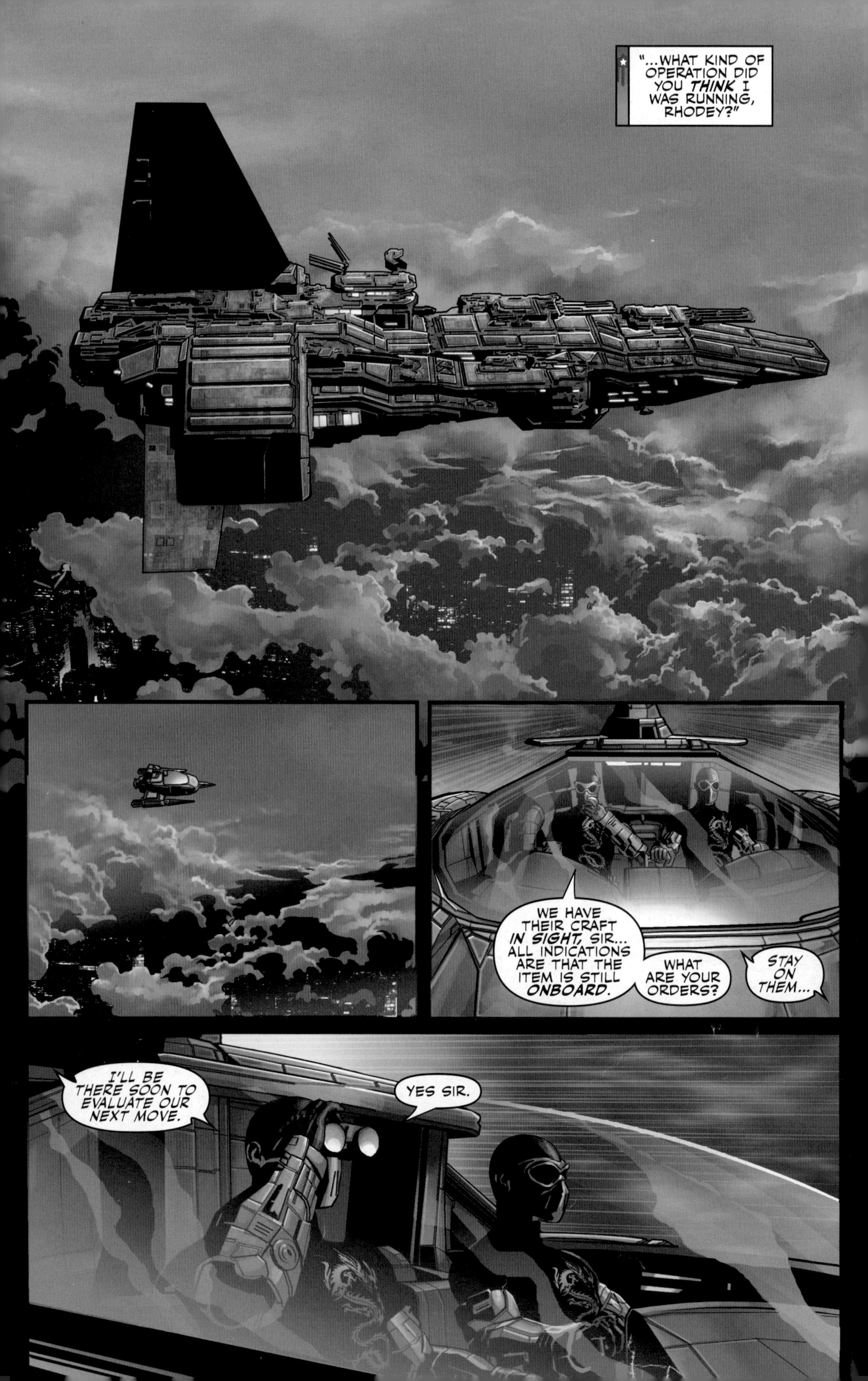
"...WHAT KIND OF OPERATION DID YOU *THINK* I WAS RUNNING, RHODEY?"
WE HAVE THEIR CRAFT *IN SIGHT,* SIR... ALL INDICATIONS ARE THAT THE ITEM IS STILL *ONBOARD.*
WHAT ARE YOUR ORDERS?
STAY ON THEM...
I'LL BE THERE SOON TO EVALUATE OUR NEXT MOVE.
YES SIR.

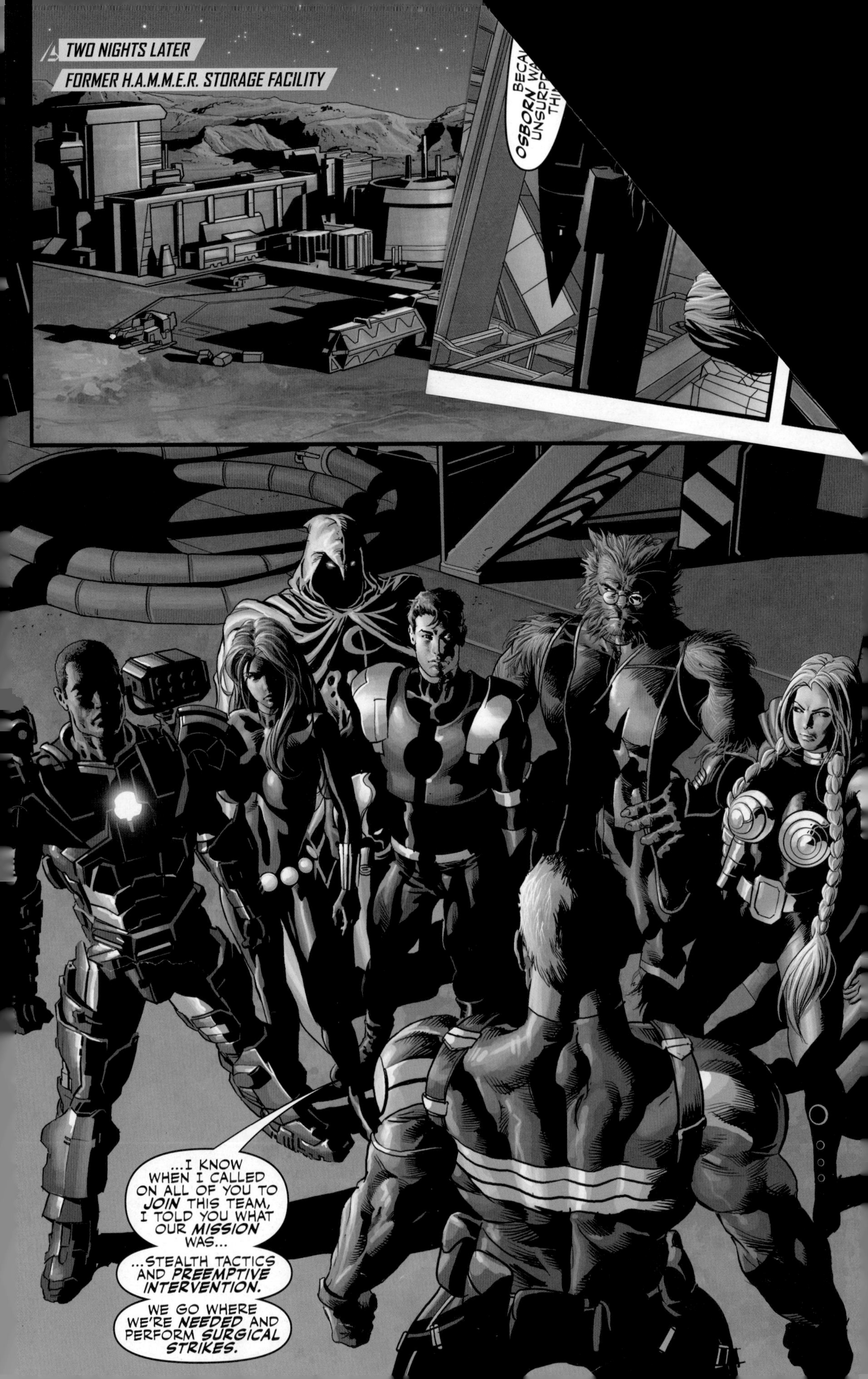
TWO NIGHTS LATER
FORMER H.A.M.M.E.R. STORAGE FACILITY
OSBORN
...I KNOW WHEN I CALLED ON ALL OF YOU TO JOIN THIS TEAM, I TOLD YOU WHAT OUR MISSION WAS...
...STEALTH TACTICS AND PREEMPTIVE INTERVENTION.
WE GO WHERE WE'RE NEEDED AND PERFORM SURGICAL STRIKES.

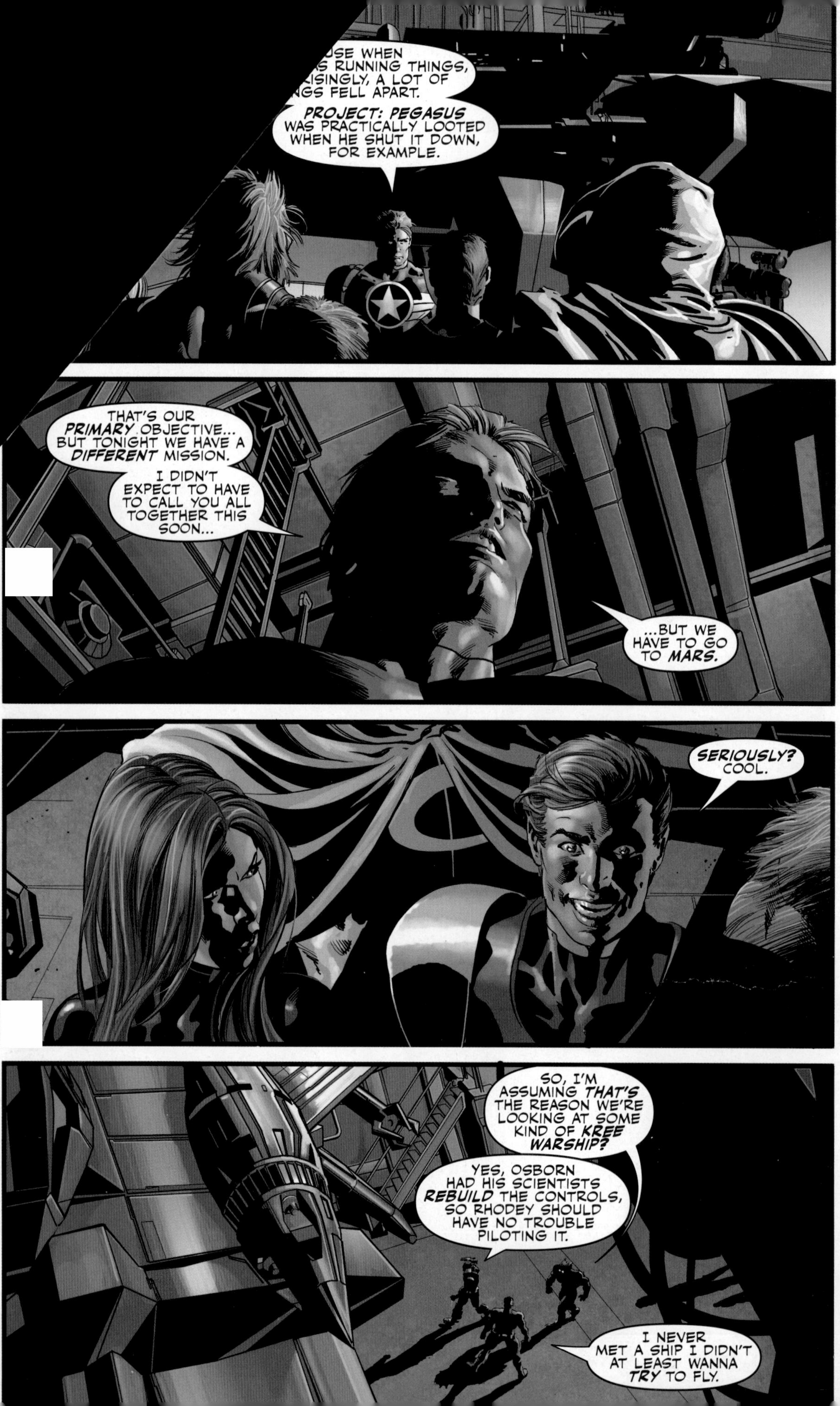
USE WHEN
RUNNING THINGS,
A LOT OF
FELL APART.
PROJECT: PEGASUS WAS PRACTICALLY LOOTED WHEN HE SHUT IT DOWN, FOR EXAMPLE.
THAT'S OUR PRIMARY OBJECTIVE... BUT TONIGHT WE HAVE A DIFFERENT MISSION.
I DIDN'T EXPECT TO HAVE TO CALL YOU ALL TOGETHER THIS SOON...
...BUT WE HAVE TO GO TO MARS.
SERIOUSLY? COOL.
SO, I'M ASSUMING THAT'S THE REASON WE'RE LOOKING AT SOME KIND OF KREE WARSHIP?
YES, OSBORN HAD HIS SCIENTISTS REBUILD THE CONTROLS, SO RHODEY SHOULD HAVE NO TROUBLE PILOTING IT.
I NEVER MET A SHIP I DIDN'T AT LEAST WANNA TRY TO FLY.

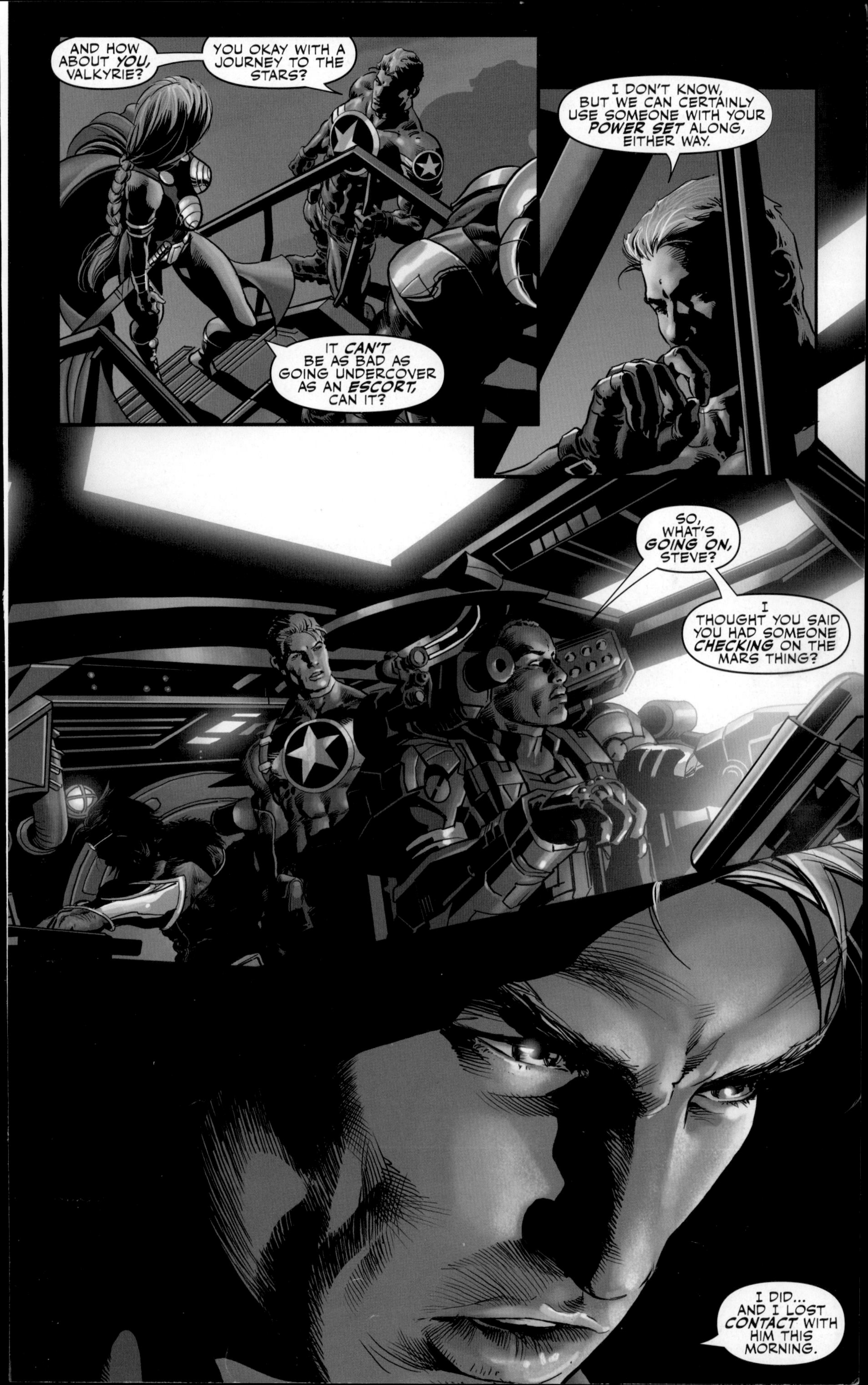
AND HOW ABOUT YOU, VALKYRIE?
YOU OKAY WITH A JOURNEY TO THE STARS?
IT CAN'T BE AS BAD AS GOING UNDERCOVER AS AN ESCORT, CAN IT?
I DON'T KNOW, BUT WE CAN CERTAINLY USE SOMEONE WITH YOUR POWER SET ALONG, EITHER WAY.
SO, WHAT'S GOING ON, STEVE?
I THOUGHT YOU SAID YOU HAD SOMEONE CHECKING ON THE MARS THING?
I DID... AND I LOST CONTACT WITH HIM THIS MORNING.

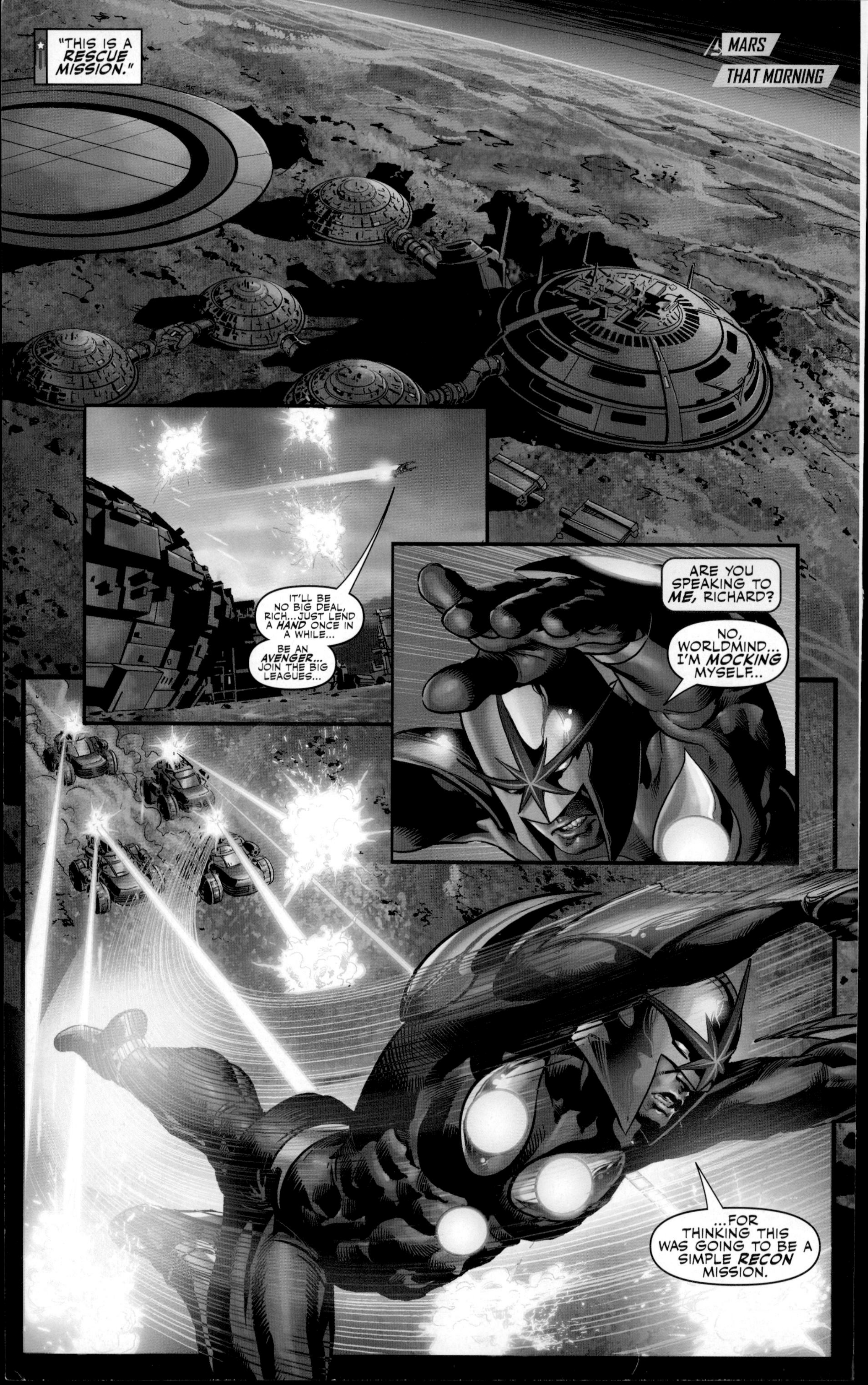
"THIS IS A RESCUE MISSION."
MARS
THAT MORNING
IT'LL BE NO BIG DEAL, RICH...JUST LEND A HAND ONCE IN A WHILE...
BE AN AVENGER... JOIN THE BIG LEAGUES...
ARE YOU SPEAKING TO ME, RICHARD?
NO, WORLDMIND... I'M MOCKING MYSELF...
...FOR THINKING THIS WAS GOING TO BE A SIMPLE RECON MISSION.

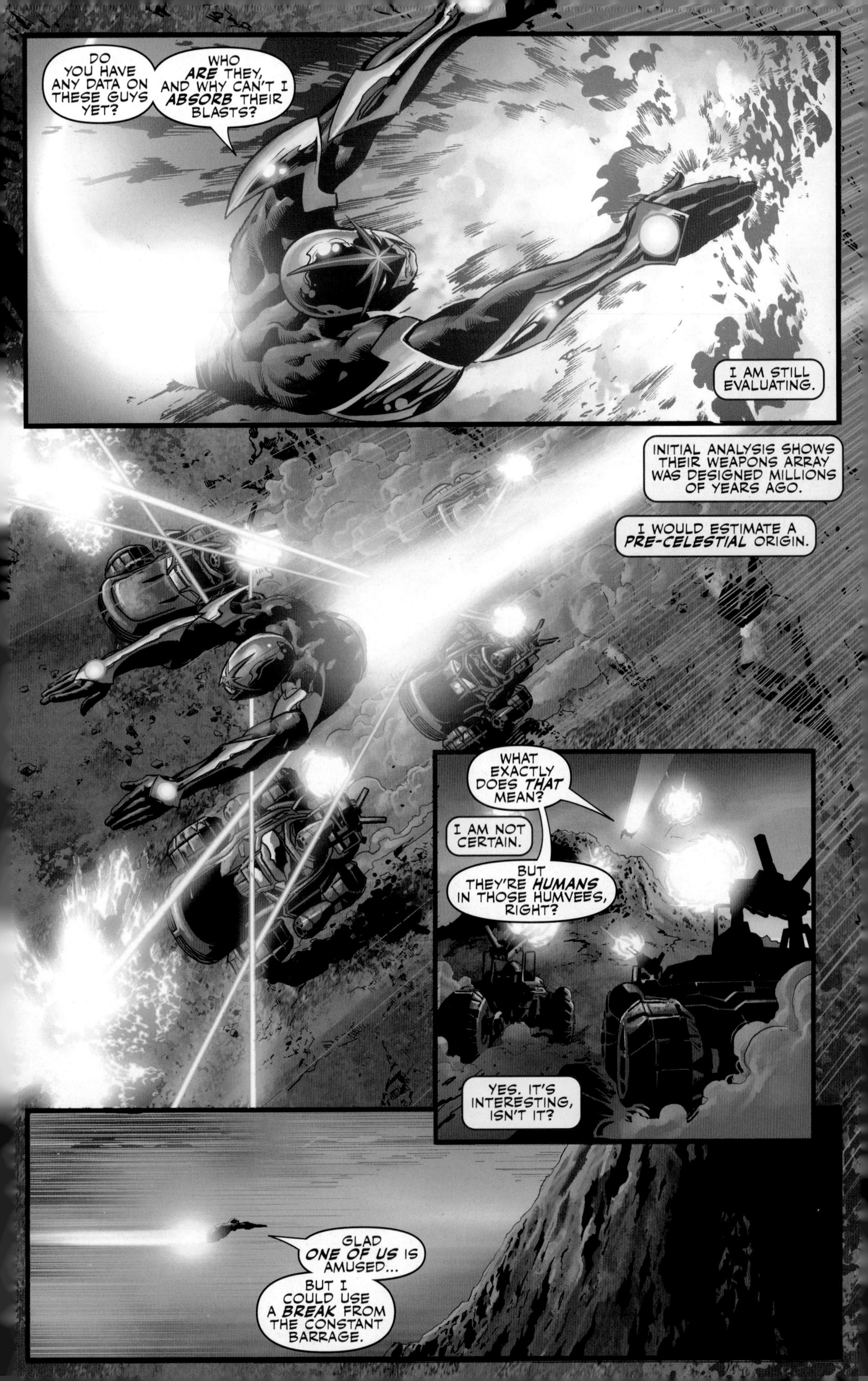
DO YOU HAVE ANY DATA ON THESE GUYS YET?
WHO ARE THEY, AND WHY CAN'T I ABSORB THEIR BLASTS?
I AM STILL EVALUATING.
INITIAL ANALYSIS SHOWS THEIR WEAPONS ARRAY WAS DESIGNED MILLIONS OF YEARS AGO.
I WOULD ESTIMATE A PRE-CELESTIAL ORIGIN.
WHAT EXACTLY DOES THAT MEAN?
I AM NOT CERTAIN.
BUT THEY'RE HUMANS IN THOSE HUMVEES, RIGHT?
YES. IT'S INTERESTING, ISN'T IT?
GLAD ONE OF US IS AMUSED...
BUT I COULD USE A BREAK FROM THE CONSTANT BARRAGE.

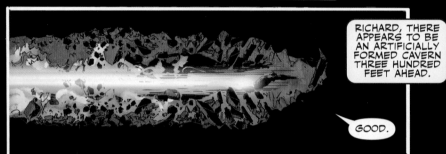

RICHARD, THERE APPEARS TO BE AN ARTIFICIALLY FORMED CAVERN THREE HUNDRED FEET AHEAD.

GOOD.

WE CAN *REGROUP* AND CONTACT THE *AVENGERS*...

...AND...

...WHAT THE *HELL*...?

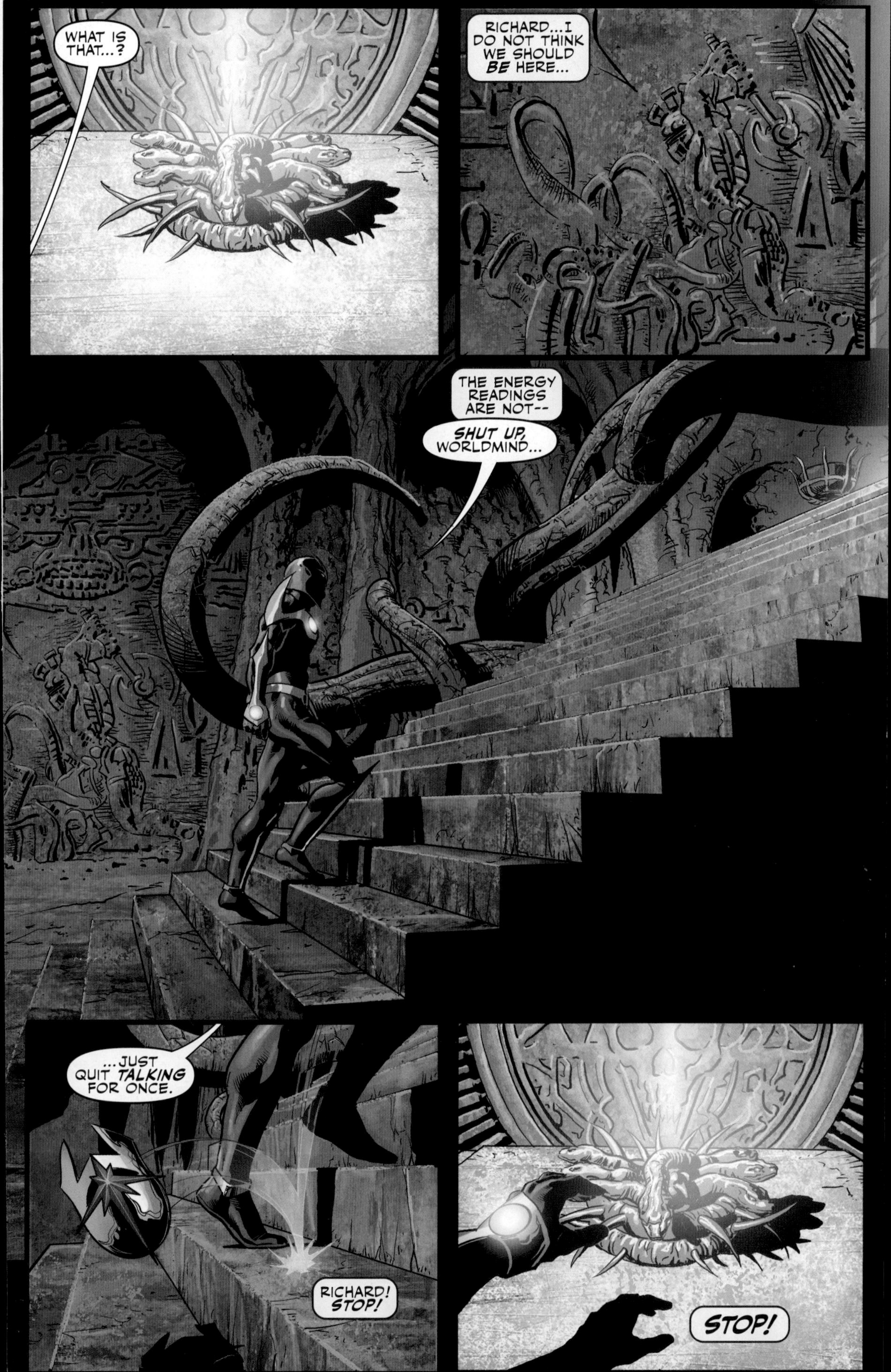
WHAT IS THAT...?
RICHARD...I DO NOT THINK WE SHOULD BE HERE...
THE ENERGY READINGS ARE NOT--
SHUT UP, WORLDMIND...
...JUST QUIT TALKING FOR ONCE.
RICHARD! STOP!
STOP!

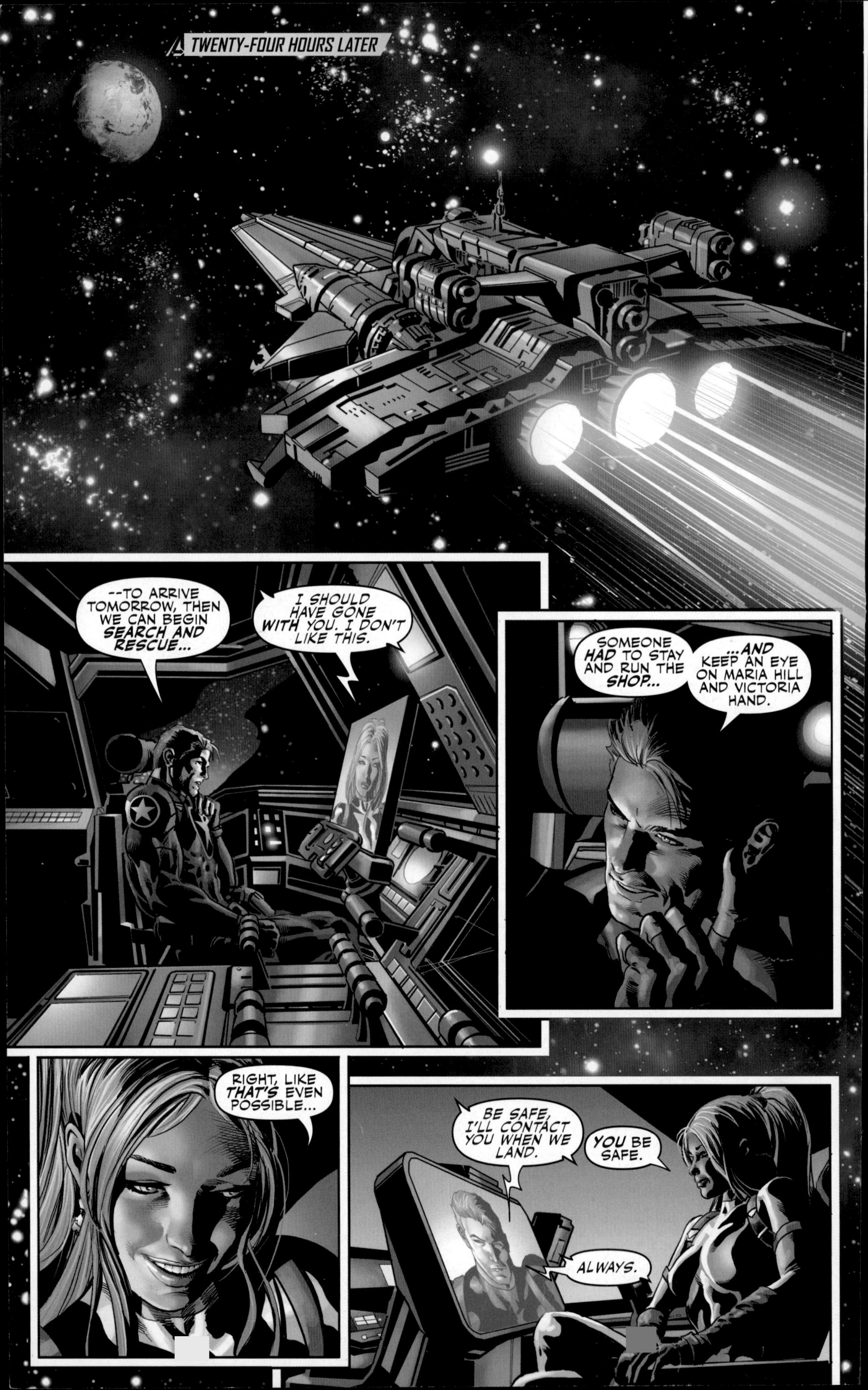
TWENTY-FOUR HOURS LATER
--TO ARRIVE TOMORROW, THEN WE CAN BEGIN SEARCH AND RESCUE...
I SHOULD HAVE GONE WITH YOU. I DON'T LIKE THIS.
SOMEONE HAD TO STAY AND RUN THE SHOP...
...AND KEEP AN EYE ON MARIA HILL AND VICTORIA HAND.
RIGHT, LIKE THAT'S EVEN POSSIBLE...
BE SAFE, I'LL CONTACT YOU WHEN WE LAND.
YOU BE SAFE.
ALWAYS.

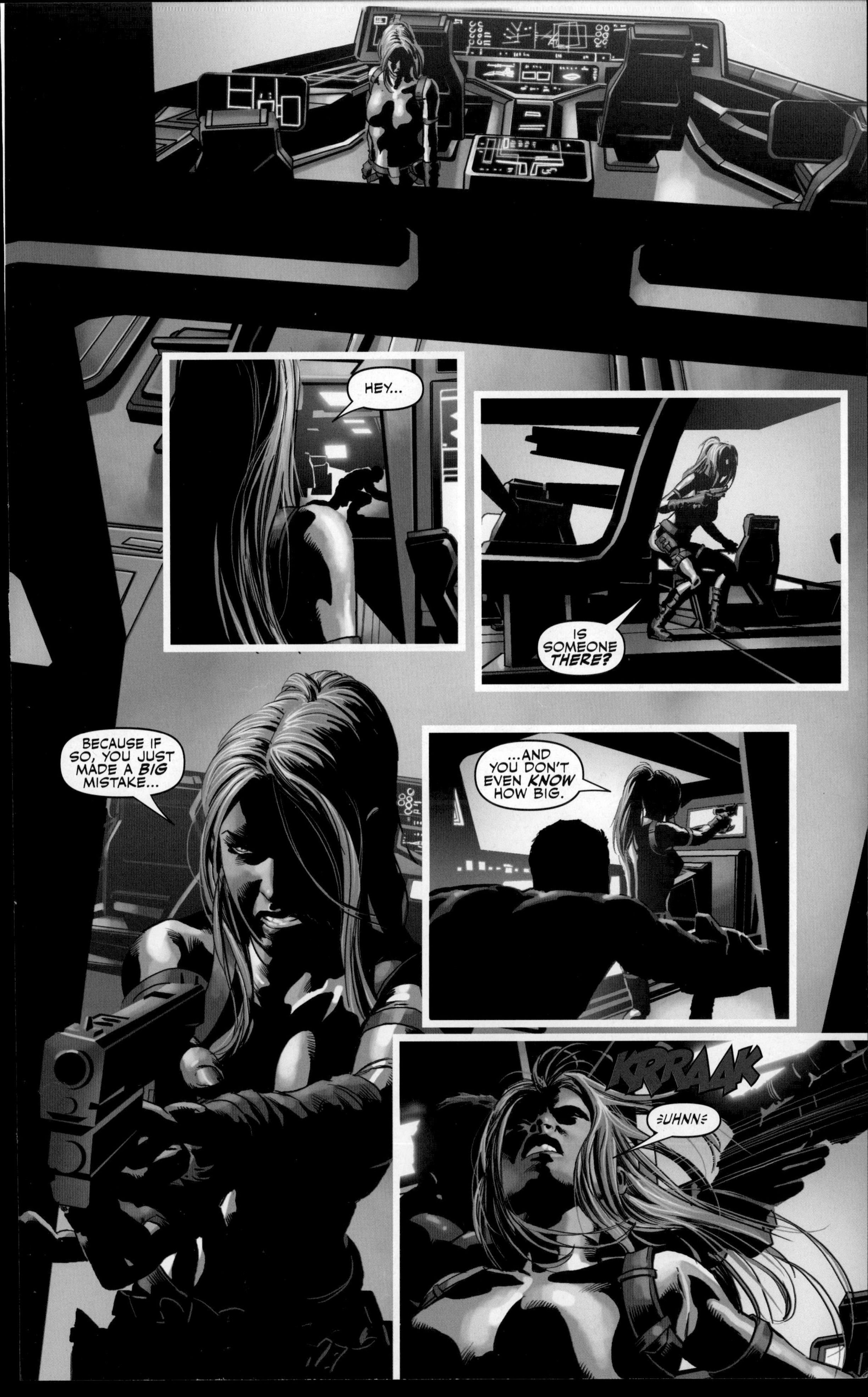

HEY...
IS SOMEONE THERE?
BECAUSE IF SO, YOU JUST MADE A BIG MISTAKE...
...AND YOU DON'T EVEN KNOW HOW BIG.
KRRAAK
UHNN

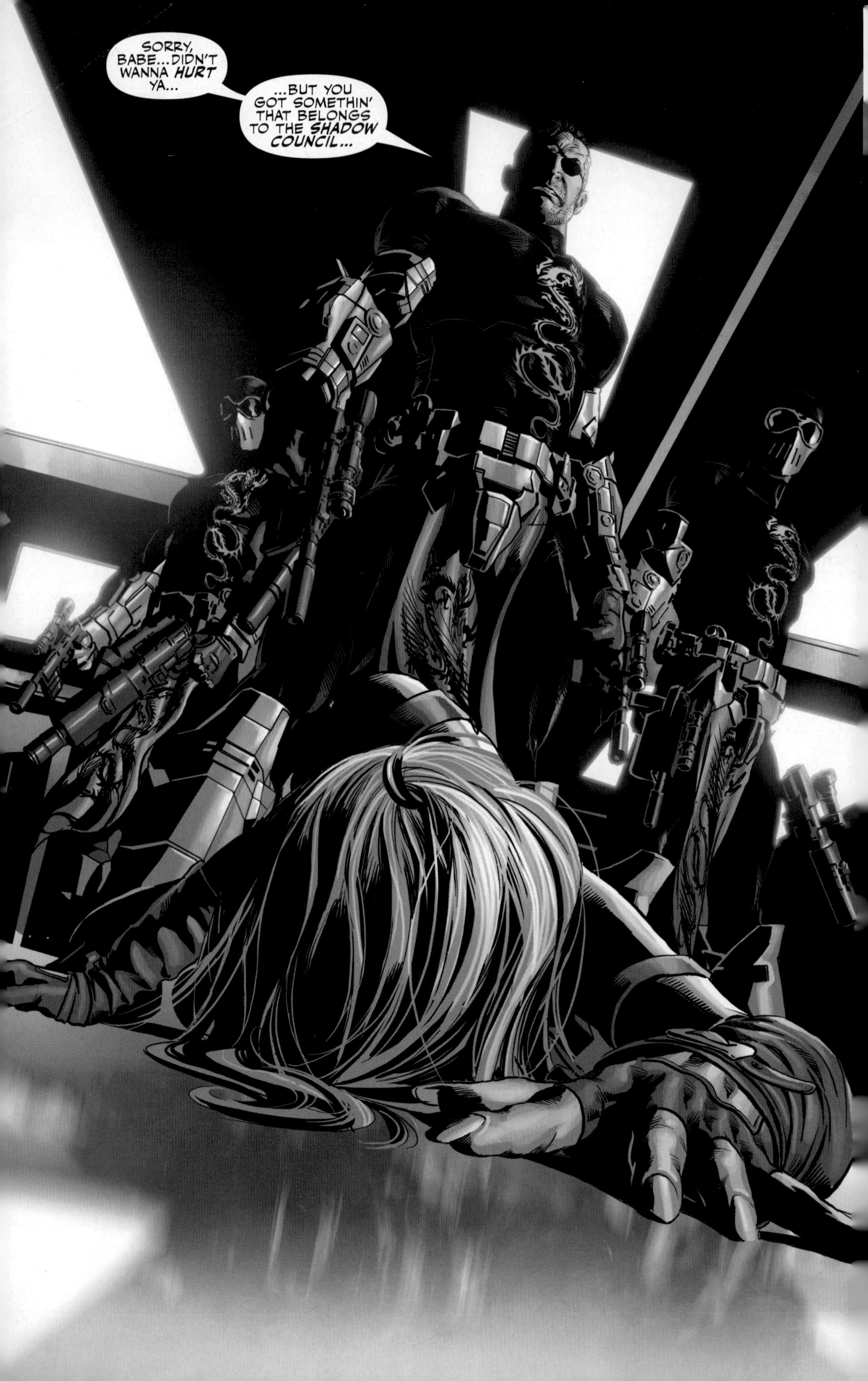
SORRY, BABE...DIDN'T WANNA *HURT* YA...
...BUT YOU GOT SOMETHIN' THAT BELONGS TO THE *SHADOW COUNCIL*...

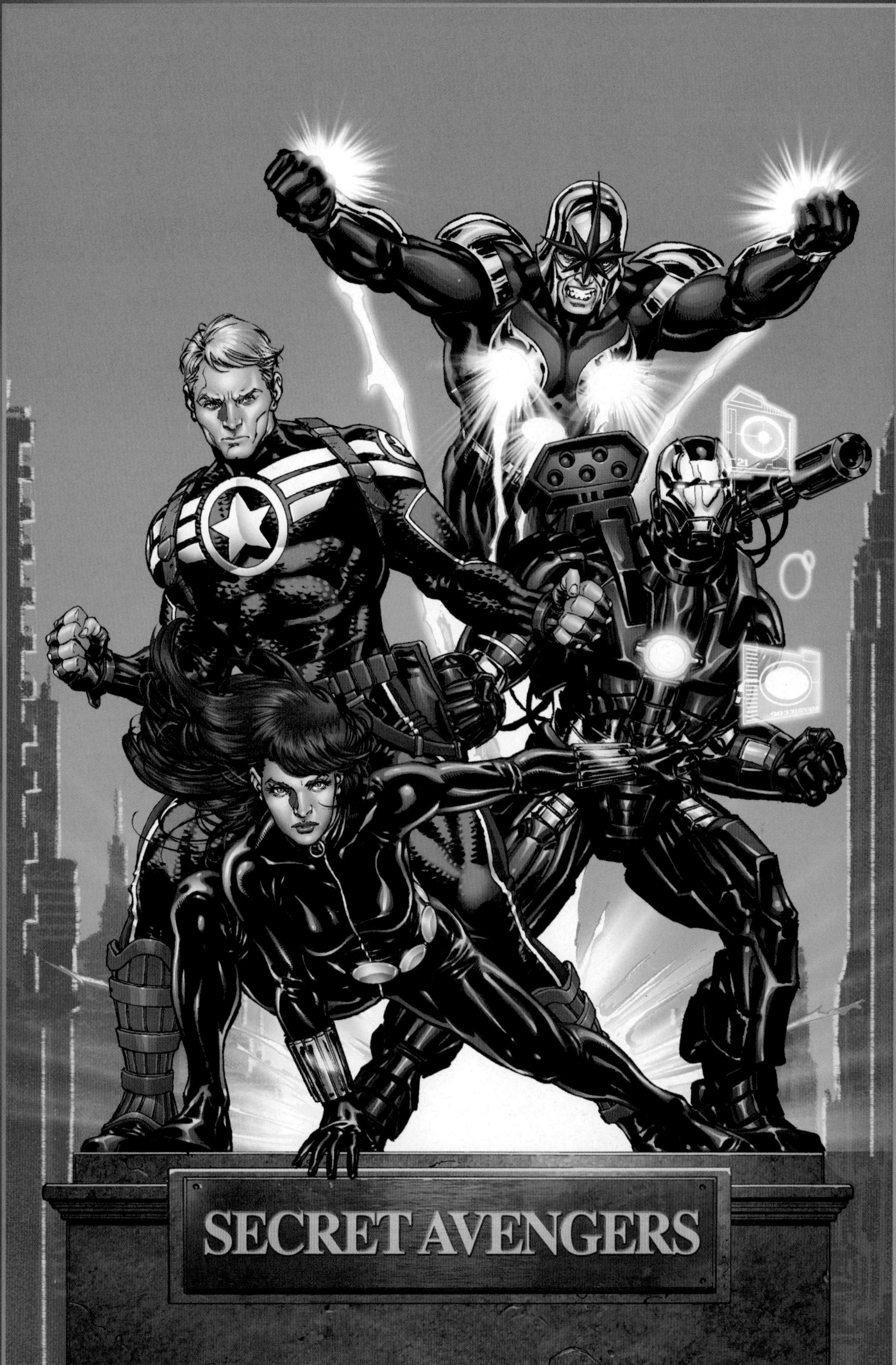
SECRET AVENGERS

**#1 HEROIC AGE VARIANT BY DAVID YARDIN & THOMAS MASON**

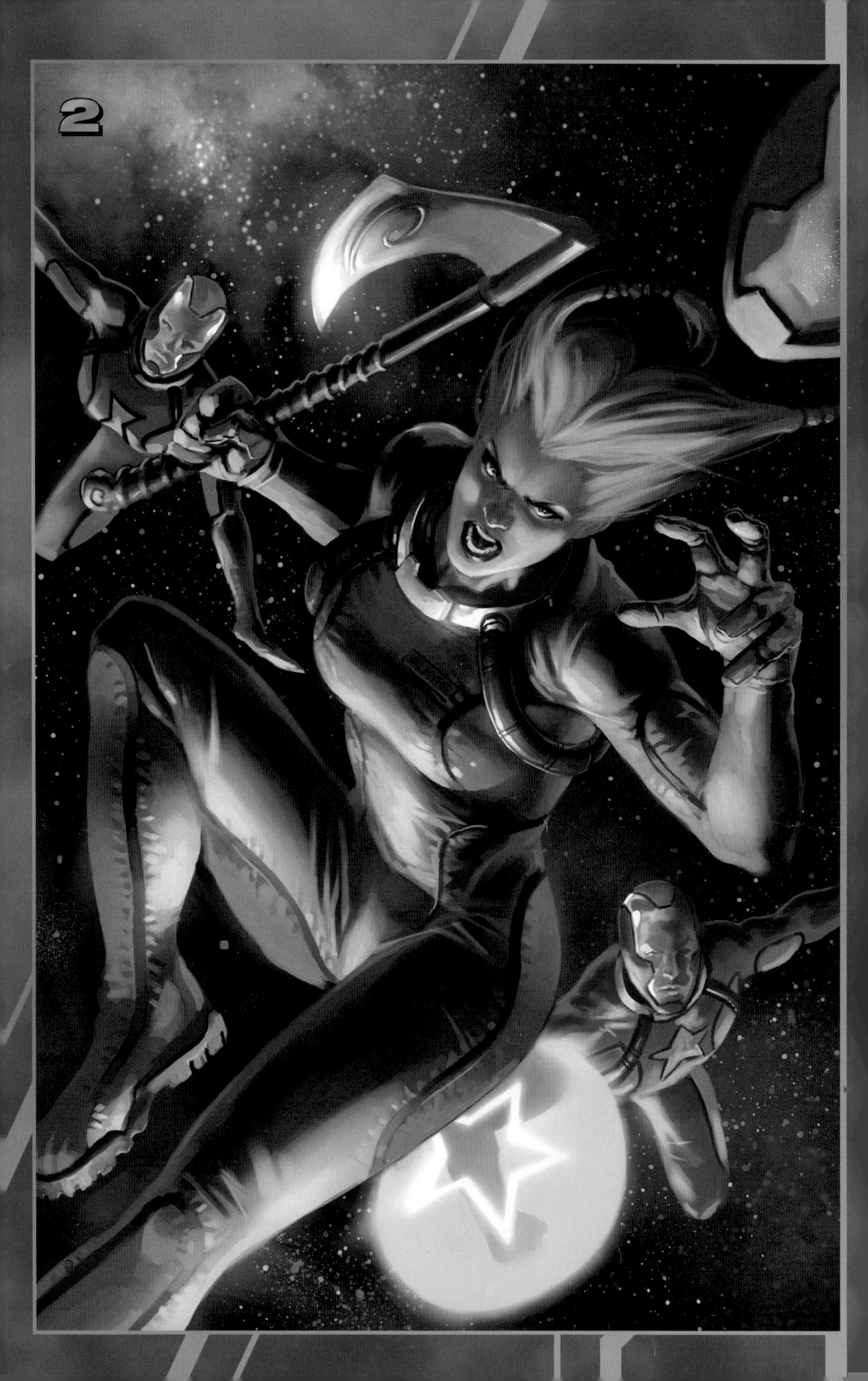
2

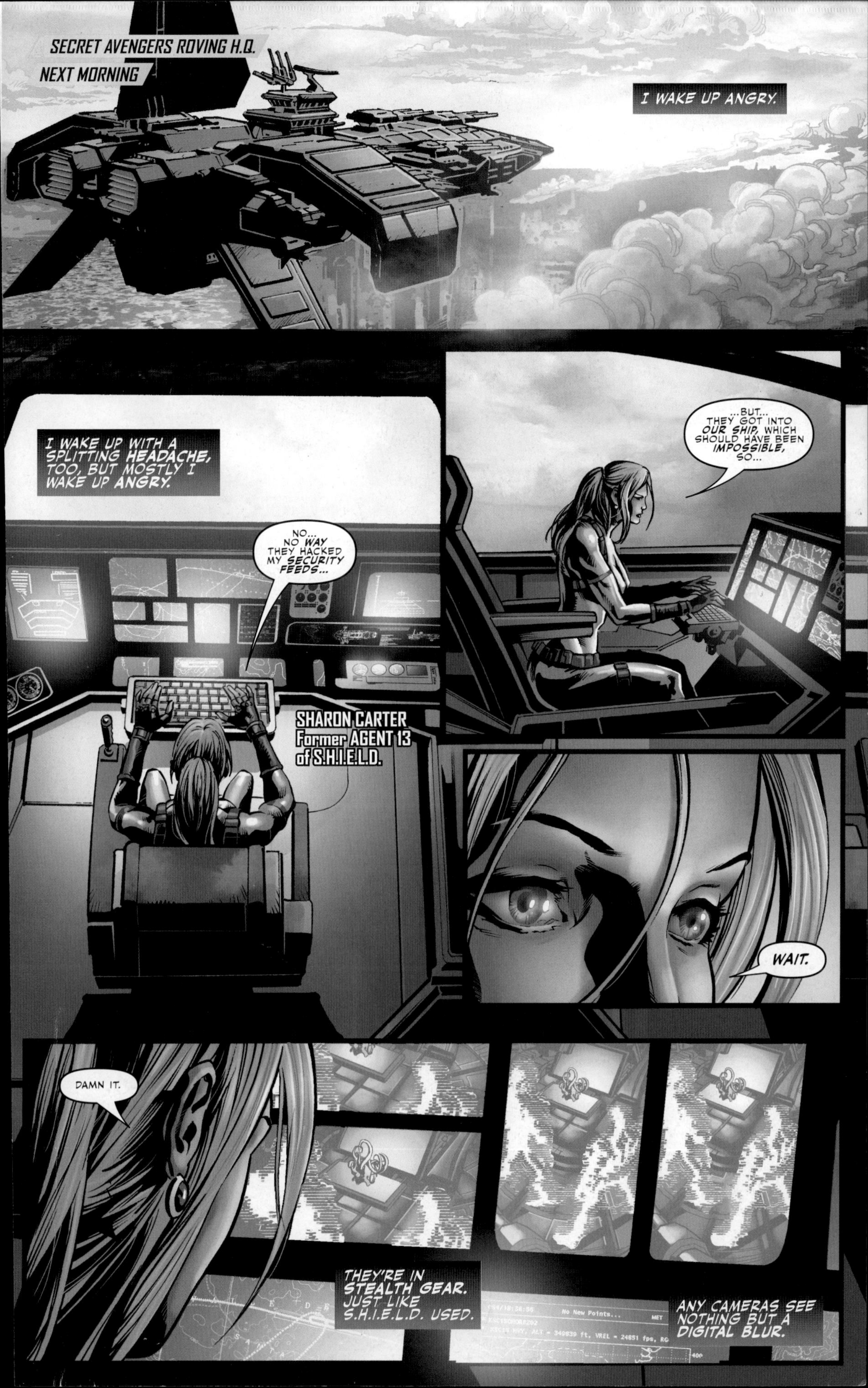
SECRET AVENGERS ROVING H.Q.
NEXT MORNING
I WAKE UP ANGRY.
I WAKE UP WITH A SPLITTING HEADACHE, TOO, BUT MOSTLY I WAKE UP ANGRY.
NO... NO WAY THEY HACKED MY SECURITY FEEDS...
SHARON CARTER Former AGENT 13 of S.H.I.E.L.D.
...BUT... THEY GOT INTO OUR SHIP, WHICH SHOULD HAVE BEEN IMPOSSIBLE, SO...
WAIT.
DAMN IT.
THEY'RE IN STEALTH GEAR. JUST LIKE S.H.I.E.L.D. USED.
ANY CAMERAS SEE NOTHING BUT A DIGITAL BLUR.

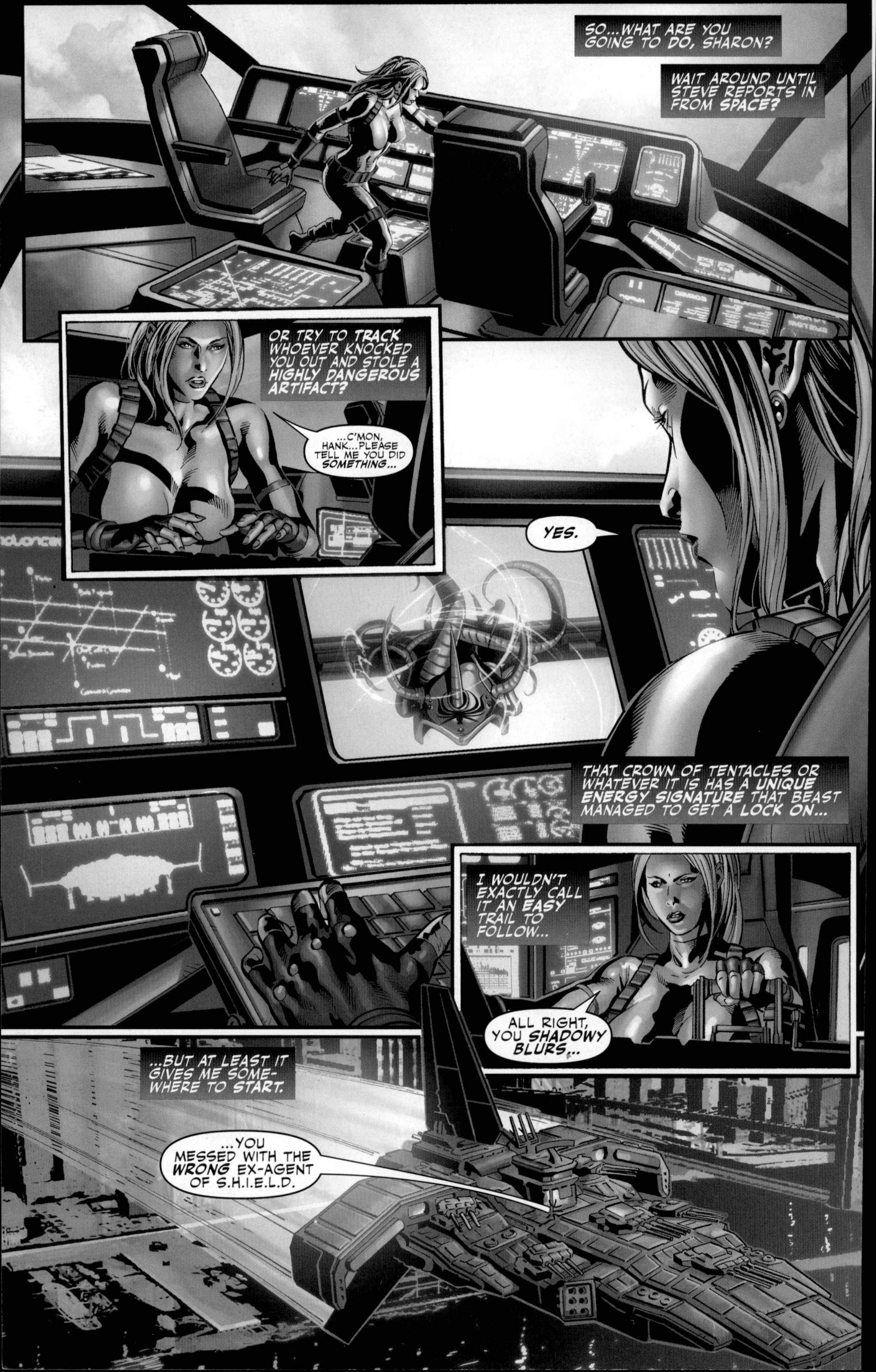
SO...WHAT ARE YOU GOING TO DO, SHARON?
WAIT AROUND UNTIL STEVE REPORTS IN FROM SPACE?
OR TRY TO TRACK WHOEVER KNOCKED YOU OUT AND STOLE A HIGHLY DANGEROUS ARTIFACT?
...C'MON, HANK...PLEASE TELL ME YOU DID SOMETHING...
YES.
THAT CROWN OF TENTACLES OR WHATEVER IT IS HAS A UNIQUE ENERGY SIGNATURE THAT BEAST MANAGED TO GET A LOCK ON...
I WOULDN'T EXACTLY CALL IT AN EASY TRAIL TO FOLLOW...
ALL RIGHT, YOU SHADOWY BLURS...
...BUT AT LEAST IT GIVES ME SOME-WHERE TO START.
...YOU MESSED WITH THE WRONG EX-AGENT OF S.H.I.E.L.D.

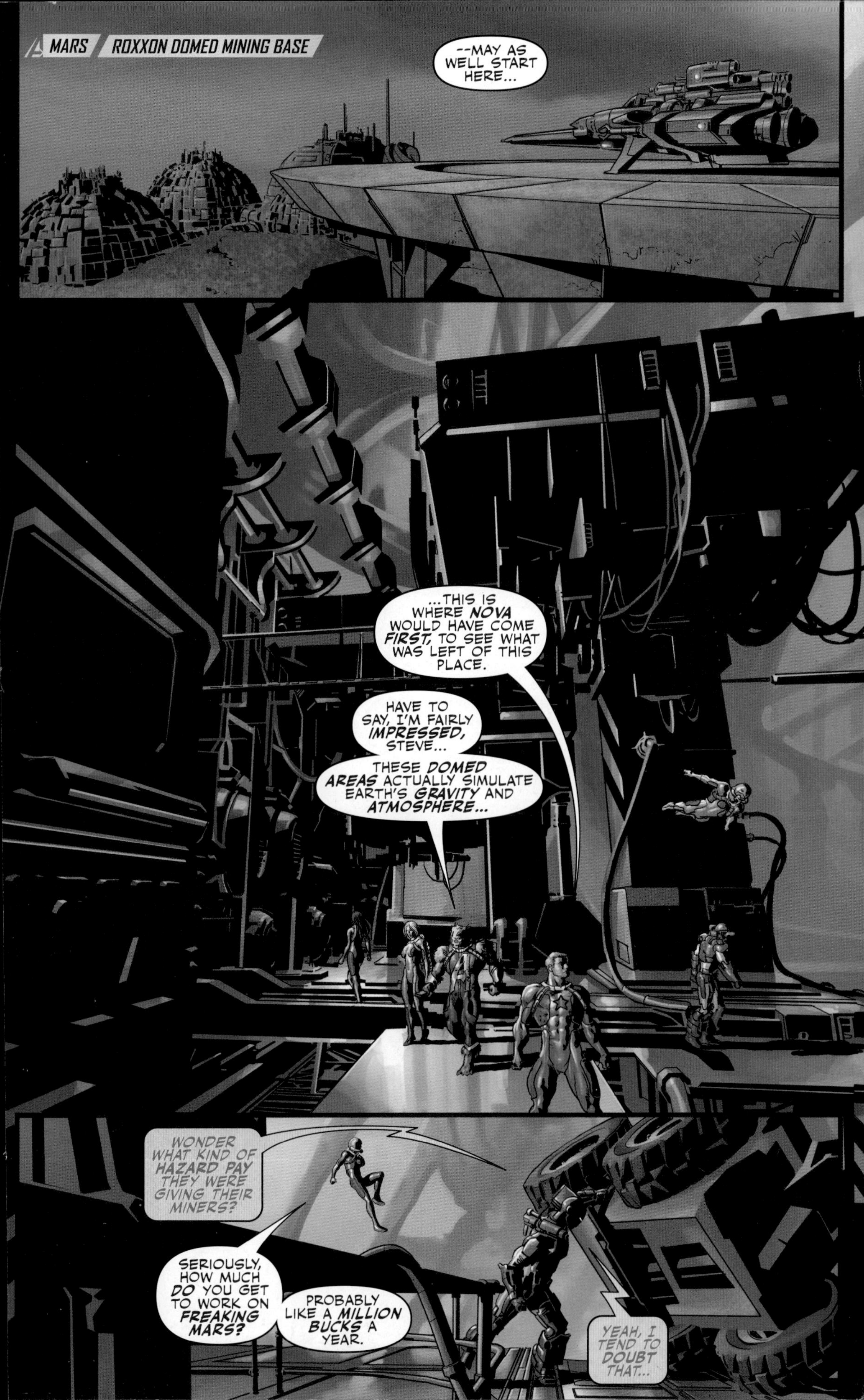
MARS
ROXXON DOMED MINING BASE
--MAY AS WELL START HERE...
...THIS IS WHERE NOVA WOULD HAVE COME FIRST, TO SEE WHAT WAS LEFT OF THIS PLACE.
HAVE TO SAY, I'M FAIRLY IMPRESSED, STEVE...
THESE DOMED AREAS ACTUALLY SIMULATE EARTH'S GRAVITY AND ATMOSPHERE...
WONDER WHAT KIND OF HAZARD PAY THEY WERE GIVING THEIR MINERS?
SERIOUSLY, HOW MUCH DO YOU GET TO WORK ON FREAKING MARS?
PROBABLY LIKE A MILLION BUCKS A YEAR.
YEAH, I TEND TO DOUBT THAT...

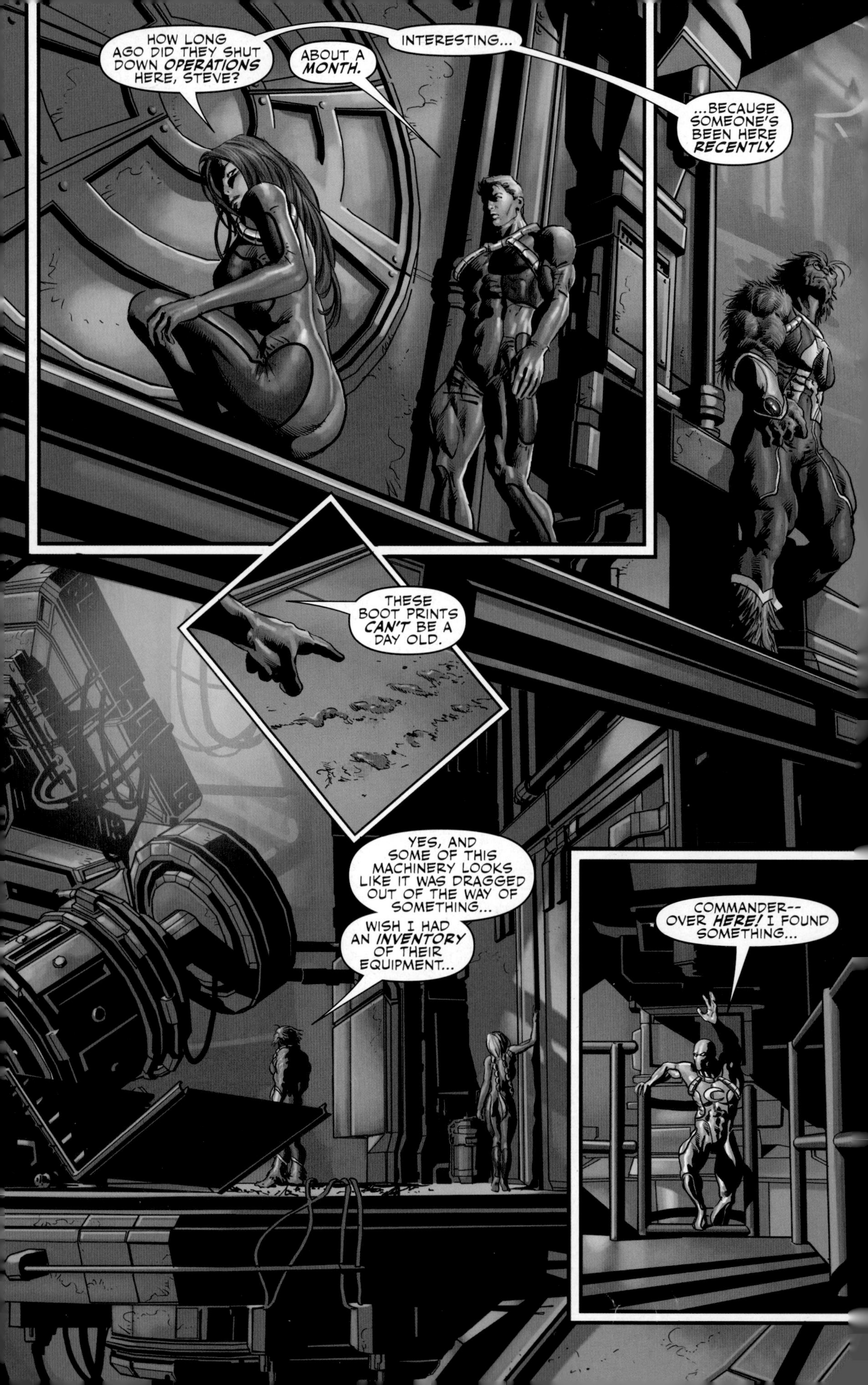
HOW LONG AGO DID THEY SHUT DOWN *OPERATIONS* HERE, STEVE?
ABOUT A *MONTH.*
INTERESTING...
...BECAUSE SOMEONE'S BEEN HERE *RECENTLY.*
THESE BOOT PRINTS *CAN'T* BE A DAY OLD.
YES, AND SOME OF THIS MACHINERY LOOKS LIKE IT WAS DRAGGED OUT OF THE WAY OF SOMETHING...
WISH I HAD AN *INVENTORY* OF THEIR EQUIPMENT...
COMMANDER-- OVER *HERE!* I FOUND SOMETHING...

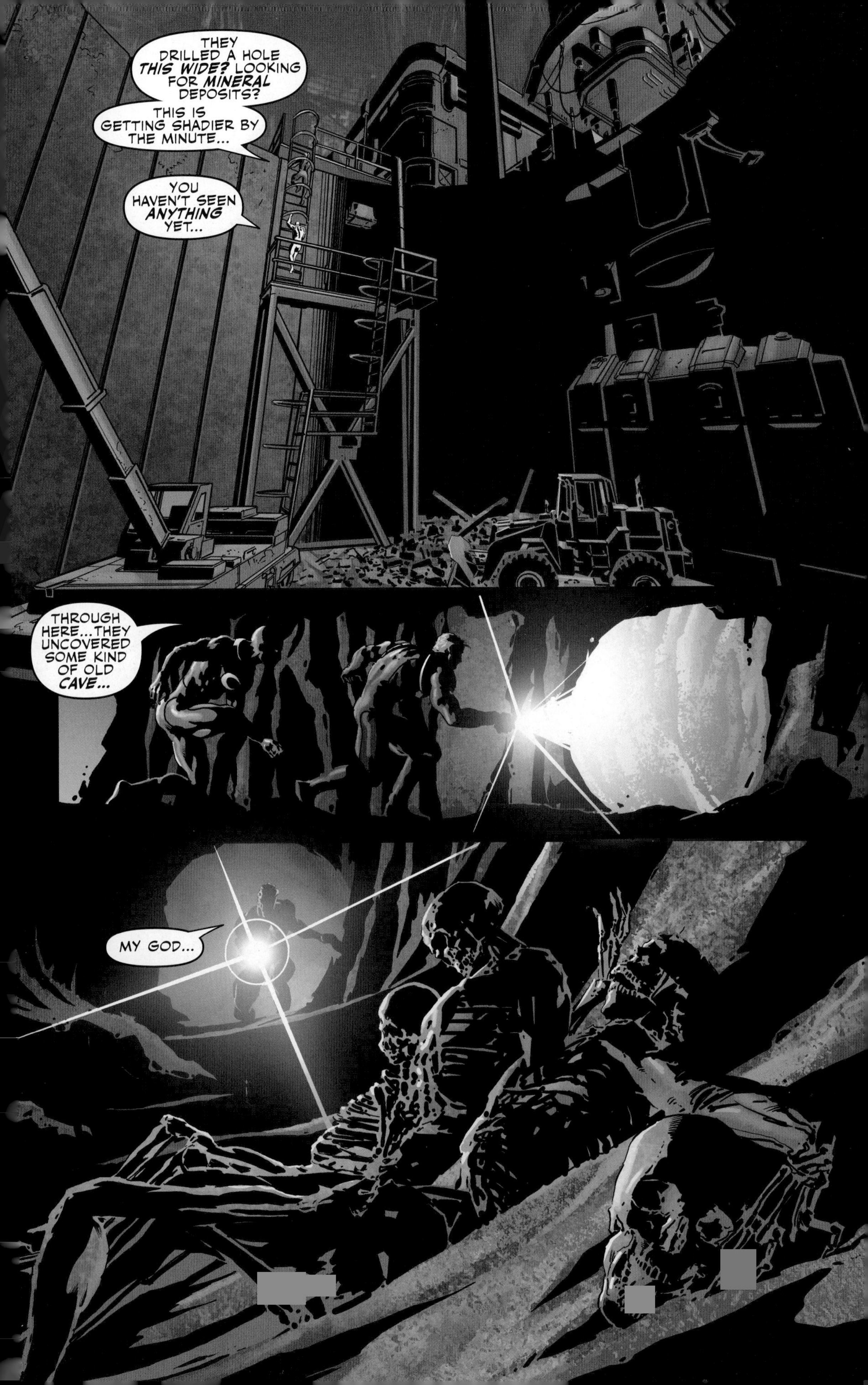
THEY DRILLED A HOLE THIS WIDE? LOOKING FOR MINERAL DEPOSITS?
THIS IS GETTING SHADIER BY THE MINUTE...
YOU HAVEN'T SEEN ANYTHING YET...
THROUGH HERE...THEY UNCOVERED SOME KIND OF OLD CAVE...
MY GOD...

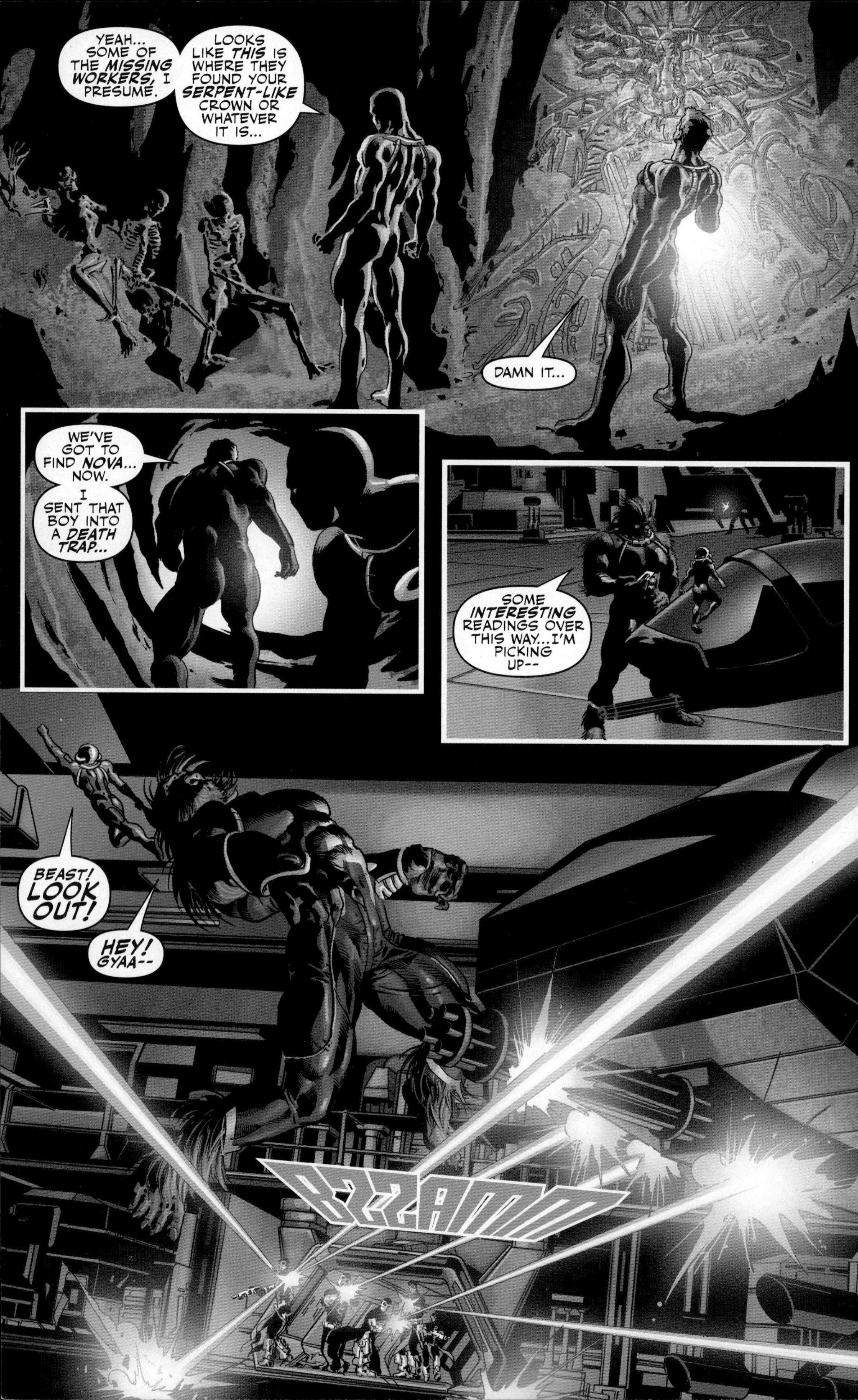
YEAH... SOME OF THE MISSING WORKERS, I PRESUME.
LOOKS LIKE THIS IS WHERE THEY FOUND YOUR SERPENT-LIKE CROWN OR WHATEVER IT IS...
DAMN IT...
WE'VE GOT TO FIND NOVA... NOW.
I SENT THAT BOY INTO A DEATH TRAP...
SOME INTERESTING READINGS OVER THIS WAY...I'M PICKING UP--
BEAST! LOOK OUT!
HEY! GYAA--
BZZAMM

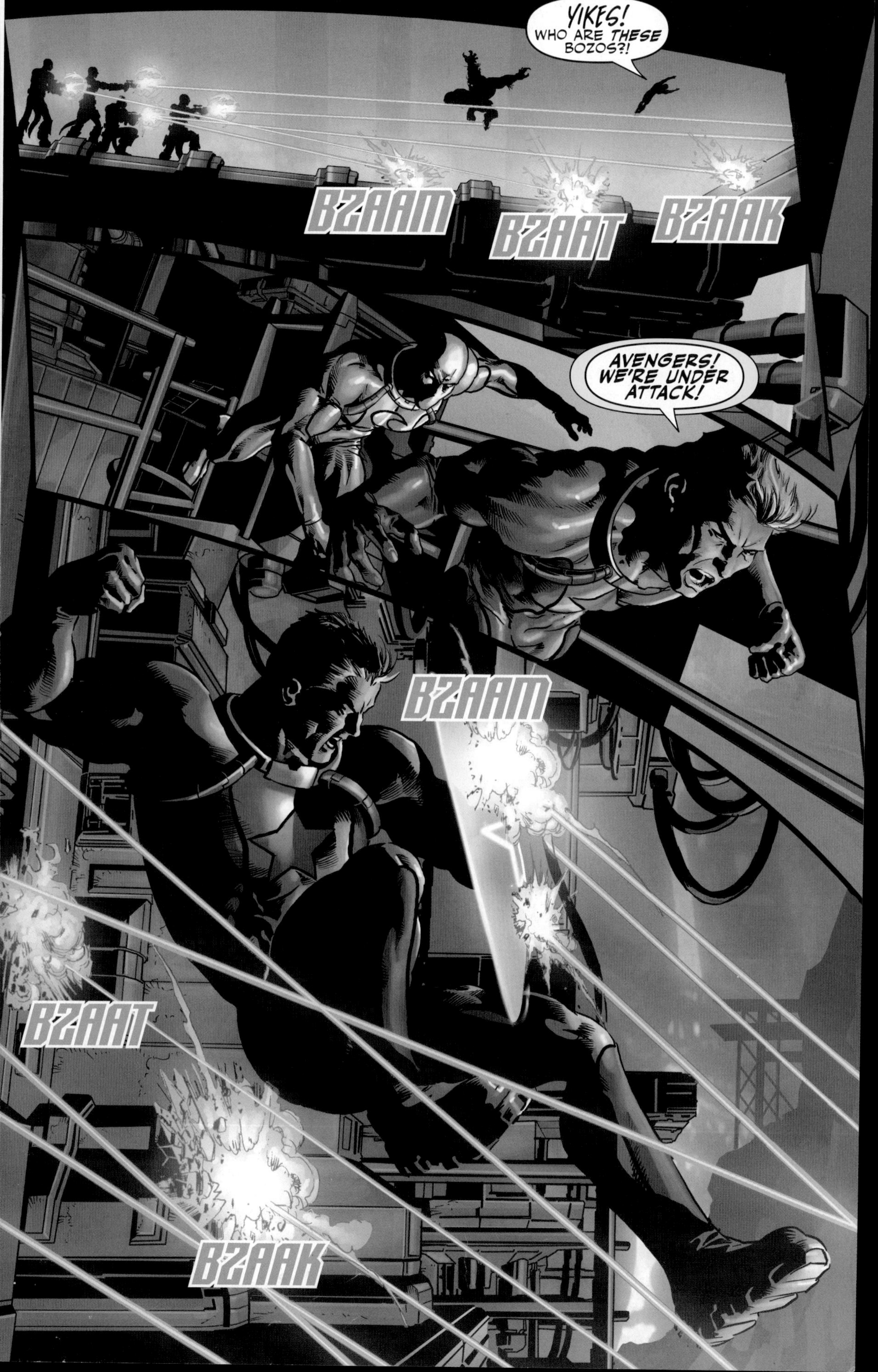
YIKES! WHO ARE THESE BOZOS?!
BZAAM
BZAAT
BZAAK
AVENGERS! WE'RE UNDER ATTACK!
BZAAM
BZAAT
BZAAK

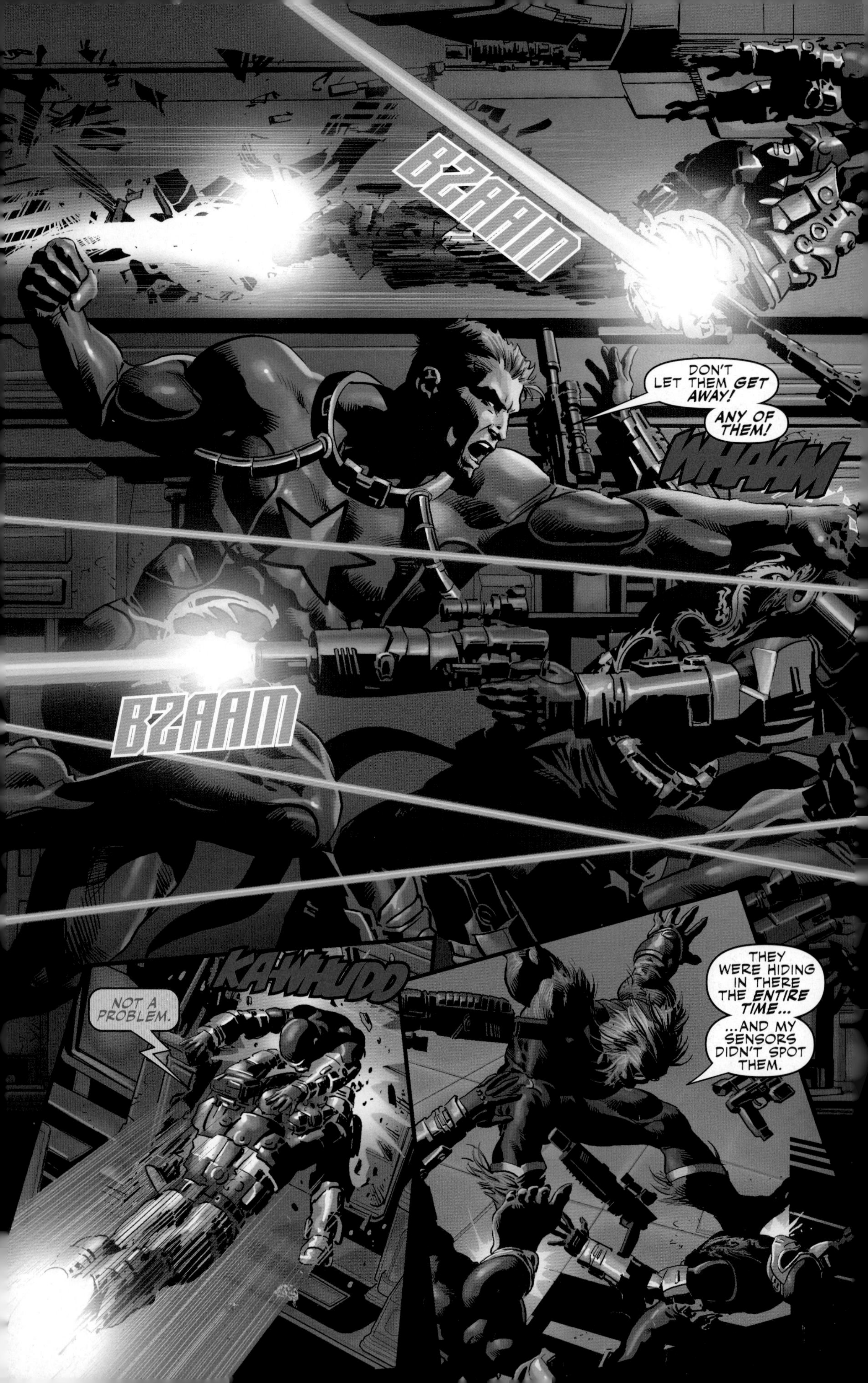
BZAAM
DON'T LET THEM GET AWAY!
ANY OF THEM!
WHAAM
BZAAM
KA-WHUDD
NOT A PROBLEM.
THEY WERE HIDING IN THERE THE ENTIRE TIME...
...AND MY SENSORS DIDN'T SPOT THEM.

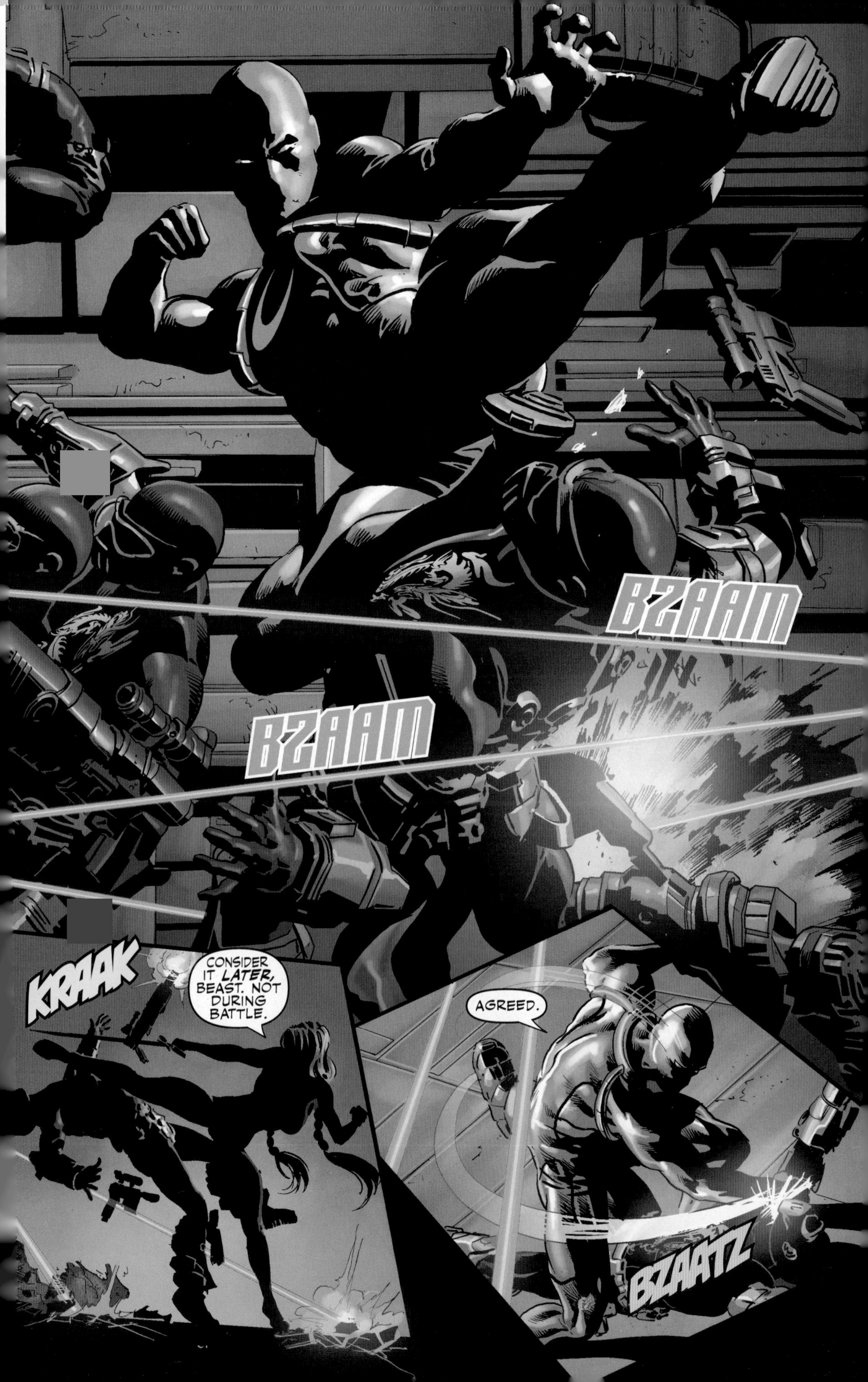
BZAAM
BZAAM
KRAAK
CONSIDER IT LATER, BEAST. NOT DURING BATTLE.
AGREED.
BZAATZ

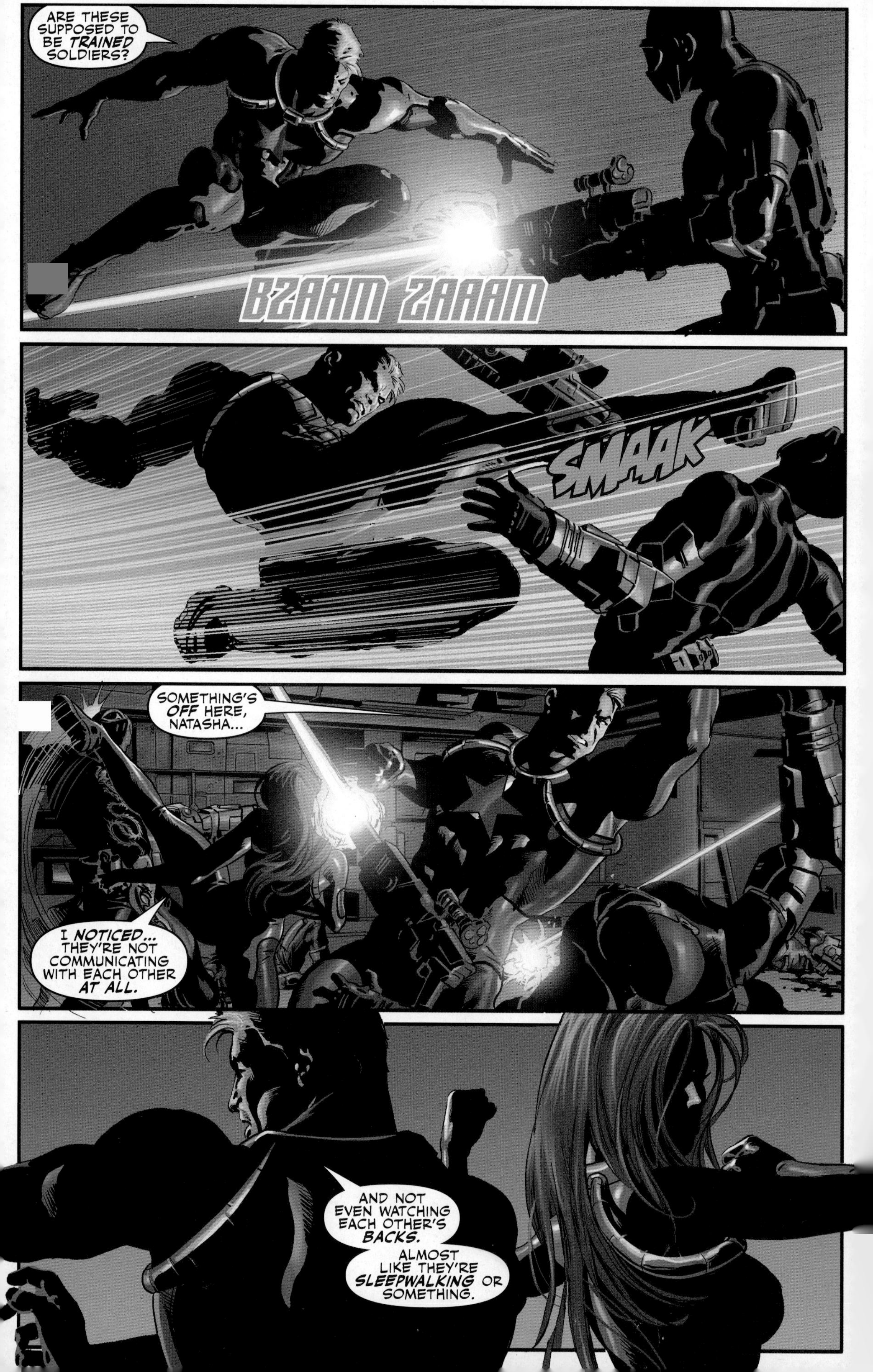

ARE THESE SUPPOSED TO BE *TRAINED* SOLDIERS?
BZAAM ZAAAM
SMAAK
SOMETHING'S *OFF* HERE, NATASHA...
I *NOTICED*... THEY'RE NOT COMMUNICATING WITH EACH OTHER *AT ALL.*
AND NOT EVEN WATCHING EACH OTHER'S *BACKS.*
ALMOST LIKE THEY'RE *SLEEPWALKING* OR SOMETHING.

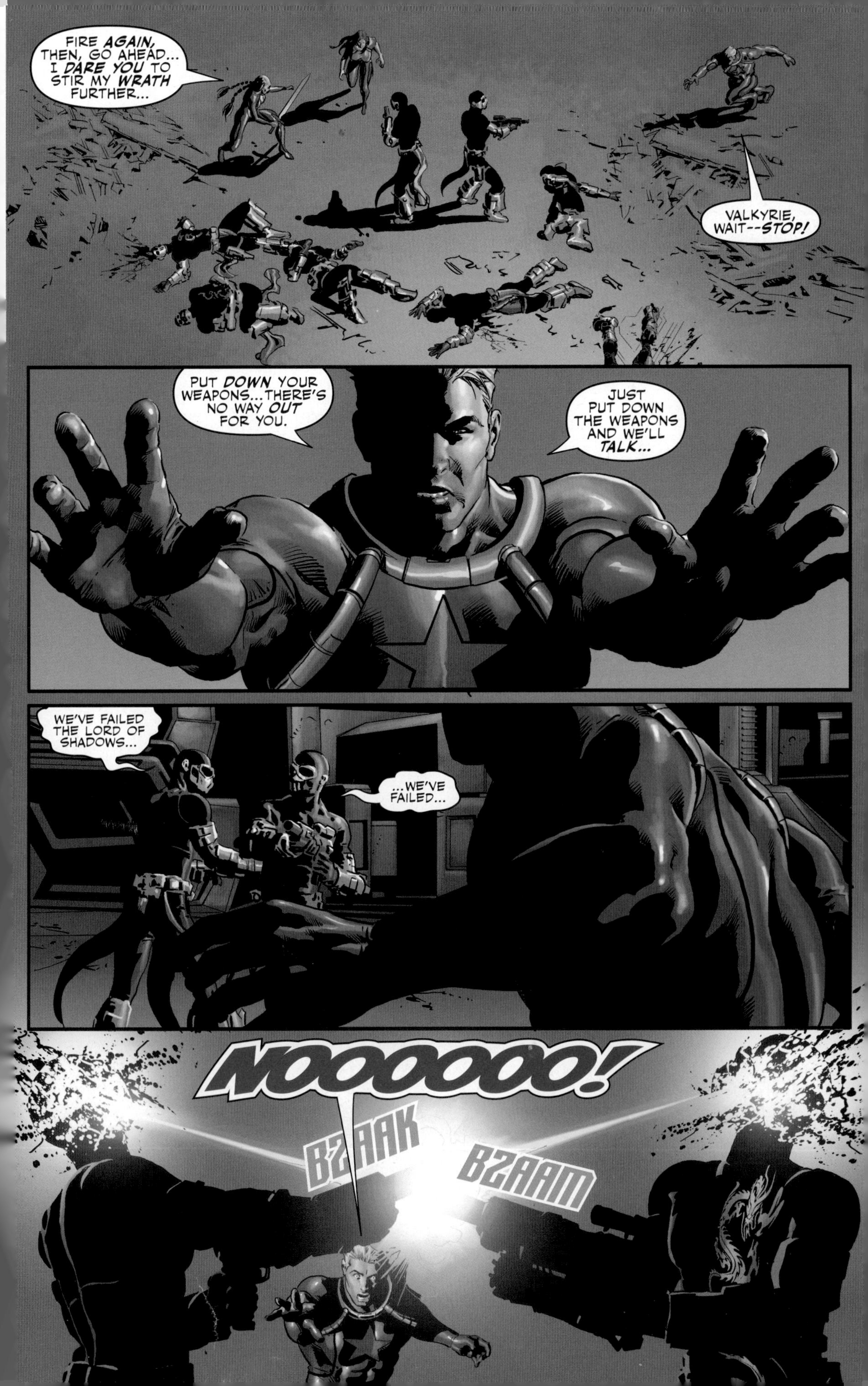
FIRE AGAIN, THEN, GO AHEAD... I DARE YOU TO STIR MY WRATH FURTHER...
VALKYRIE, WAIT--STOP!
PUT DOWN YOUR WEAPONS...THERE'S NO WAY OUT FOR YOU.
JUST PUT DOWN THE WEAPONS AND WE'LL TALK...
WE'VE FAILED THE LORD OF SHADOWS...
...WE'VE FAILED...
NOOOOOO!
BZAAK
BZAAM

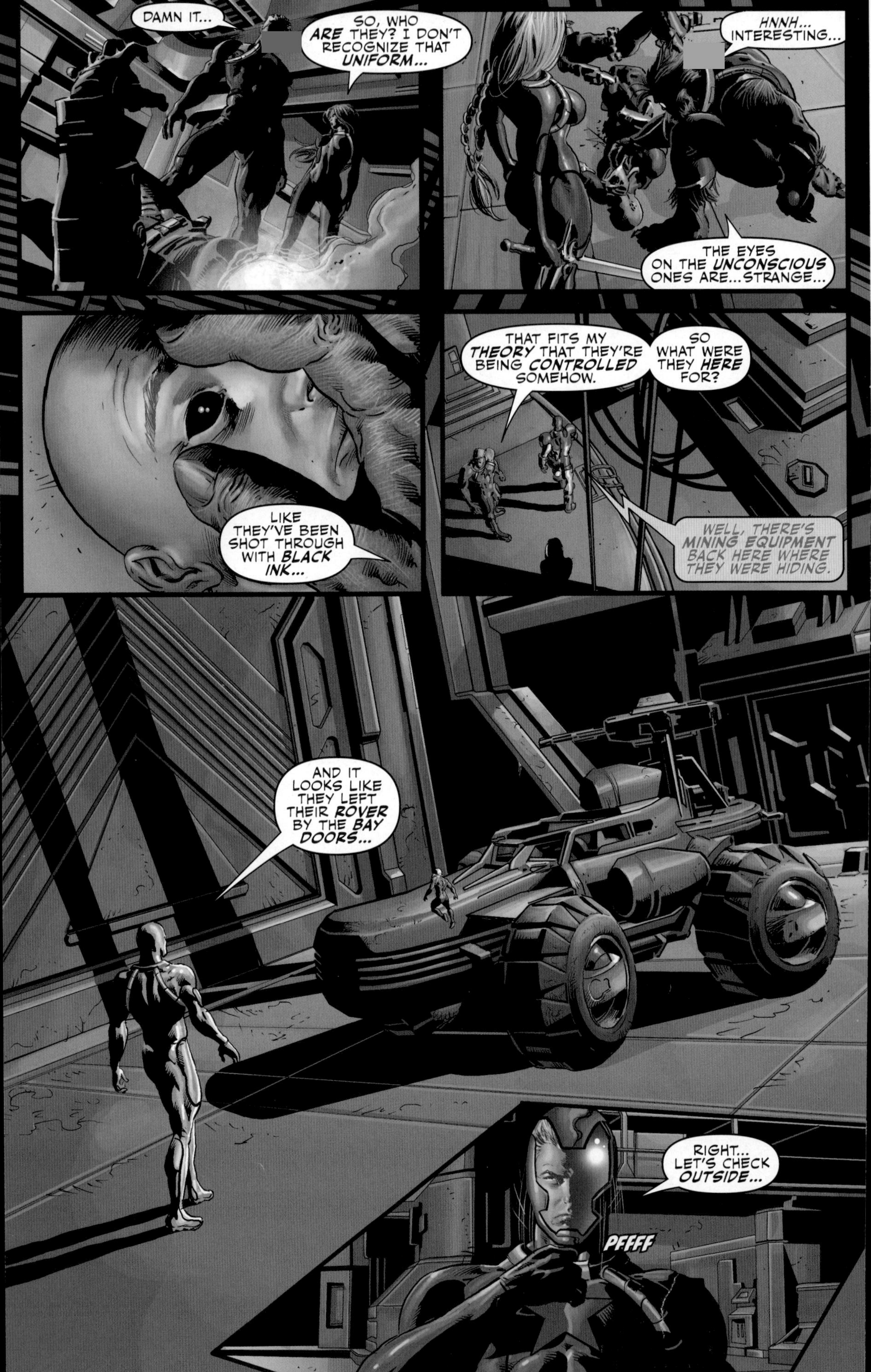
DAMN IT...
SO, WHO ARE THEY? I DON'T RECOGNIZE THAT UNIFORM...
HNNH... INTERESTING...
THE EYES ON THE UNCONSCIOUS ONES ARE... STRANGE...
LIKE THEY'VE BEEN SHOT THROUGH WITH BLACK INK...
THAT FITS MY THEORY THAT THEY'RE BEING CONTROLLED SOMEHOW.
SO WHAT WERE THEY HERE FOR?
WELL, THERE'S MINING EQUIPMENT BACK HERE WHERE THEY WERE HIDING.
AND IT LOOKS LIKE THEY LEFT THEIR ROVER BY THE BAY DOORS...
RIGHT... LET'S CHECK OUTSIDE...
PFFFF

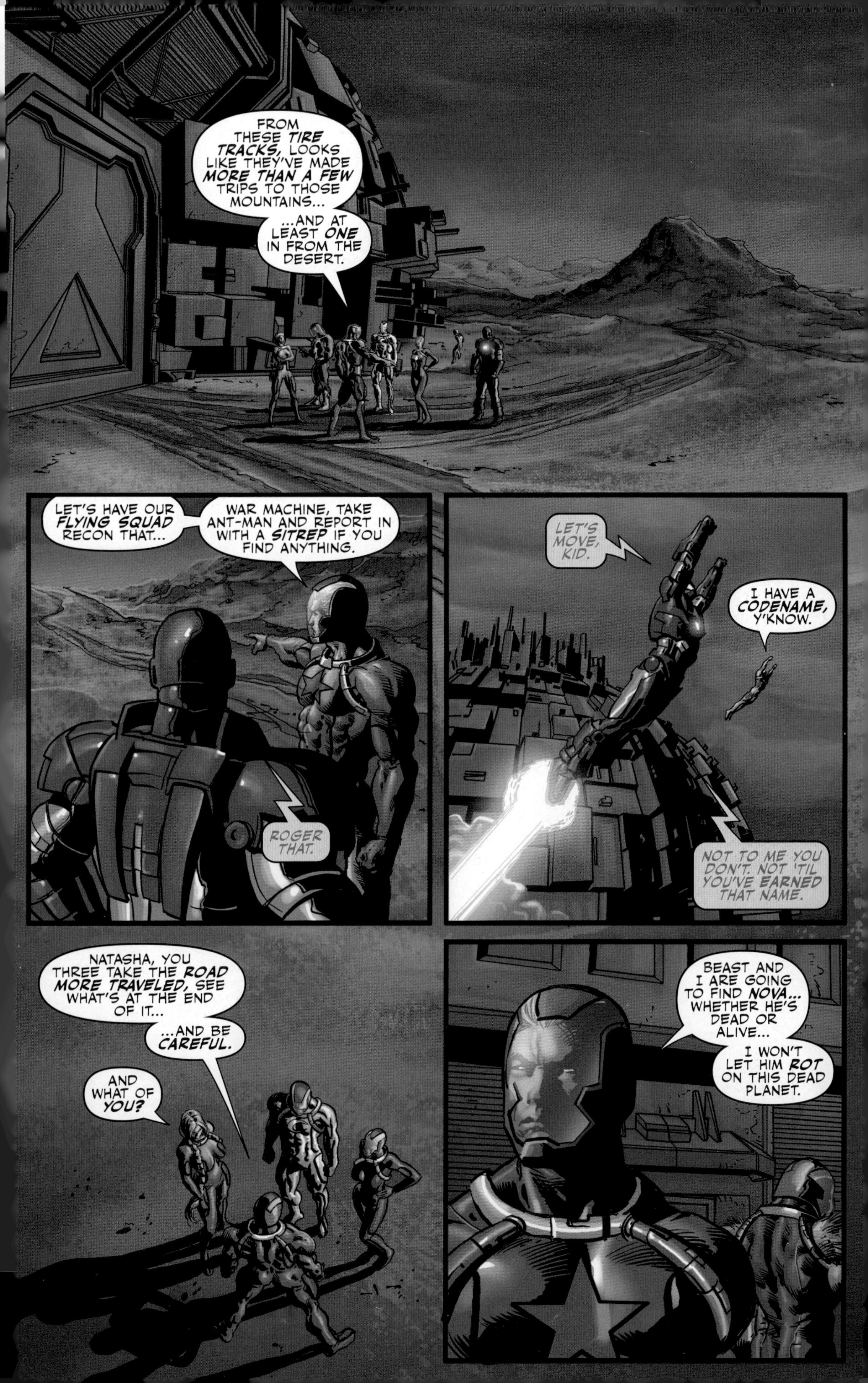
FROM THESE TIRE TRACKS, LOOKS LIKE THEY'VE MADE MORE THAN A FEW TRIPS TO THOSE MOUNTAINS...
...AND AT LEAST ONE IN FROM THE DESERT.
LET'S HAVE OUR FLYING SQUAD RECON THAT...
WAR MACHINE, TAKE ANT-MAN AND REPORT IN WITH A SITREP IF YOU FIND ANYTHING.
ROGER THAT.
LET'S MOVE, KID.
I HAVE A CODENAME, Y'KNOW.
NOT TO ME YOU DON'T. NOT 'TIL YOU'VE EARNED THAT NAME.
NATASHA, YOU THREE TAKE THE ROAD MORE TRAVELED, SEE WHAT'S AT THE END OF IT...
...AND BE CAREFUL.
AND WHAT OF YOU?
BEAST AND I ARE GOING TO FIND NOVA... WHETHER HE'S DEAD OR ALIVE...
I WON'T LET HIM ROT ON THIS DEAD PLANET.

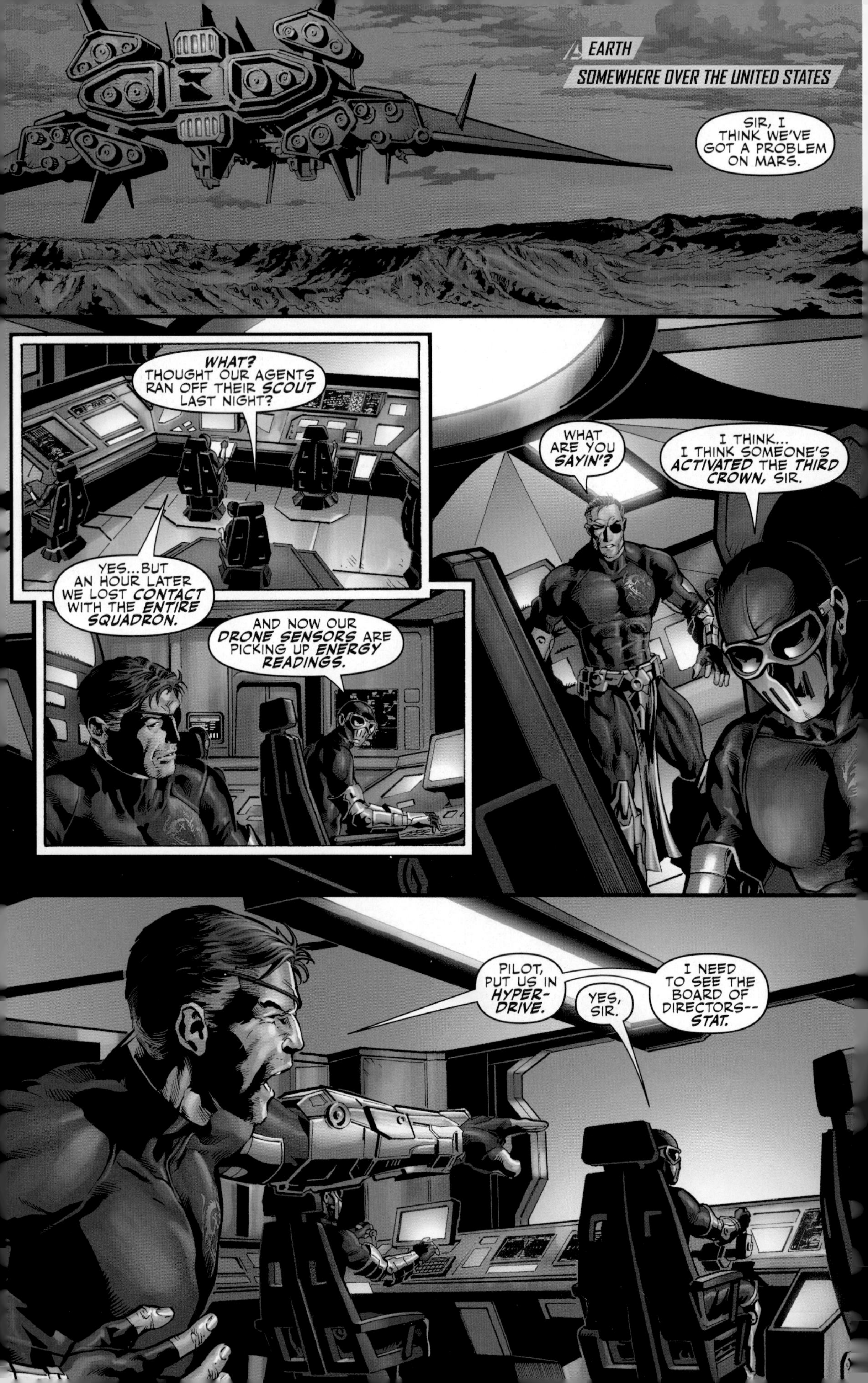
EARTH
SOMEWHERE OVER THE UNITED STATES
SIR, I THINK WE'VE GOT A PROBLEM ON MARS.
WHAT? THOUGHT OUR AGENTS RAN OFF THEIR SCOUT LAST NIGHT?
YES...BUT AN HOUR LATER WE LOST CONTACT WITH THE ENTIRE SQUADRON.
AND NOW OUR DRONE SENSORS ARE PICKING UP ENERGY READINGS.
WHAT ARE YOU SAYIN'?
I THINK... I THINK SOMEONE'S ACTIVATED THE THIRD CROWN, SIR.
PILOT, PUT US IN HYPER-DRIVE.
YES, SIR.
I NEED TO SEE THE BOARD OF DIRECTORS--STAT.

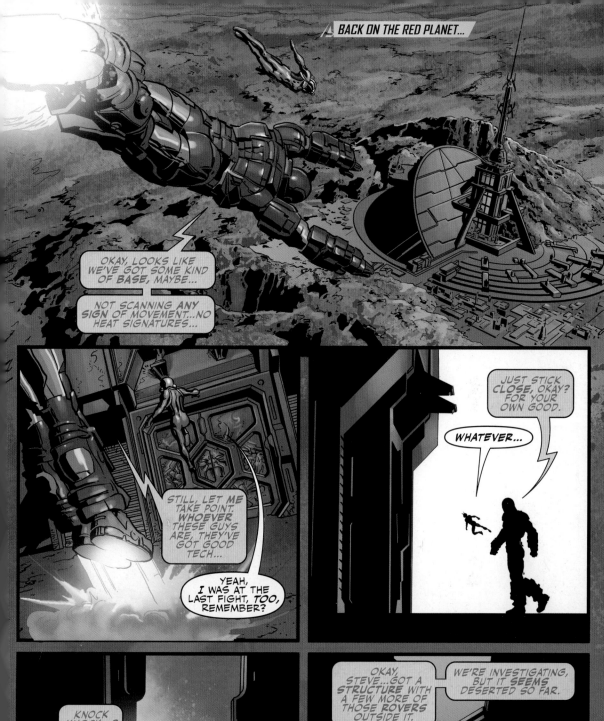

OKAY, LOOKS LIKE WE'VE GOT SOME KIND OF *BASE*, MAYBE...

NOT SCANNING ANY SIGN OF MOVEMENT...NO HEAT SIGNATURES...

JUST STICK *CLOSE*, OKAY? FOR YOUR OWN GOOD.

*WHATEVER*...

STILL, LET ME TAKE POINT. *WHOEVER* THESE GUYS ARE, THEY'VE GOT GOOD TECH...

YEAH, I WAS AT THE LAST FIGHT, *TOO*, REMEMBER?

KNOCK KNOCK...?

KREEEEKKK

OKAY, STEVE...GOT A STRUCTURE WITH A FEW MORE OF THOSE *ROVERS* OUTSIDE IT.

WE'RE INVESTIGATING, BUT IT *SEEMS* DESERTED SO FAR.

ROGER THAT. GATHER ANY *INTEL* YOU CAN ON OUR NEW FRIENDS...

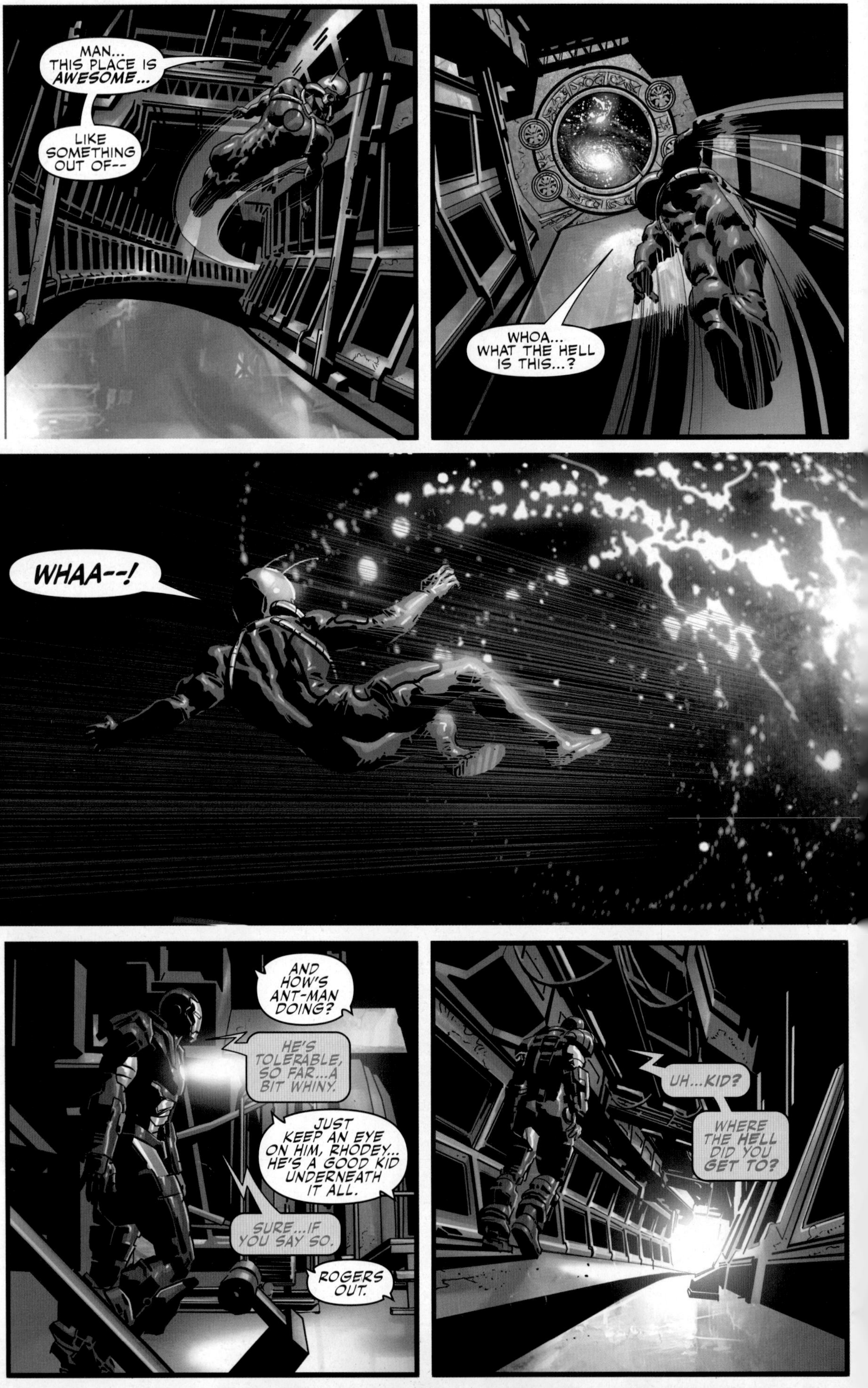
MAN... THIS PLACE IS AWESOME...
LIKE SOMETHING OUT OF--
WHOA... WHAT THE HELL IS THIS...?
WHAA--!
AND HOW'S ANT-MAN DOING?
HE'S TOLERABLE, SO FAR...A BIT WHINY.
JUST KEEP AN EYE ON HIM, RHODEY... HE'S A GOOD KID UNDERNEATH IT ALL.
SURE...IF YOU SAY SO.
ROGERS OUT.
UH...KID?
WHERE THE HELL DID YOU GET TO?

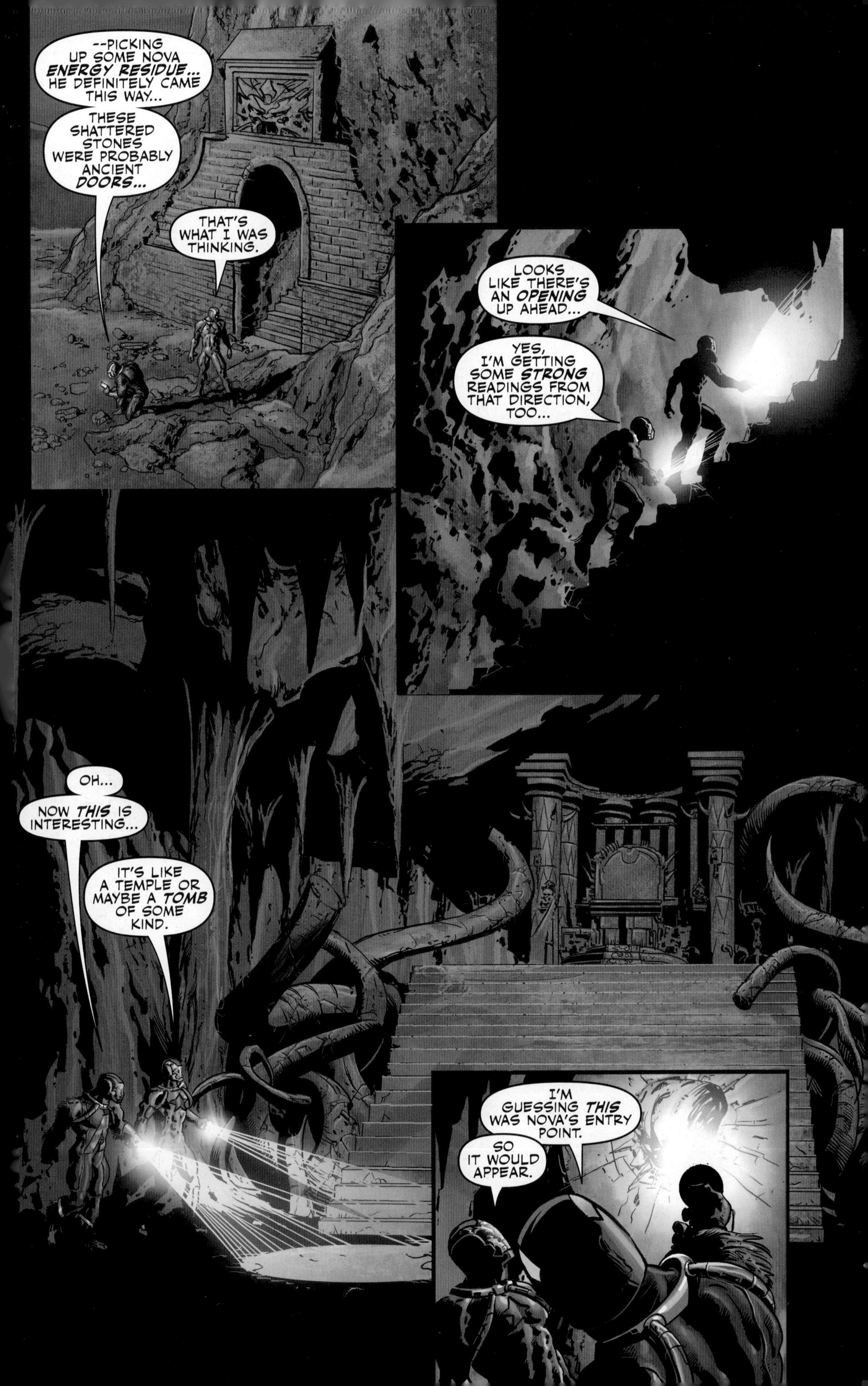
--PICKING UP SOME NOVA ENERGY RESIDUE... HE DEFINITELY CAME THIS WAY...
THESE SHATTERED STONES WERE PROBABLY ANCIENT DOORS...
THAT'S WHAT I WAS THINKING.
LOOKS LIKE THERE'S AN OPENING UP AHEAD...
YES, I'M GETTING SOME STRONG READINGS FROM THAT DIRECTION, TOO...
OH...
NOW THIS IS INTERESTING...
IT'S LIKE A TEMPLE OR MAYBE A TOMB OF SOME KIND.
I'M GUESSING THIS WAS NOVA'S ENTRY POINT.
SO IT WOULD APPEAR.

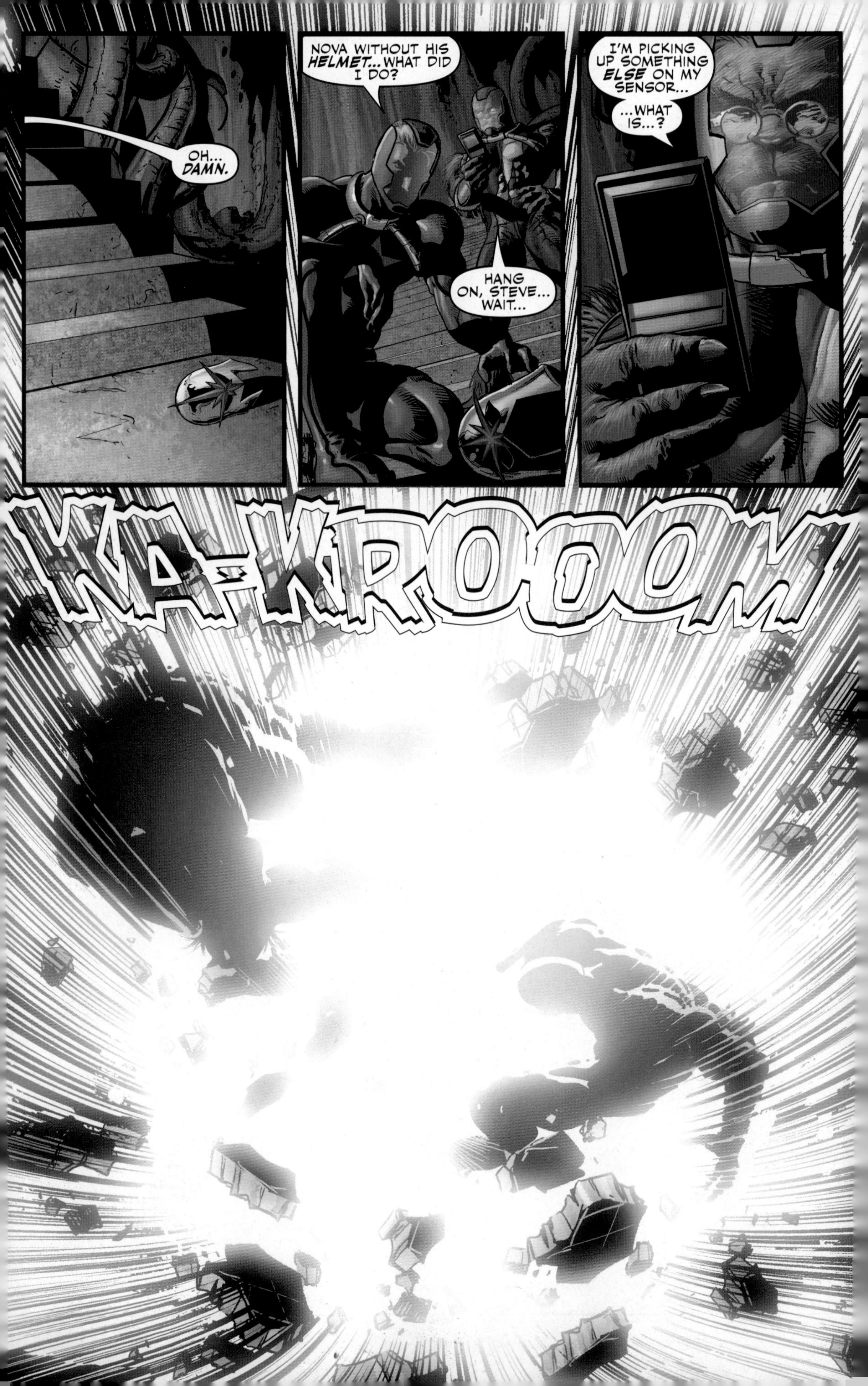
OH... DAMN.
NOVA WITHOUT HIS HELMET... WHAT DID I DO?
HANG ON, STEVE... WAIT...
I'M PICKING UP SOMETHING ELSE ON MY SENSOR...
...WHAT IS...?
KA-KROOOM

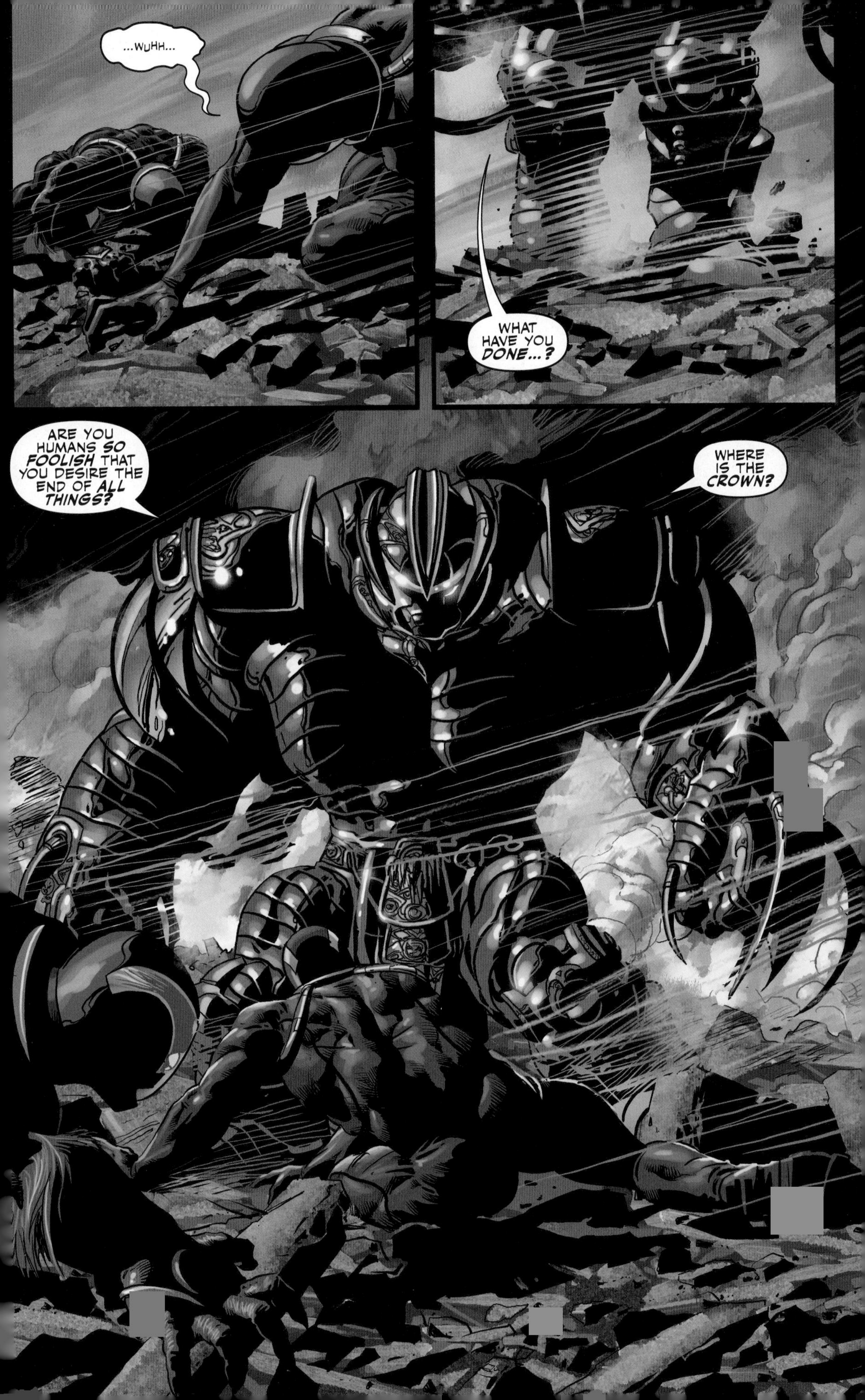
...WUHH...
WHAT HAVE YOU DONE...?
ARE YOU HUMANS SO FOOLISH THAT YOU DESIRE THE END OF ALL THINGS?
WHERE IS THE CROWN?

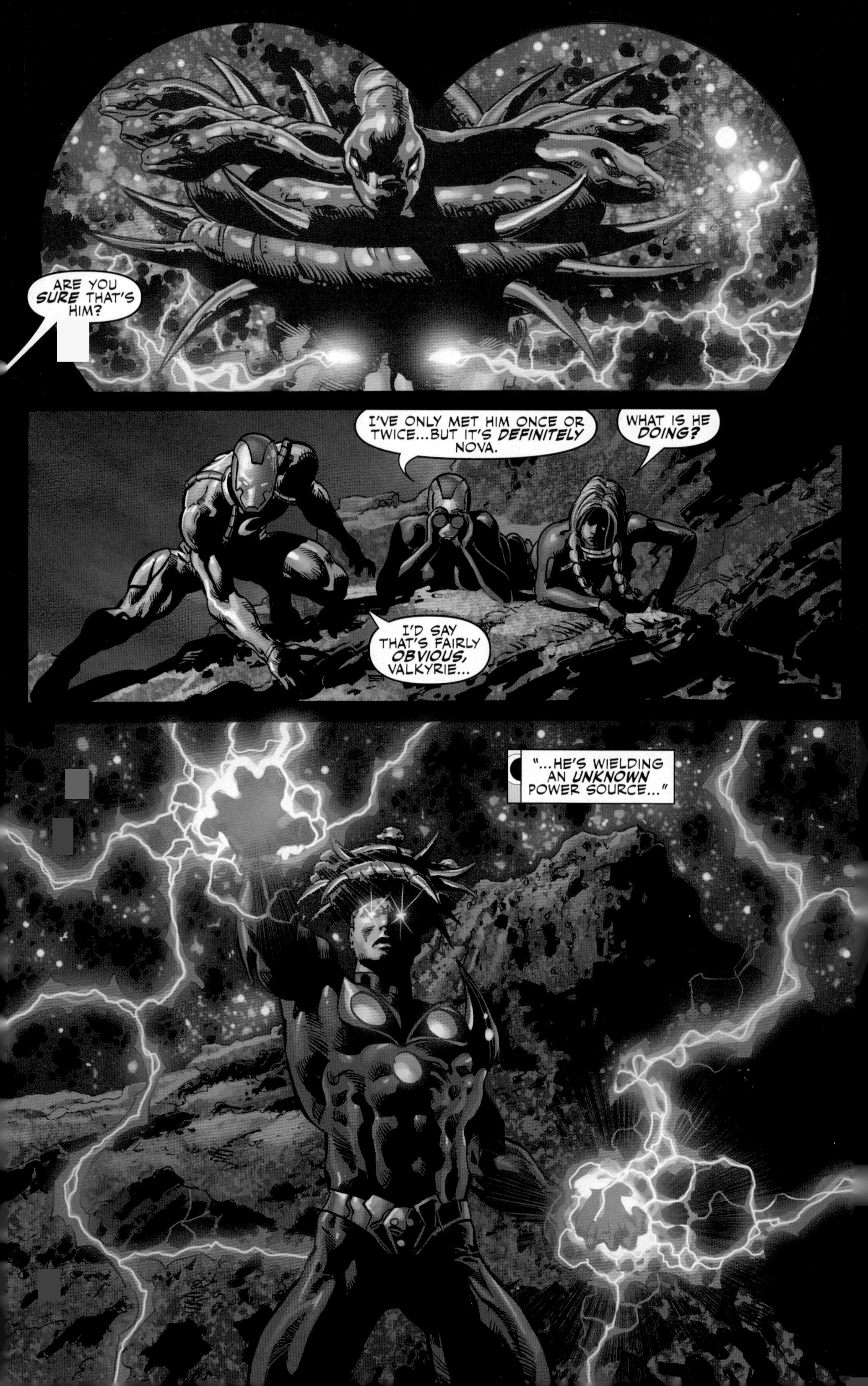
ARE YOU SURE THAT'S HIM?
I'VE ONLY MET HIM ONCE OR TWICE...BUT IT'S DEFINITELY NOVA.
WHAT IS HE DOING?
I'D SAY THAT'S FAIRLY OBVIOUS, VALKYRIE...
"...HE'S WIELDING AN UNKNOWN POWER SOURCE..."

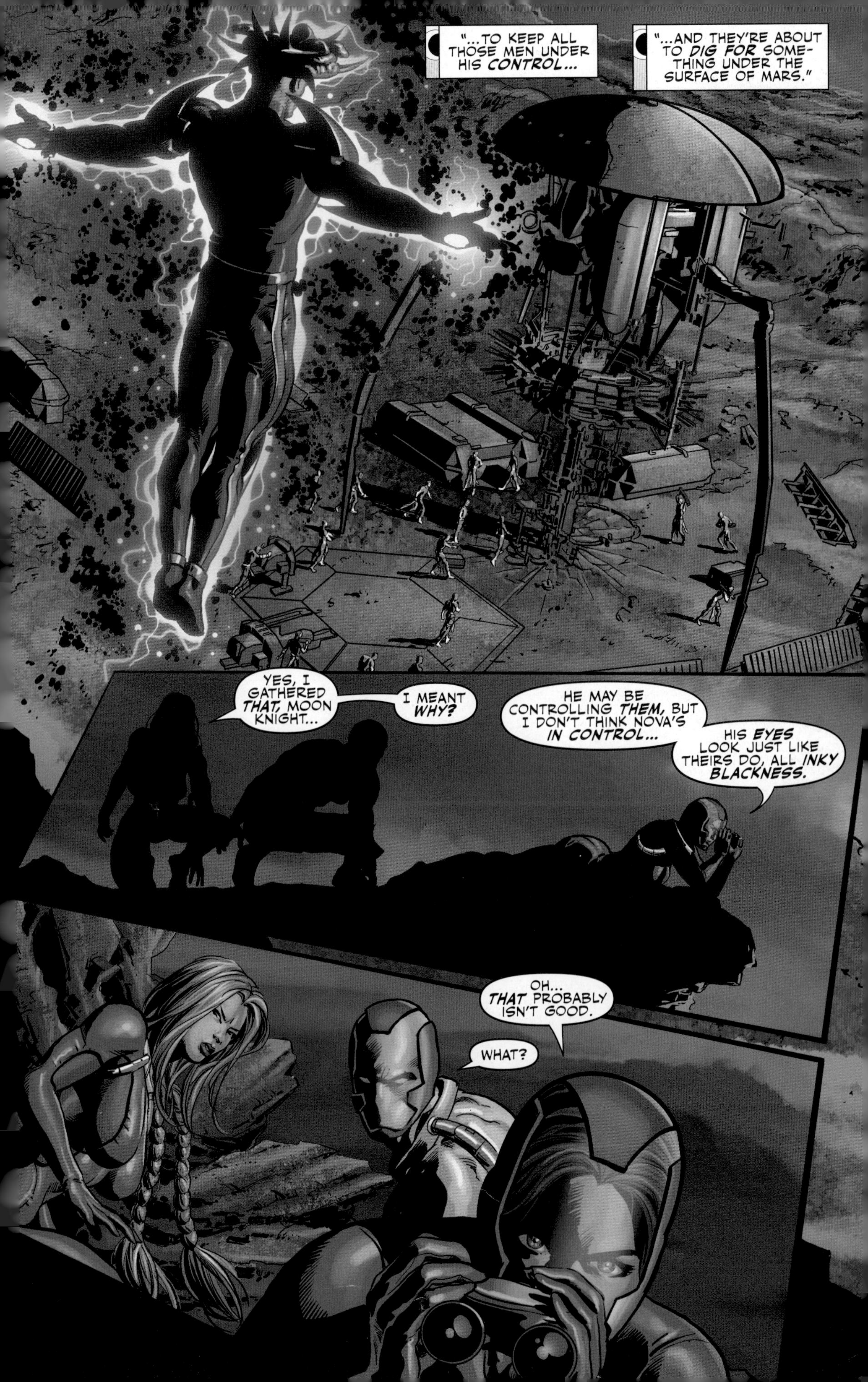
"...TO KEEP ALL THOSE MEN UNDER HIS CONTROL..."
"...AND THEY'RE ABOUT TO DIG FOR SOMETHING UNDER THE SURFACE OF MARS."
YES, I GATHERED THAT, MOON KNIGHT...
I MEANT WHY?
HE MAY BE CONTROLLING THEM, BUT I DON'T THINK NOVA'S IN CONTROL...
HIS EYES LOOK JUST LIKE THEIRS DO, ALL INKY BLACKNESS.
OH... THAT PROBABLY ISN'T GOOD.
WHAT?

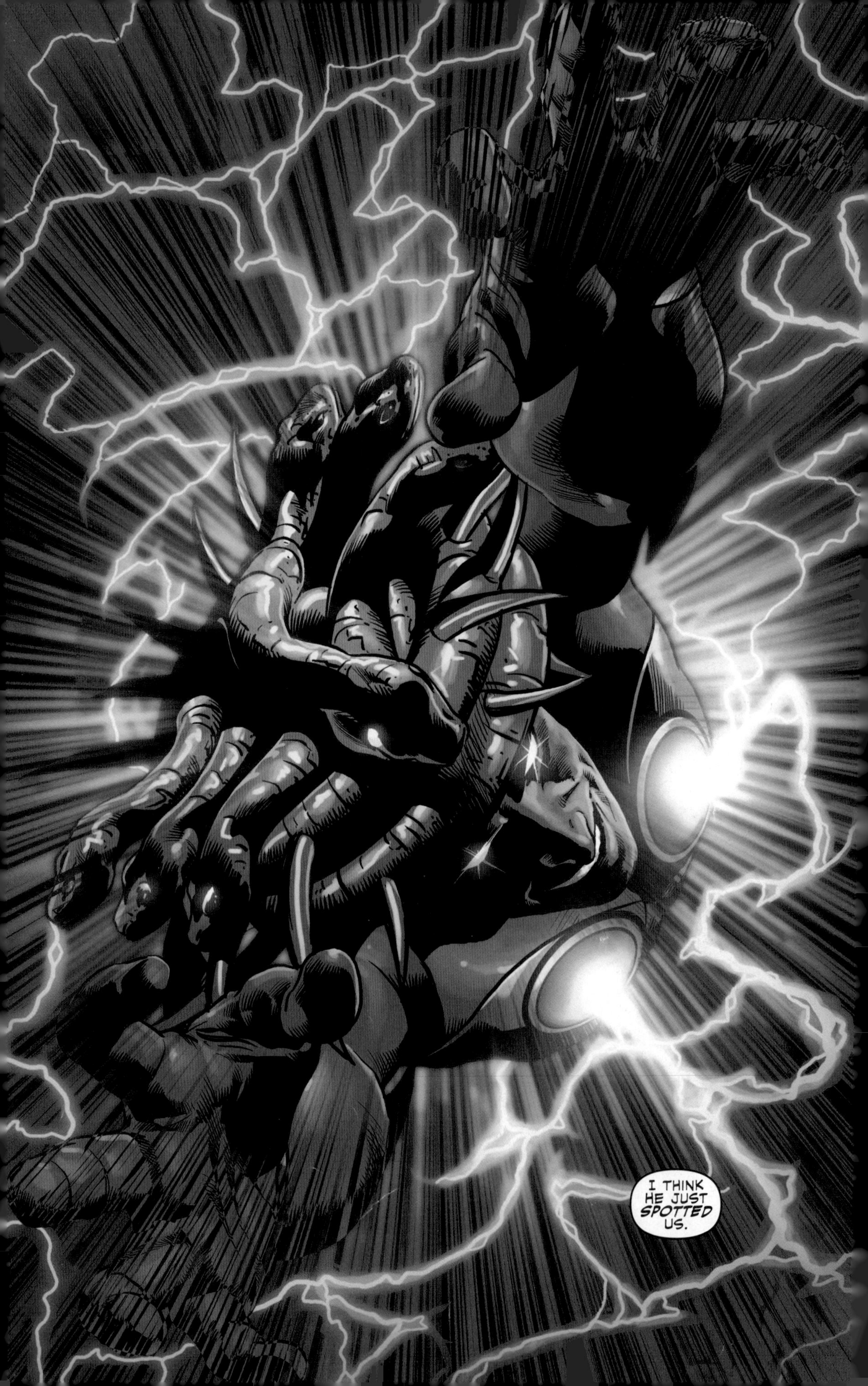
I THINK HE JUST SPOTTED US.

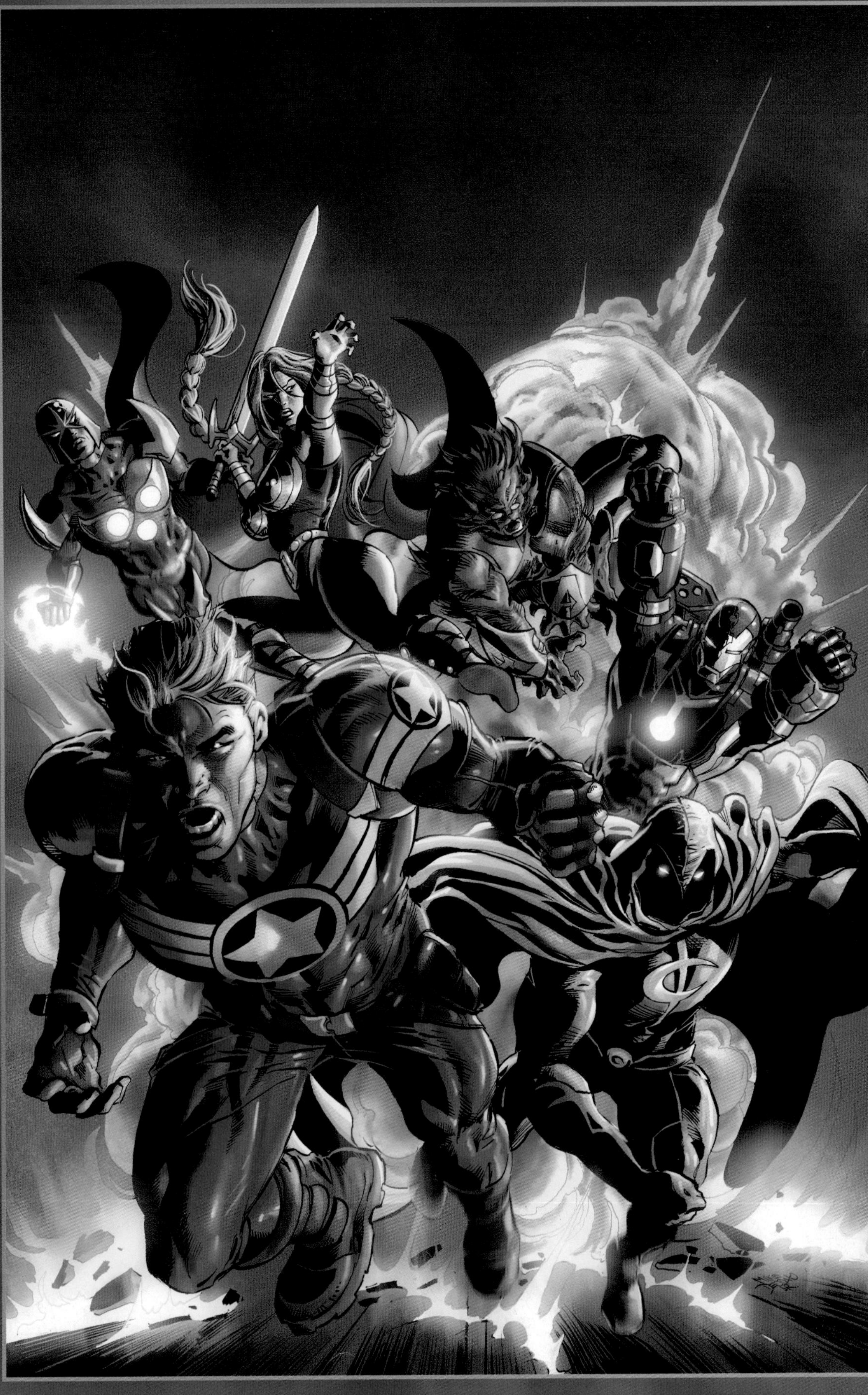

**#2 VARIANT BY MIKE DEODATO & RAIN BEREDO**

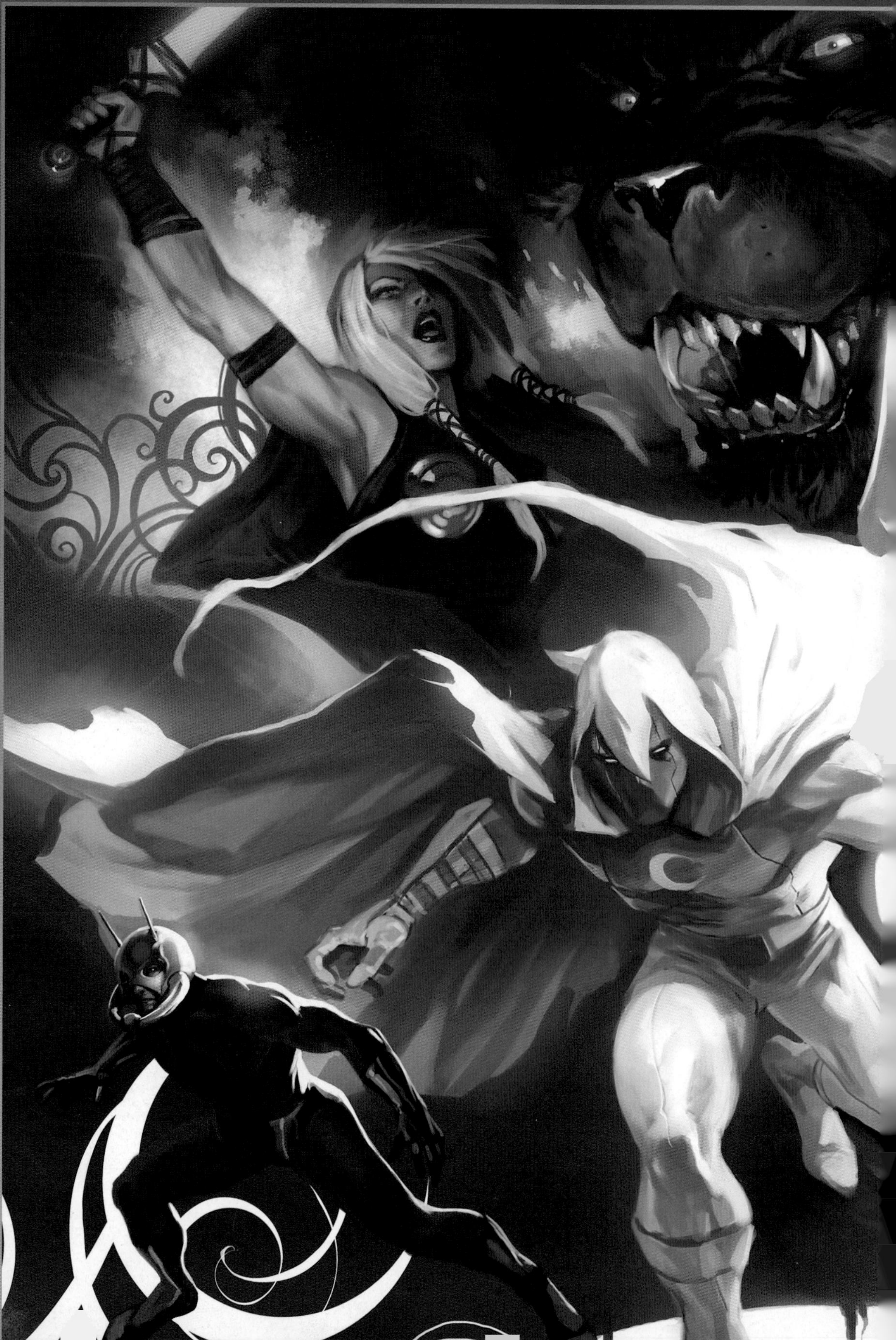

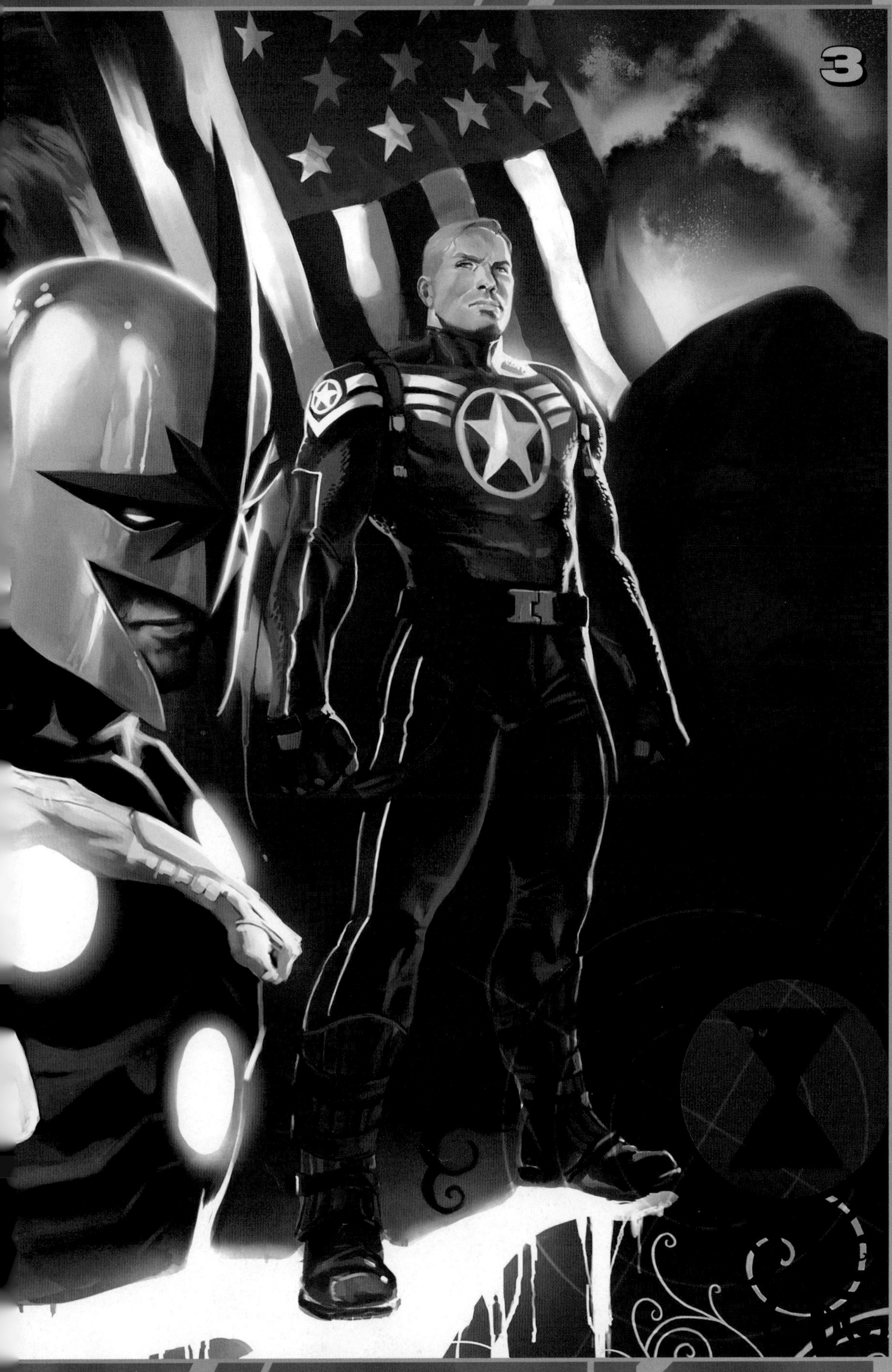
3

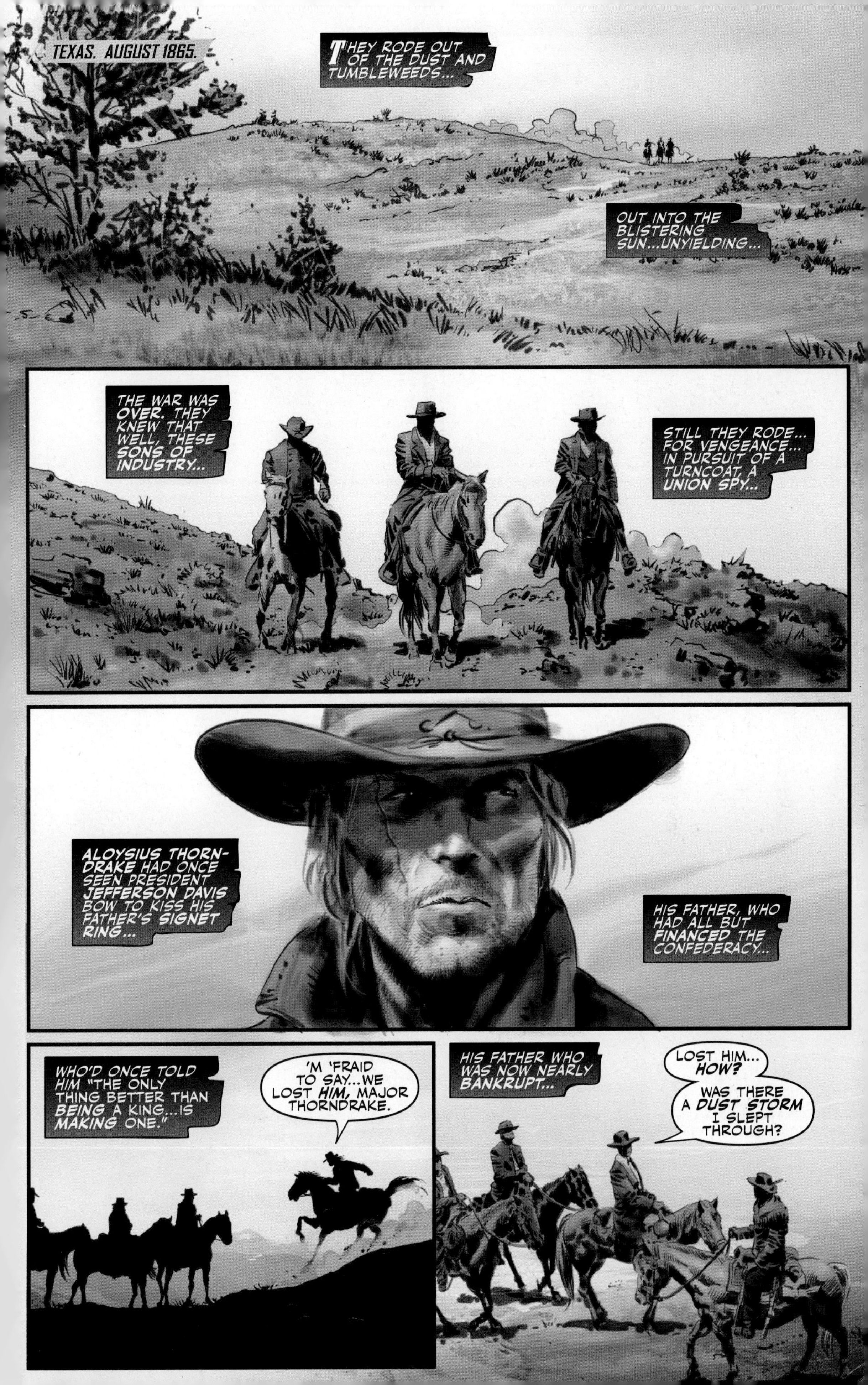
TEXAS. AUGUST 1865.
THEY RODE OUT OF THE DUST AND TUMBLEWEEDS...
OUT INTO THE BLISTERING SUN...UNYIELDING...
THE WAR WAS OVER. THEY KNEW THAT WELL, THESE SONS OF INDUSTRY...
STILL THEY RODE... FOR VENGEANCE... IN PURSUIT OF A TURNCOAT, A UNION SPY...
ALOYSIUS THORNDRAKE HAD ONCE SEEN PRESIDENT JEFFERSON DAVIS BOW TO KISS HIS FATHER'S SIGNET RING...
HIS FATHER, WHO HAD ALL BUT FINANCED THE CONFEDERACY...
WHO'D ONCE TOLD HIM "THE ONLY THING BETTER THAN BEING A KING...IS MAKING ONE."
'M 'FRAID TO SAY...WE LOST HIM, MAJOR THORNDRAKE.
HIS FATHER WHO WAS NOW NEARLY BANKRUPT...
LOST HIM... HOW?
WAS THERE A DUST STORM I SLEPT THROUGH?

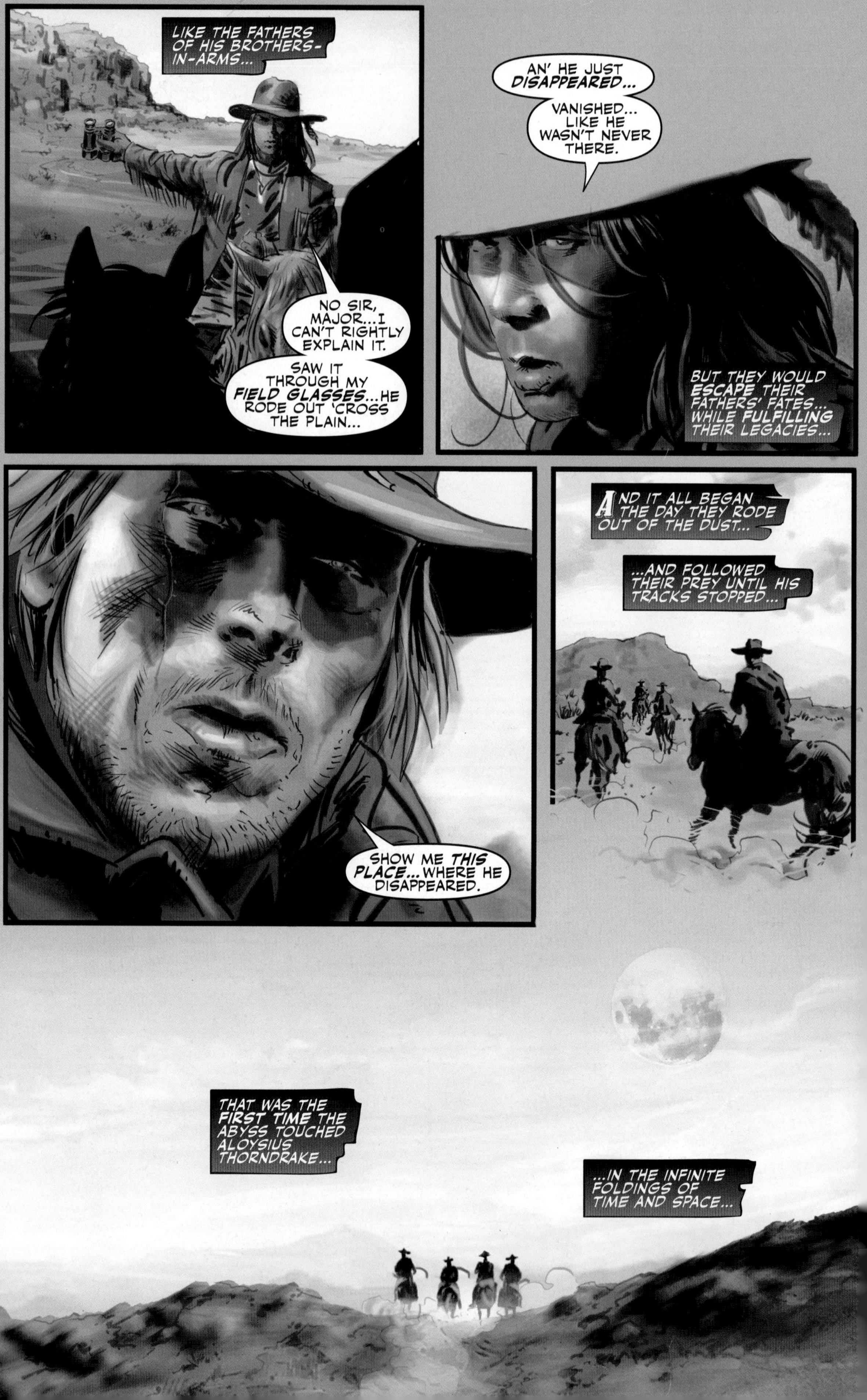
LIKE THE FATHERS OF HIS BROTHERS-IN-ARMS...
NO SIR, MAJOR...I CAN'T RIGHTLY EXPLAIN IT.
SAW IT THROUGH MY FIELD GLASSES...HE RODE OUT 'CROSS THE PLAIN...
AN' HE JUST DISAPPEARED...
VANISHED... LIKE HE WASN'T NEVER THERE.
BUT THEY WOULD ESCAPE THEIR FATHERS' FATES... WHILE FULFILLING THEIR LEGACIES...
SHOW ME THIS PLACE...WHERE HE DISAPPEARED.
AND IT ALL BEGAN THE DAY THEY RODE OUT OF THE DUST...
...AND FOLLOWED THEIR PREY UNTIL HIS TRACKS STOPPED...
THAT WAS THE FIRST TIME THE ABYSS TOUCHED ALOYSIUS THORNDRAKE...
...IN THE INFINITE FOLDINGS OF TIME AND SPACE...

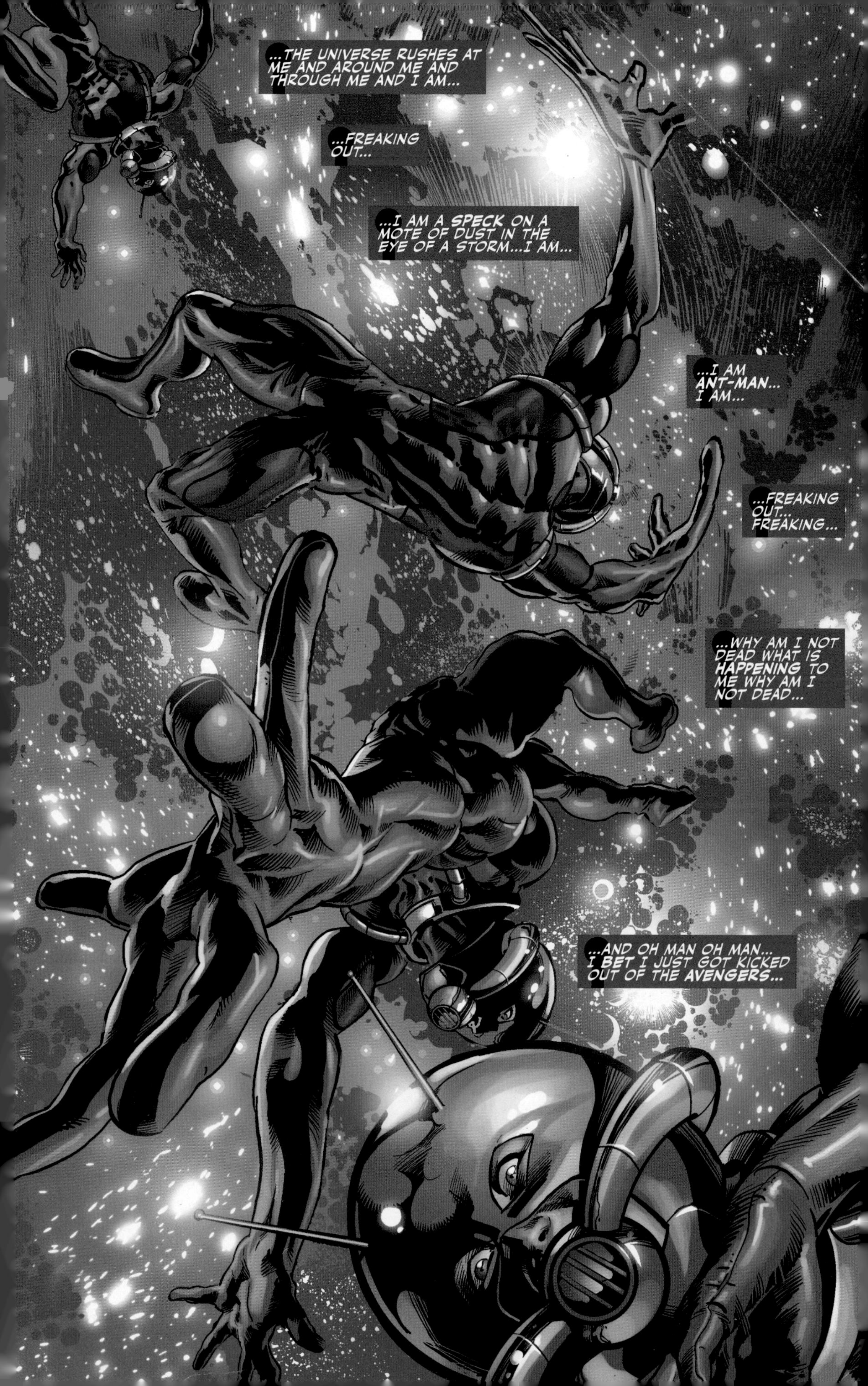
...THE UNIVERSE RUSHES AT ME AND AROUND ME AND THROUGH ME AND I AM...
...FREAKING OUT...
...I AM A SPECK ON A MOTE OF DUST IN THE EYE OF A STORM...I AM...
...I AM ANT-MAN... I AM...
...FREAKING OUT... FREAKING...
...WHY AM I NOT DEAD WHAT IS HAPPENING TO ME WHY AM I NOT DEAD...
...AND OH MAN OH MAN... I BET I JUST GOT KICKED OUT OF THE AVENGERS...

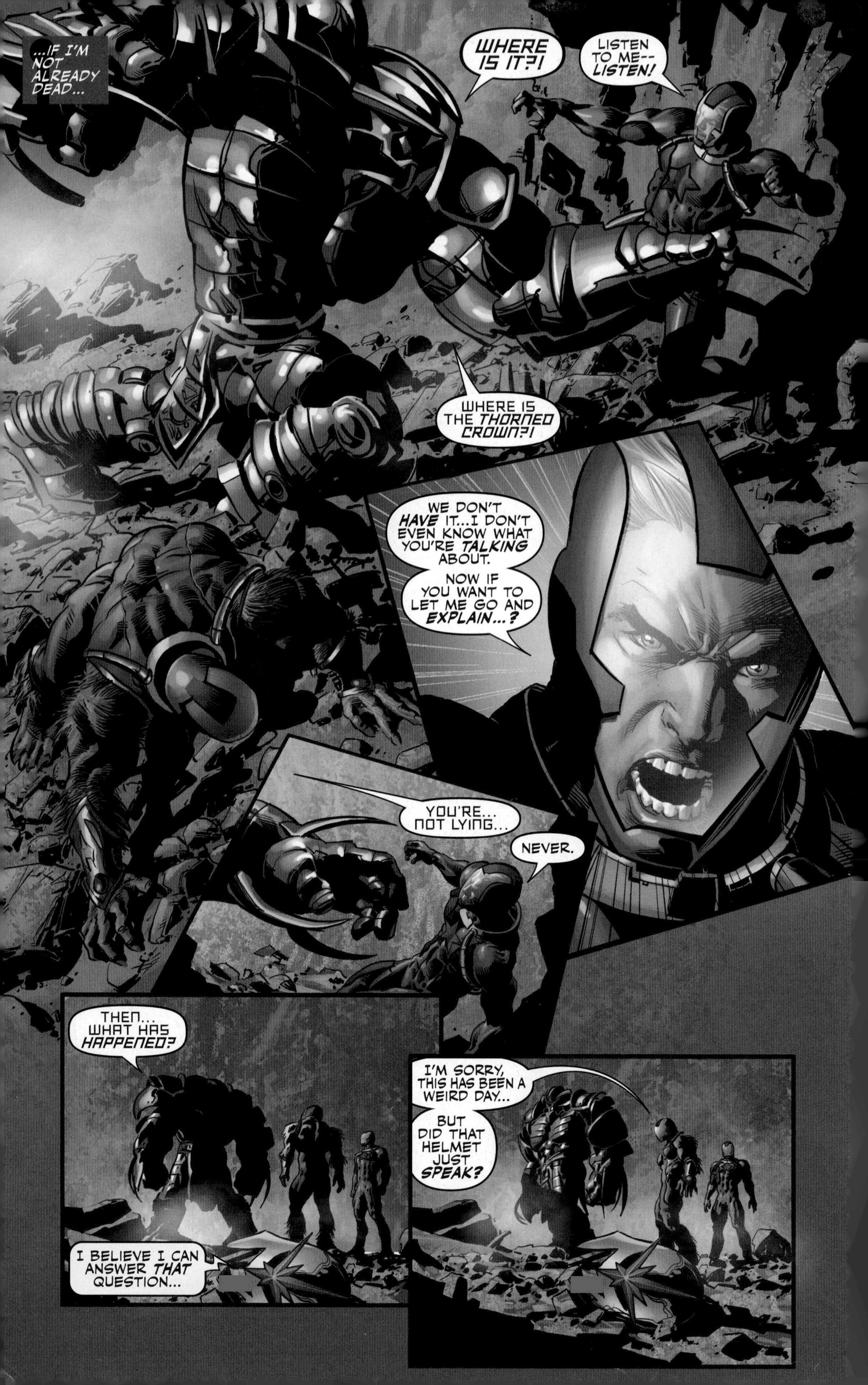
...IF I'M NOT ALREADY DEAD...
WHERE IS IT?!
LISTEN TO ME-- LISTEN!
WHERE IS THE THORNED CROWN?!
WE DON'T HAVE IT...I DON'T EVEN KNOW WHAT YOU'RE TALKING ABOUT.
NOW IF YOU WANT TO LET ME GO AND EXPLAIN...?
YOU'RE... NOT LYING...
NEVER.
THEN... WHAT HAS HAPPENED?
I BELIEVE I CAN ANSWER THAT QUESTION...
I'M SORRY, THIS HAS BEEN A WEIRD DAY...
BUT DID THAT HELMET JUST SPEAK?

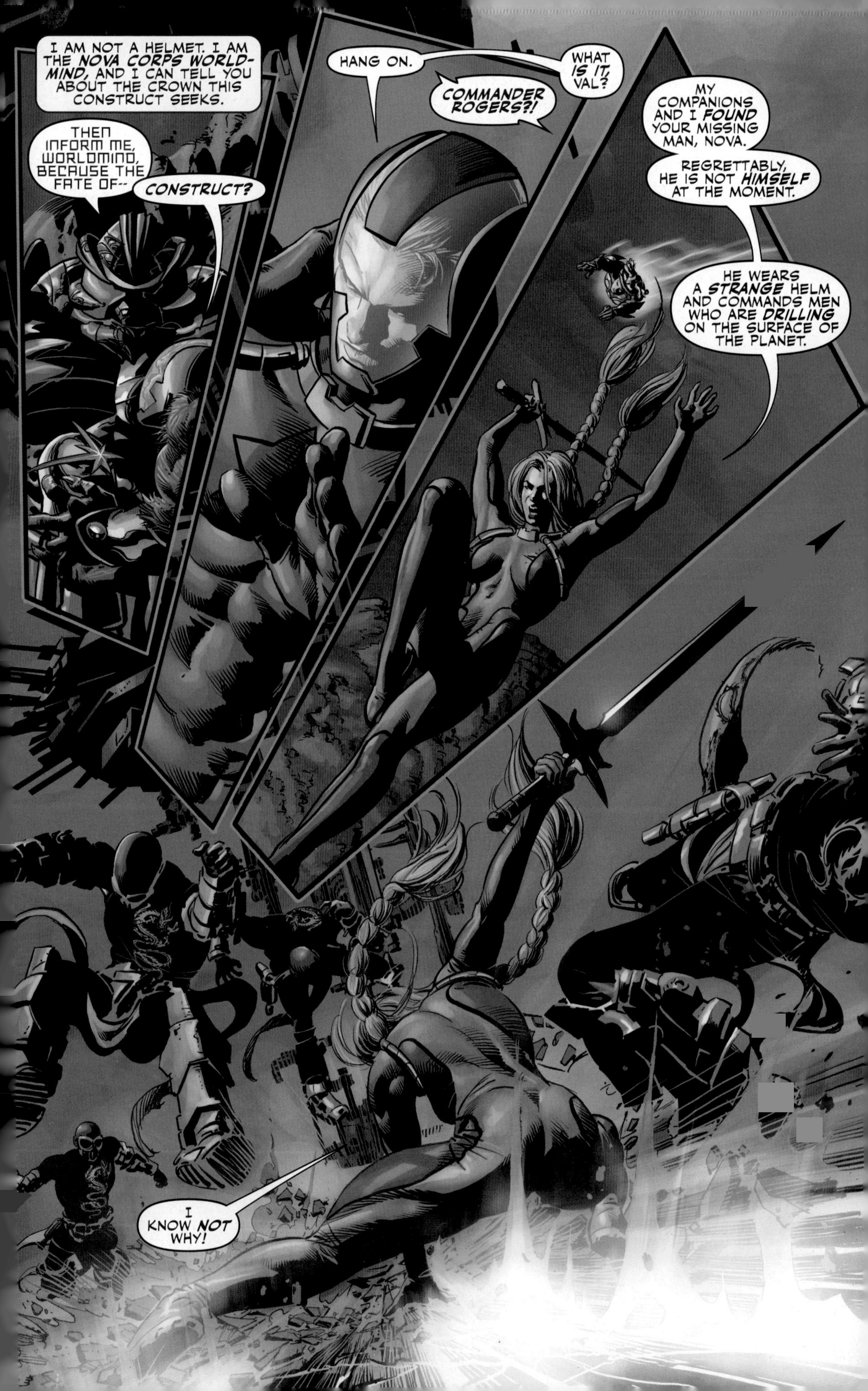

I AM NOT A HELMET. I AM THE NOVA CORPS WORLD-MIND, AND I CAN TELL YOU ABOUT THE CROWN THIS CONSTRUCT SEEKS.
THEN INFORM ME, WORLDMIND, BECAUSE THE FATE OF--
CONSTRUCT?
HANG ON.
WHAT IS IT, VAL?
COMMANDER ROGERS?!
MY COMPANIONS AND I FOUND YOUR MISSING MAN, NOVA.
REGRETTABLY, HE IS NOT HIMSELF AT THE MOMENT.
HE WEARS A STRANGE HELM AND COMMANDS MEN WHO ARE DRILLING ON THE SURFACE OF THE PLANET.
I KNOW NOT WHY!

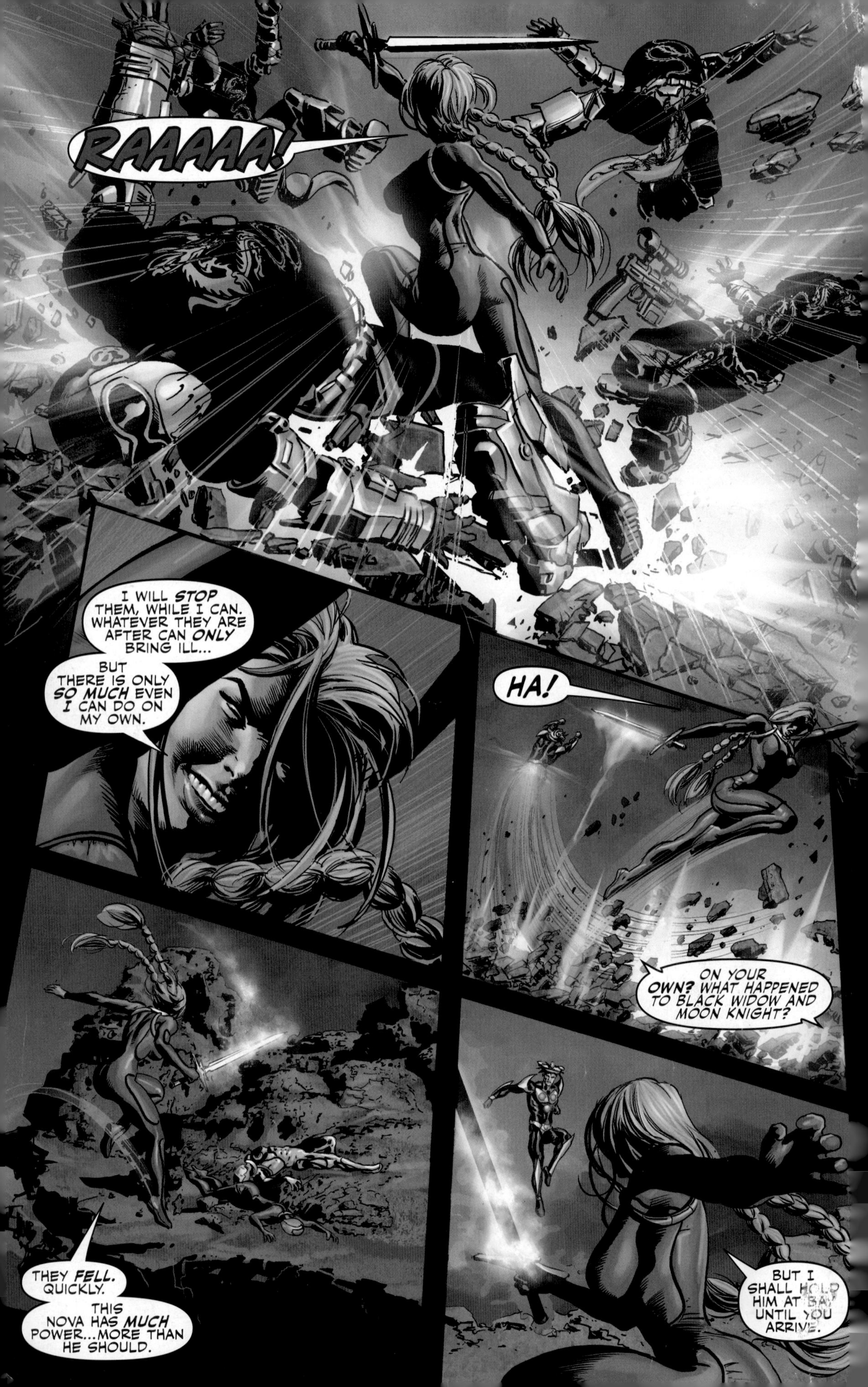
RAAAAA!
I WILL *STOP* THEM, WHILE I CAN. WHATEVER THEY ARE AFTER CAN *ONLY* BRING ILL...
BUT THERE IS ONLY *SO MUCH* EVEN *I* CAN DO ON MY OWN.
HA!
ON YOUR *OWN?* WHAT HAPPENED TO BLACK WIDOW AND MOON KNIGHT?
THEY *FELL.* QUICKLY.
THIS NOVA HAS *MUCH* POWER...MORE THAN HE SHOULD.
BUT I SHALL HOLD HIM AT BAY UNTIL YOU ARRIVE.

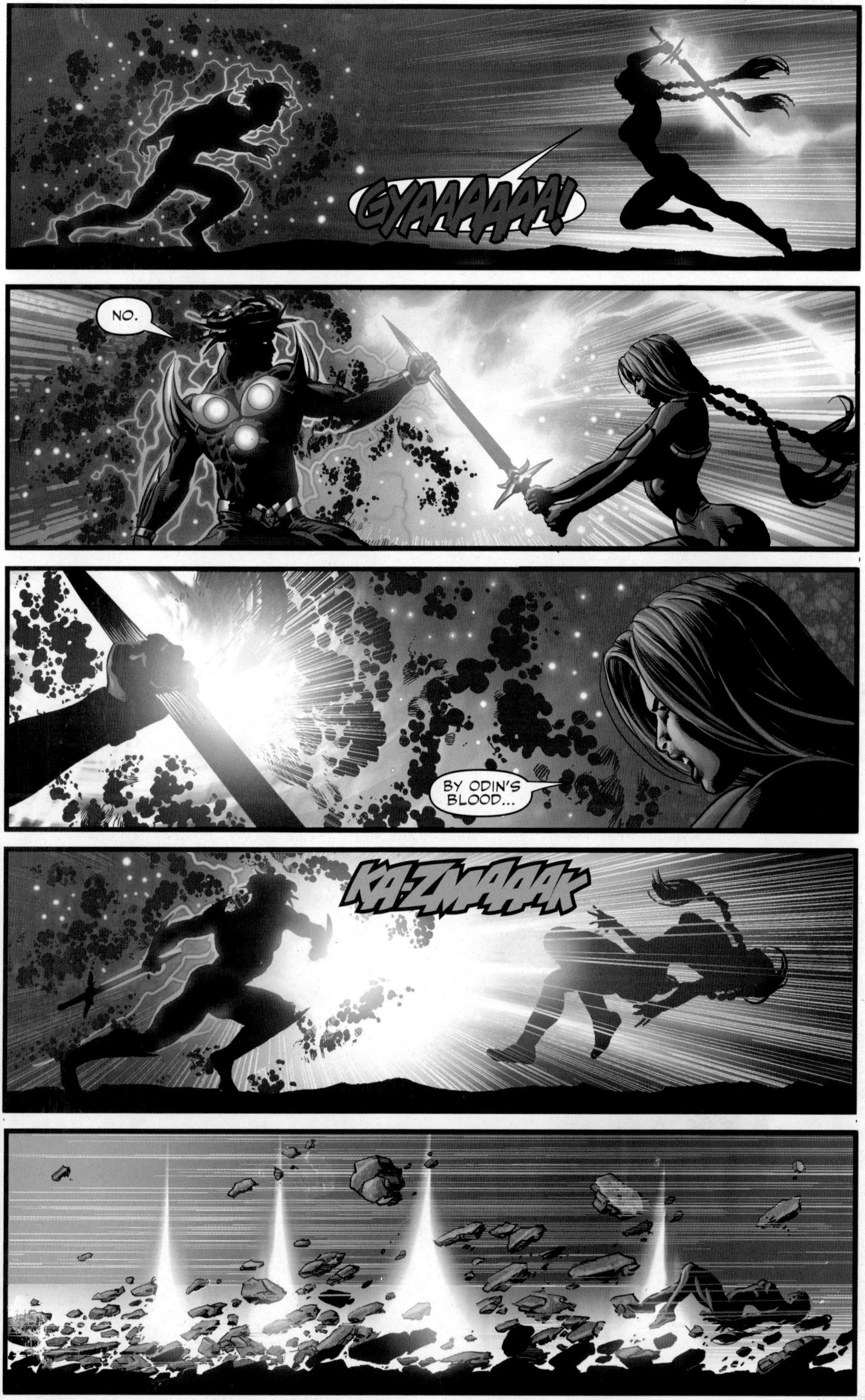
GYAAAAAA!
NO.
BY ODIN'S BLOOD...
KA-ZMAAAAK

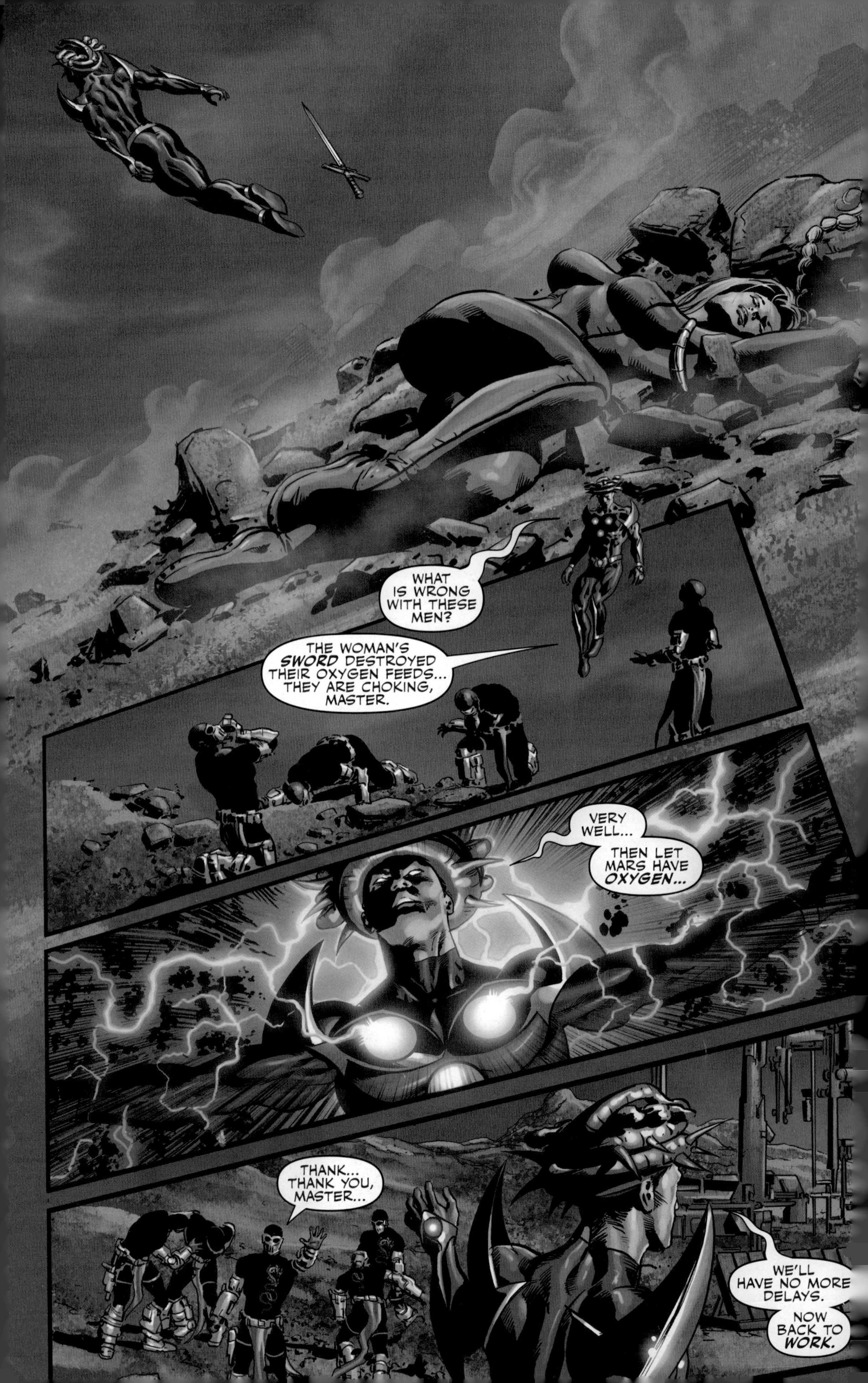
WHAT IS WRONG WITH THESE MEN?
THE WOMAN'S SWORD DESTROYED THEIR OXYGEN FEEDS... THEY ARE CHOKING, MASTER.
VERY WELL...
THEN LET MARS HAVE OXYGEN...
THANK... THANK YOU, MASTER...
WE'LL HAVE NO MORE DELAYS.
NOW BACK TO WORK.

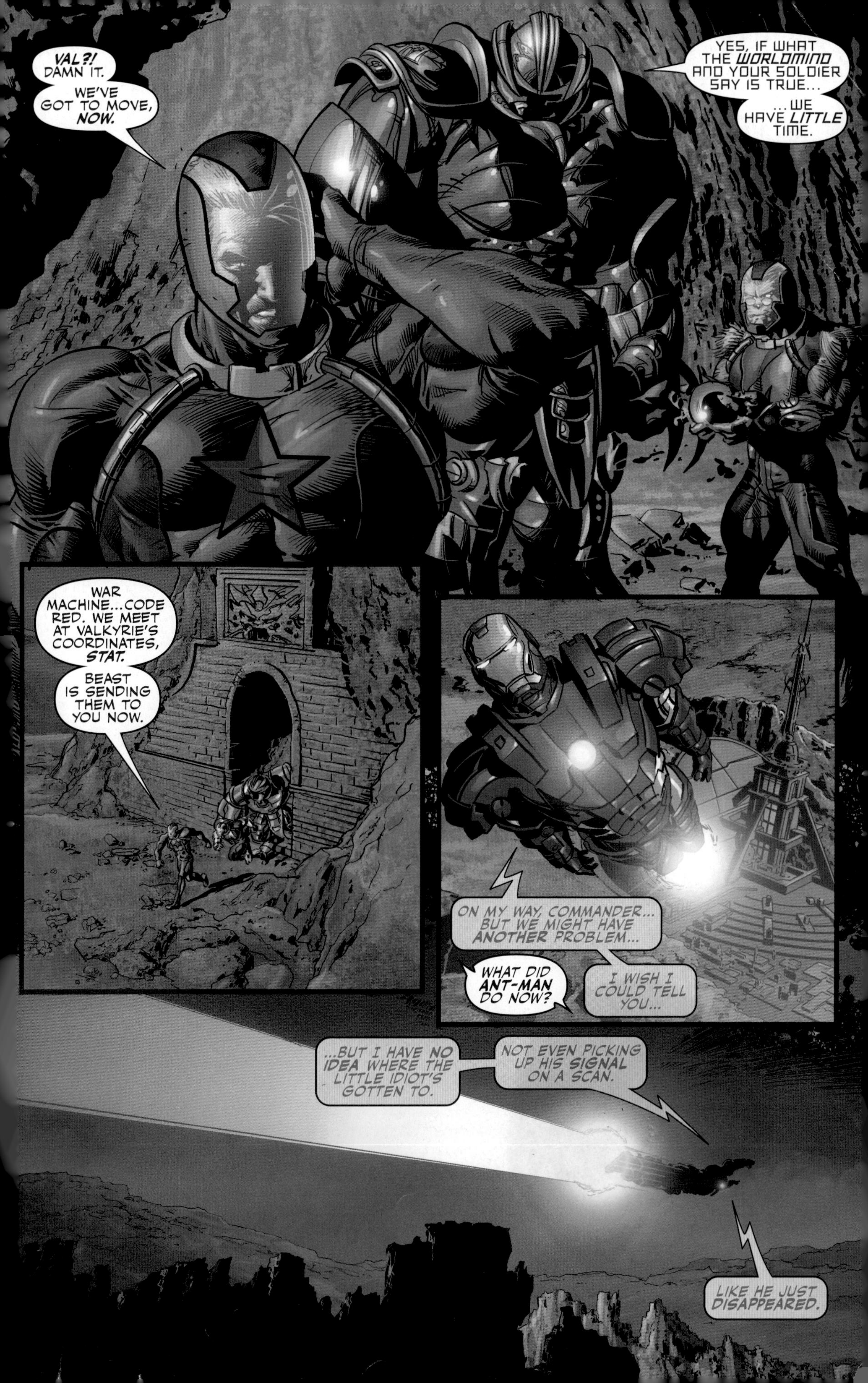
VAL?! DAMN IT.
WE'VE GOT TO MOVE, NOW.
YES, IF WHAT THE WORLDMIND AND YOUR SOLDIER SAY IS TRUE...
...WE HAVE LITTLE TIME.
WAR MACHINE...CODE RED. WE MEET AT VALKYRIE'S COORDINATES, STAT.
BEAST IS SENDING THEM TO YOU NOW.
ON MY WAY, COMMANDER... BUT WE MIGHT HAVE ANOTHER PROBLEM...
WHAT DID ANT-MAN DO NOW?
I WISH I COULD TELL YOU...
...BUT I HAVE NO IDEA WHERE THE LITTLE IDIOT'S GOTTEN TO.
NOT EVEN PICKING UP HIS SIGNAL ON A SCAN.
LIKE HE JUST DISAPPEARED.

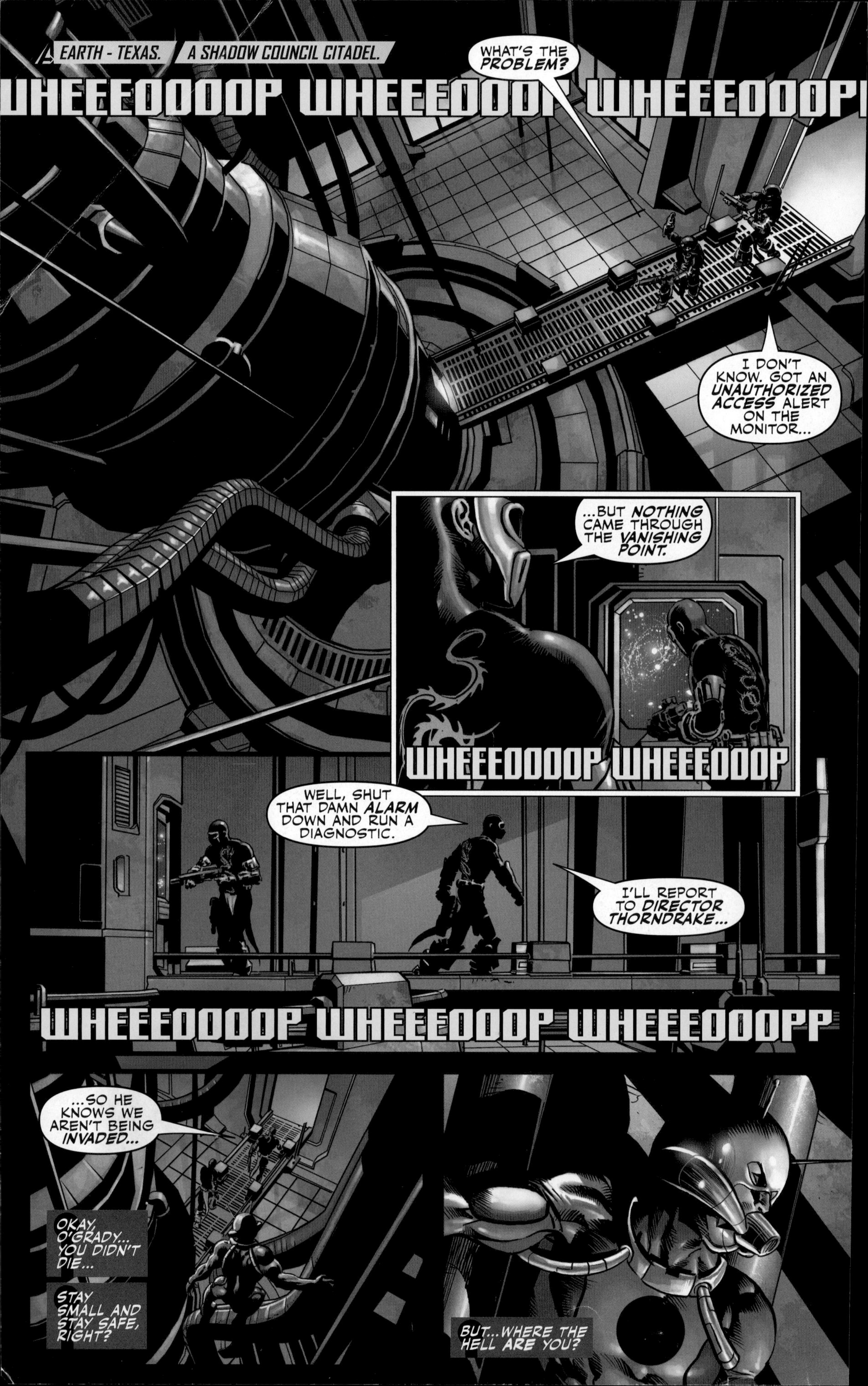
EARTH - TEXAS.
A SHADOW COUNCIL CITADEL.
WHAT'S THE PROBLEM?
WHEEEOOOOP WHEEEOOOP WHEEEOOOP
I DON'T KNOW. GOT AN UNAUTHORIZED ACCESS ALERT ON THE MONITOR...
...BUT NOTHING CAME THROUGH THE VANISHING POINT.
WHEEEOOOOP WHEEEOOOP
WELL, SHUT THAT DAMN ALARM DOWN AND RUN A DIAGNOSTIC.
I'LL REPORT TO DIRECTOR THORNDRAKE...
WHEEEOOOOP WHEEEOOOP WHEEEOOOPP
...SO HE KNOWS WE AREN'T BEING INVADED...
OKAY, O'GRADY... YOU DIDN'T DIE...
STAY SMALL AND STAY SAFE, RIGHT?
BUT...WHERE THE HELL ARE YOU?

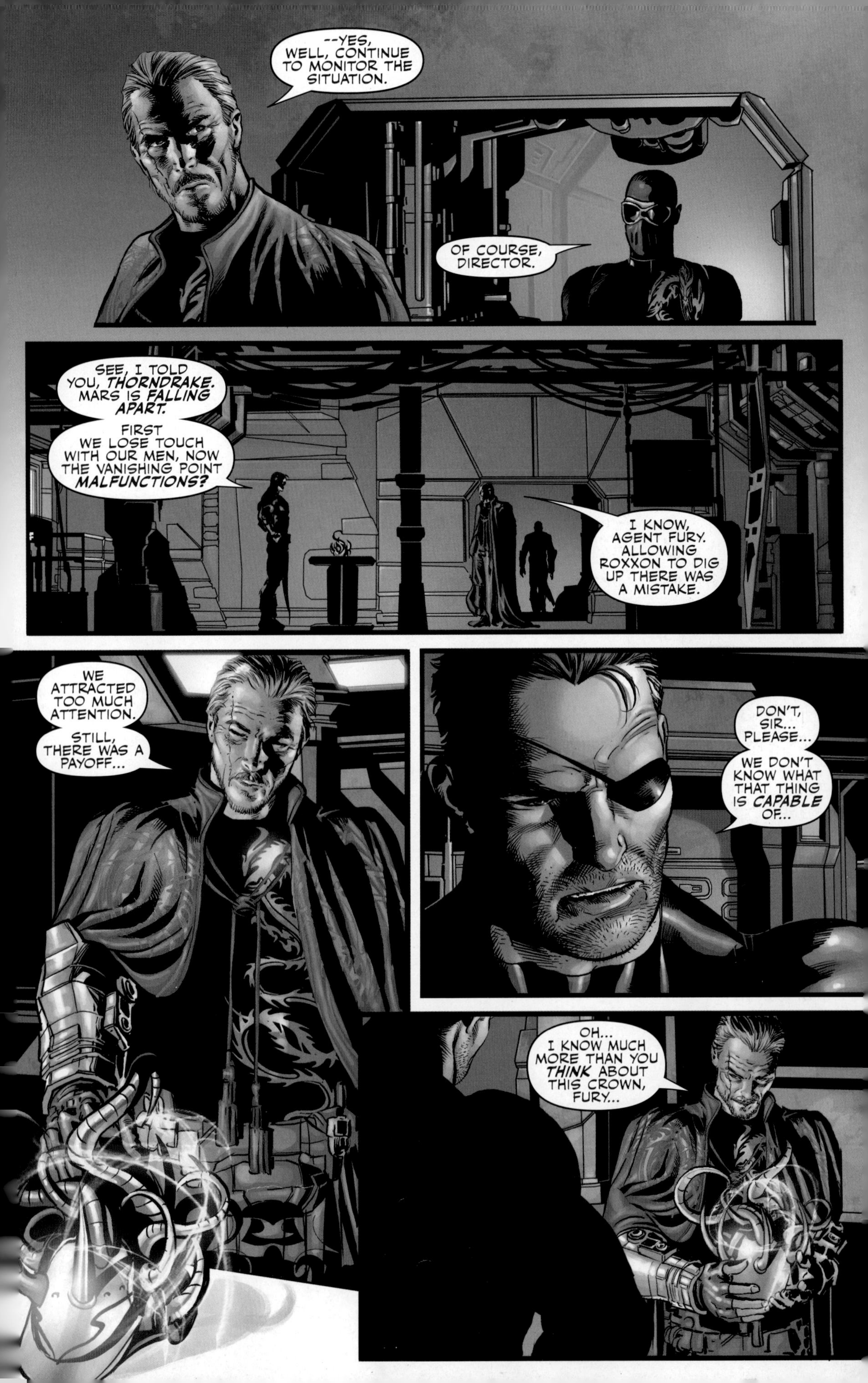
--YES, WELL, CONTINUE TO MONITOR THE SITUATION.
OF COURSE, DIRECTOR.
SEE, I TOLD YOU, THORNDRAKE. MARS IS FALLING APART.
FIRST WE LOSE TOUCH WITH OUR MEN, NOW THE VANISHING POINT MALFUNCTIONS?
I KNOW, AGENT FURY. ALLOWING ROXXON TO DIG UP THERE WAS A MISTAKE.
WE ATTRACTED TOO MUCH ATTENTION.
STILL, THERE WAS A PAYOFF...
DON'T, SIR... PLEASE...
WE DON'T KNOW WHAT THAT THING IS CAPABLE OF...
OH... I KNOW MUCH MORE THAN YOU THINK ABOUT THIS CROWN, FURY...

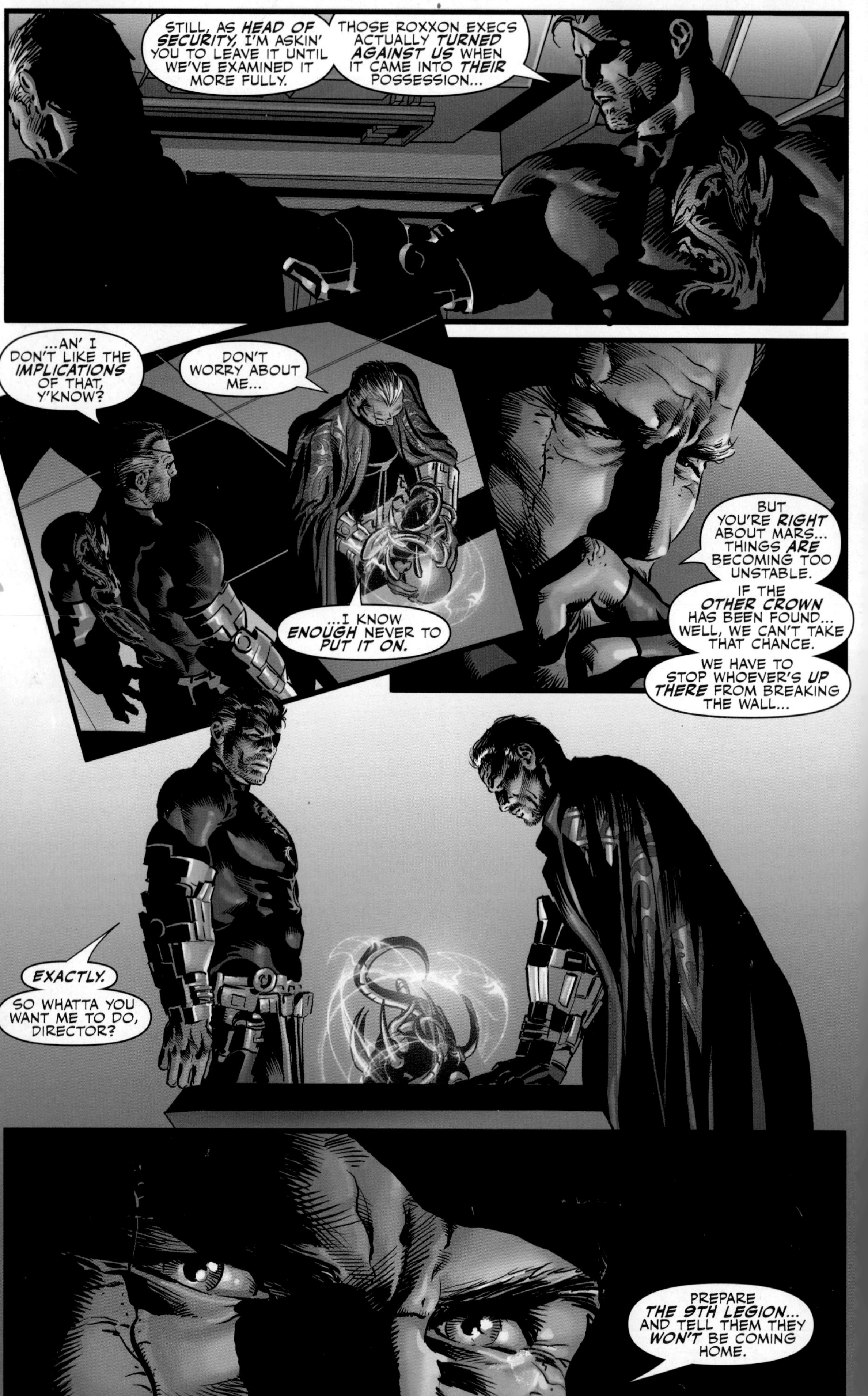
STILL, AS HEAD OF SECURITY, I'M ASKIN' YOU TO LEAVE IT UNTIL WE'VE EXAMINED IT MORE FULLY.
THOSE ROXXON EXECS ACTUALLY TURNED AGAINST US WHEN IT CAME INTO THEIR POSSESSION...
...AN' I DON'T LIKE THE IMPLICATIONS OF THAT, Y'KNOW?
DON'T WORRY ABOUT ME...
...I KNOW ENOUGH NEVER TO PUT IT ON.
BUT YOU'RE RIGHT ABOUT MARS... THINGS ARE BECOMING TOO UNSTABLE.
IF THE OTHER CROWN HAS BEEN FOUND... WELL, WE CAN'T TAKE THAT CHANCE.
WE HAVE TO STOP WHOEVER'S UP THERE FROM BREAKING THE WALL...
EXACTLY.
SO WHATTA YOU WANT ME TO DO, DIRECTOR?
PREPARE THE 9TH LEGION... AND TELL THEM THEY WON'T BE COMING HOME.

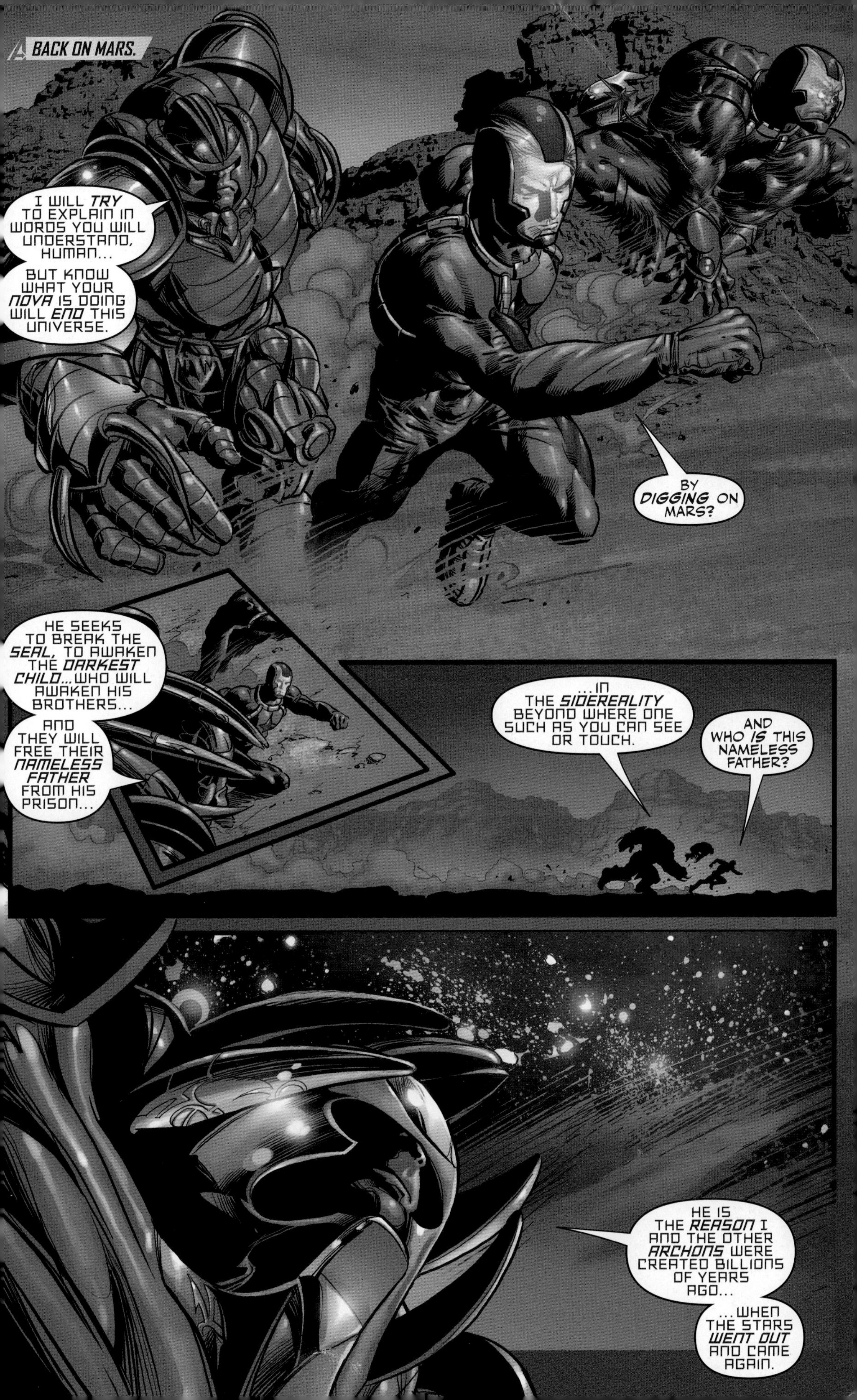
BACK ON MARS.
I WILL *TRY* TO EXPLAIN IN WORDS YOU WILL UNDERSTAND, HUMAN...
BUT KNOW WHAT YOUR *NOVA* IS DOING WILL *END* THIS UNIVERSE.
BY *DIGGING* ON MARS?
HE SEEKS TO BREAK THE *SEAL*, TO AWAKEN THE *DARKEST CHILD*...WHO WILL AWAKEN HIS BROTHERS...
AND THEY WILL FREE THEIR *NAMELESS FATHER* FROM HIS PRISON...
...IN THE *SIDEREALITY* BEYOND WHERE ONE SUCH AS YOU CAN SEE OR TOUCH.
AND WHO *IS* THIS NAMELESS FATHER?
HE IS THE *REASON* I AND THE OTHER *ARCHONS* WERE CREATED BILLIONS OF YEARS AGO...
...WHEN THE STARS *WENT OUT* AND CAME AGAIN.

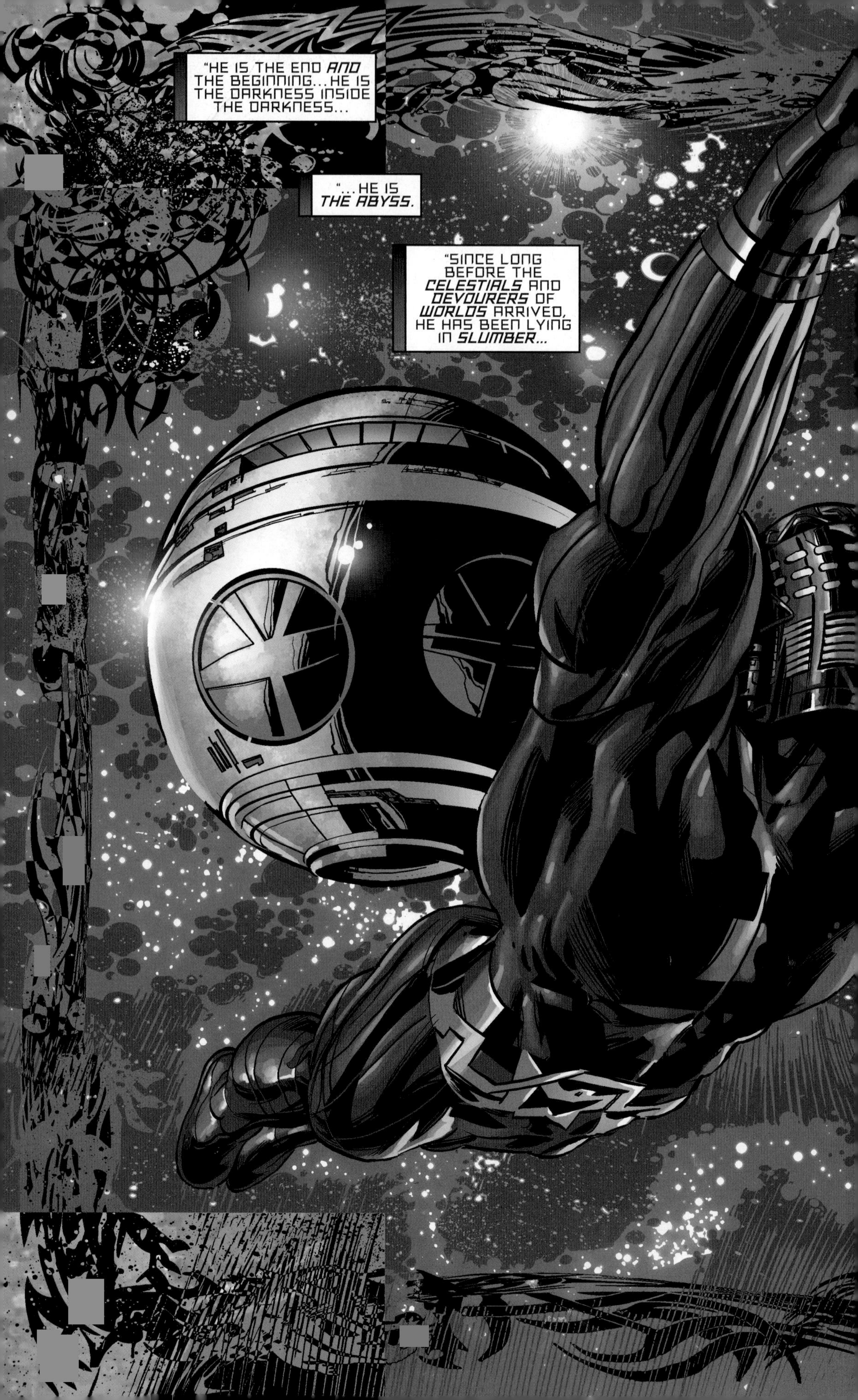
"HE IS THE END AND THE BEGINNING... HE IS THE DARKNESS INSIDE THE DARKNESS...
"...HE IS THE ABYSS.
"SINCE LONG BEFORE THE CELESTIALS AND DEVOURERS OF WORLDS ARRIVED, HE HAS BEEN LYING IN SLUMBER...

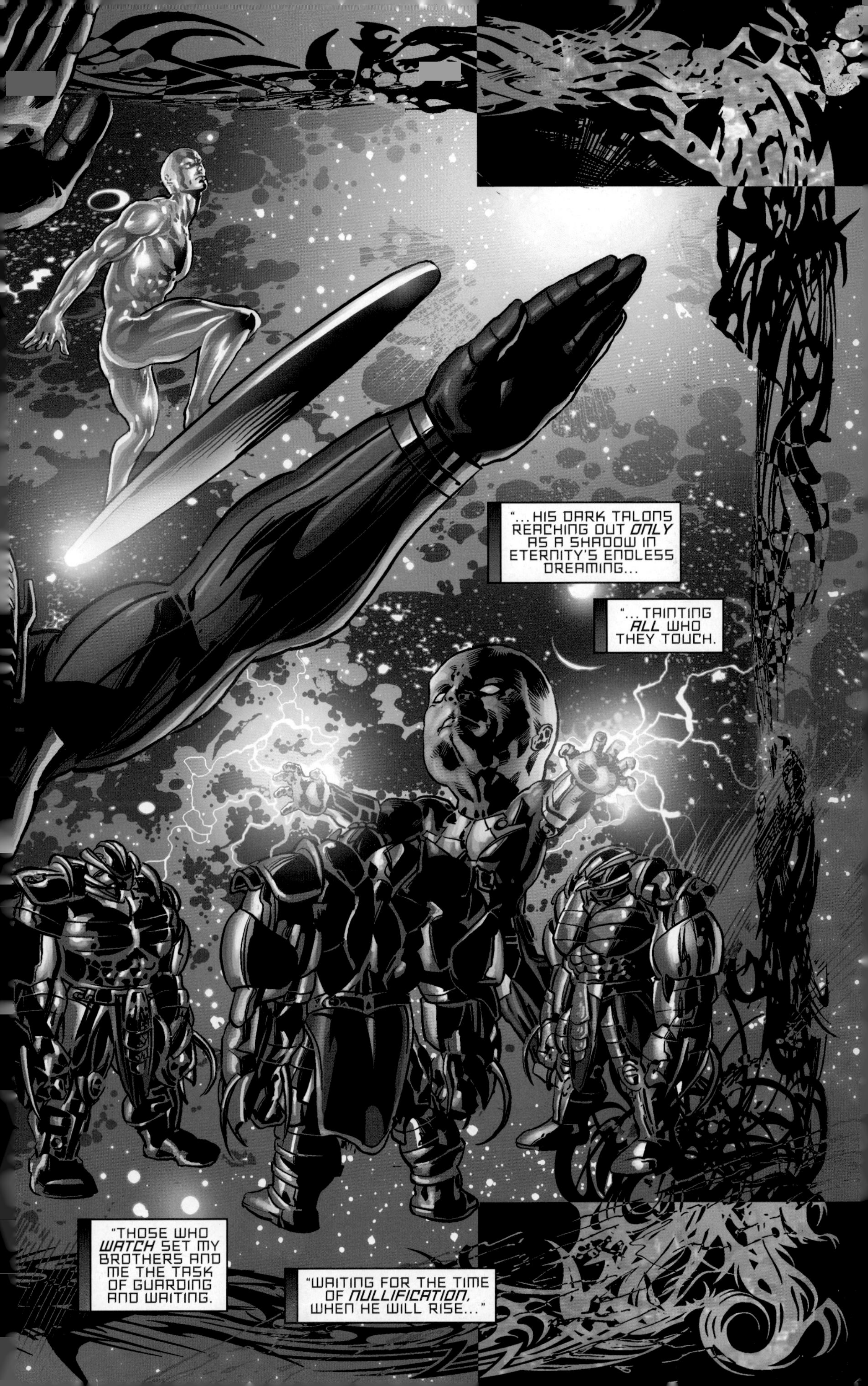
"...HIS DARK TALONS REACHING OUT ONLY AS A SHADOW IN ETERNITY'S ENDLESS DREAMING...
"...TAINTING ALL WHO THEY TOUCH.
"THOSE WHO WATCH SET MY BROTHERS AND ME THE TASK OF GUARDING AND WAITING.
"WAITING FOR THE TIME OF NULLIFICATION, WHEN HE WILL RISE..."

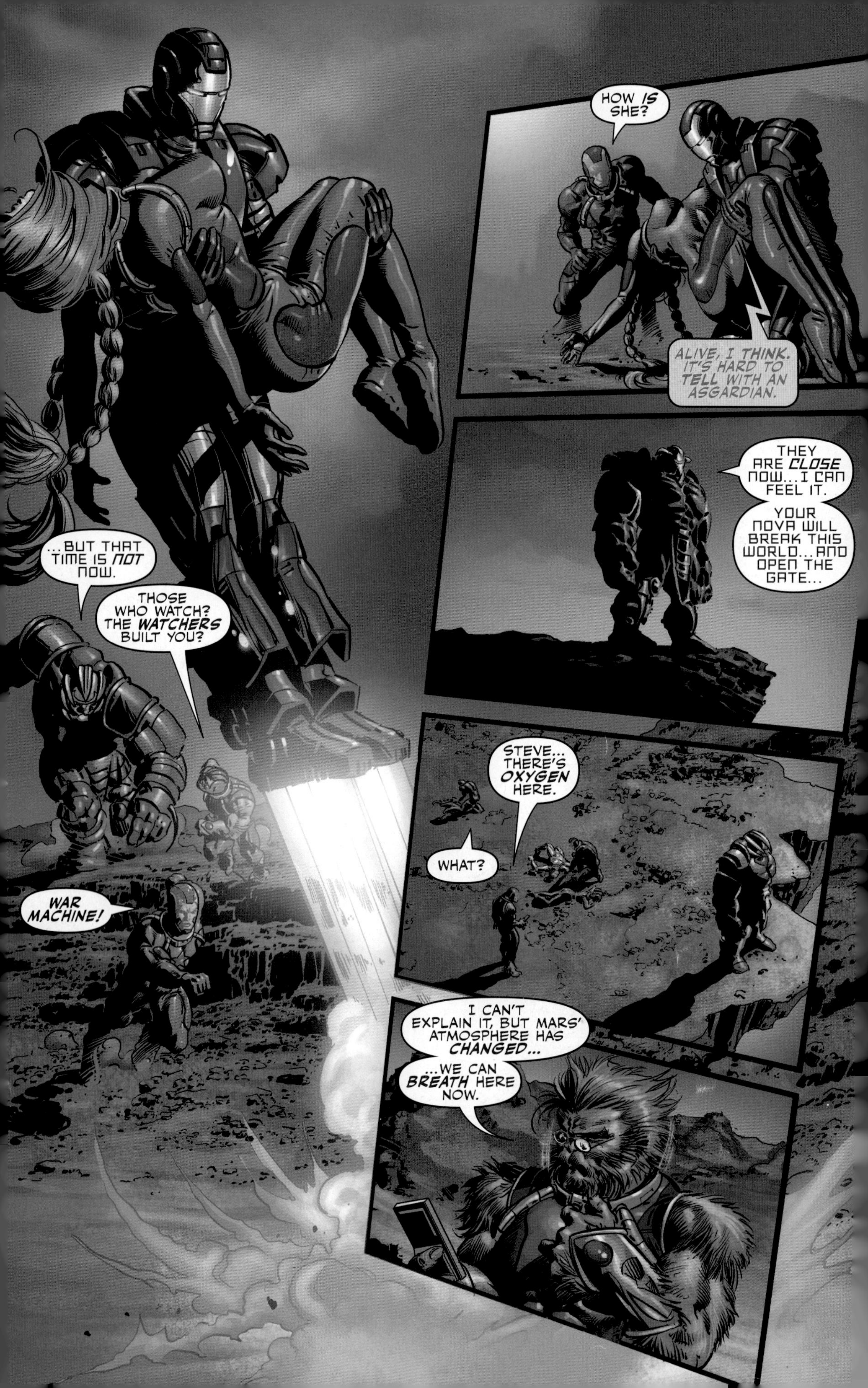

...BUT THAT TIME IS NOT NOW.
THOSE WHO WATCH? THE WATCHERS BUILT YOU?
WAR MACHINE!
HOW IS SHE?
ALIVE, I THINK. IT'S HARD TO TELL WITH AN ASGARDIAN.
THEY ARE CLOSE NOW...I CAN FEEL IT.
YOUR NOVA WILL BREAK THIS WORLD...AND OPEN THE GATE...
STEVE... THERE'S OXYGEN HERE.
WHAT?
I CAN'T EXPLAIN IT, BUT MARS' ATMOSPHERE HAS CHANGED...
...WE CAN BREATH HERE NOW.

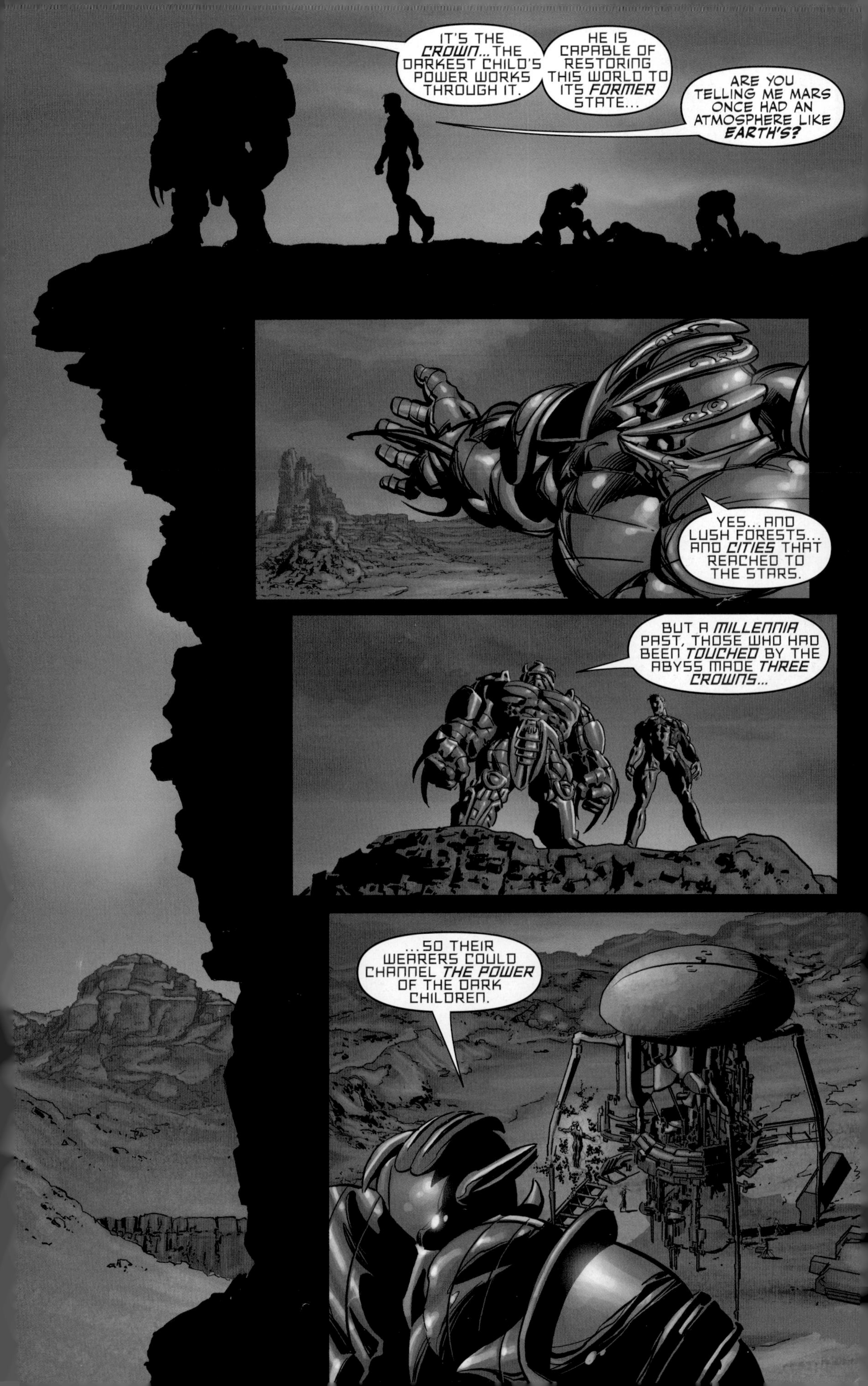
IT'S THE *CROWN*... THE DARKEST CHILD'S POWER WORKS THROUGH IT.
HE IS CAPABLE OF RESTORING THIS WORLD TO ITS *FORMER* STATE...
ARE YOU TELLING ME MARS ONCE HAD AN ATMOSPHERE LIKE *EARTH'S?*
YES... AND LUSH FORESTS... AND *CITIES* THAT REACHED TO THE STARS.
BUT A *MILLENNIA* PAST, THOSE WHO HAD BEEN *TOUCHED* BY THE ABYSS MADE *THREE CROWNS*...
...SO THEIR WEARERS COULD CHANNEL *THE POWER* OF THE DARK CHILDREN.

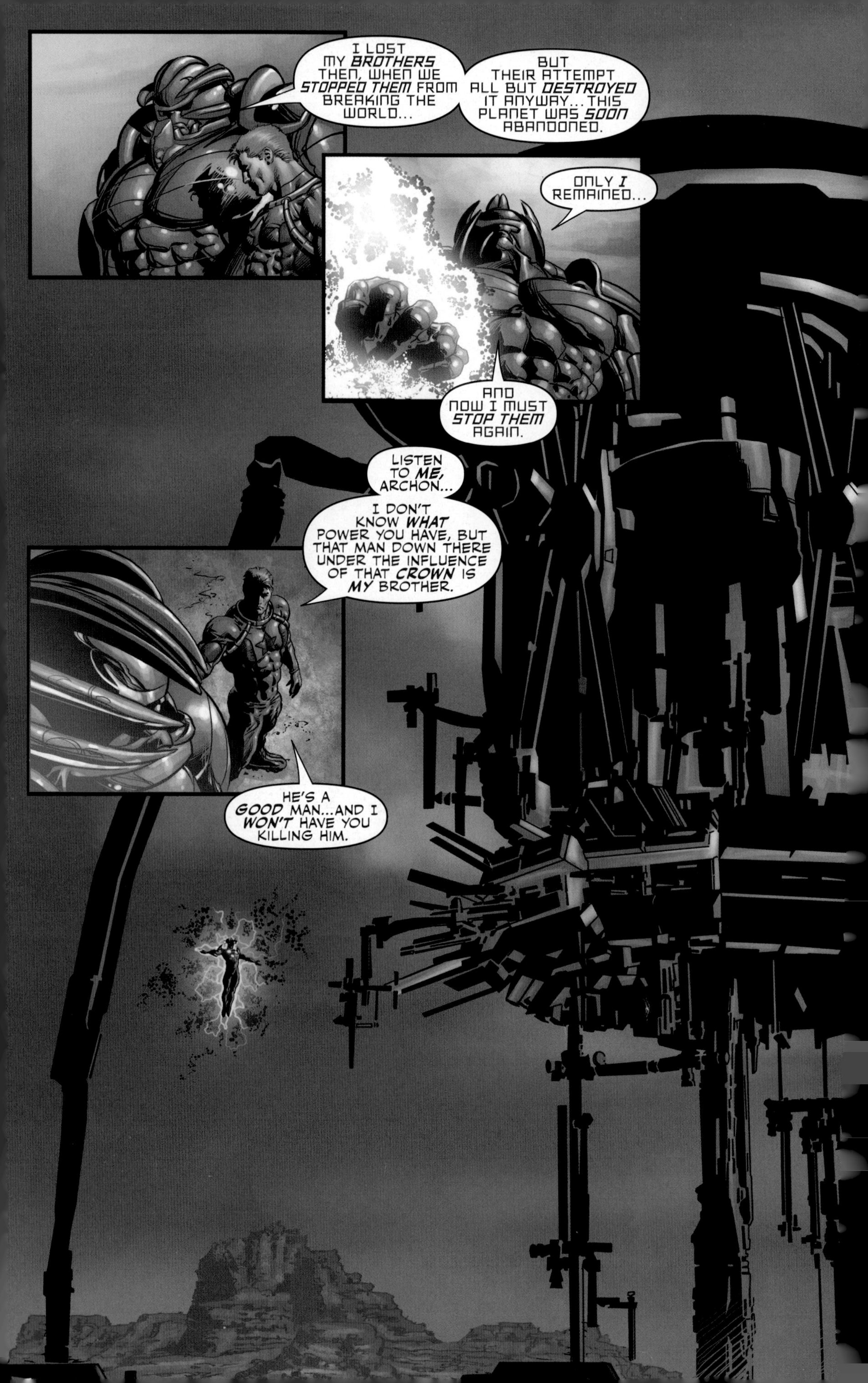
I LOST MY BROTHERS THEN, WHEN WE STOPPED THEM FROM BREAKING THE WORLD...
BUT THEIR ATTEMPT ALL BUT DESTROYED IT ANYWAY... THIS PLANET WAS SOON ABANDONED.
ONLY I REMAINED...
AND NOW I MUST STOP THEM AGAIN.
LISTEN TO ME, ARCHON...
I DON'T KNOW WHAT POWER YOU HAVE, BUT THAT MAN DOWN THERE UNDER THE INFLUENCE OF THAT CROWN IS MY BROTHER.
HE'S A GOOD MAN...AND I WON'T HAVE YOU KILLING HIM.

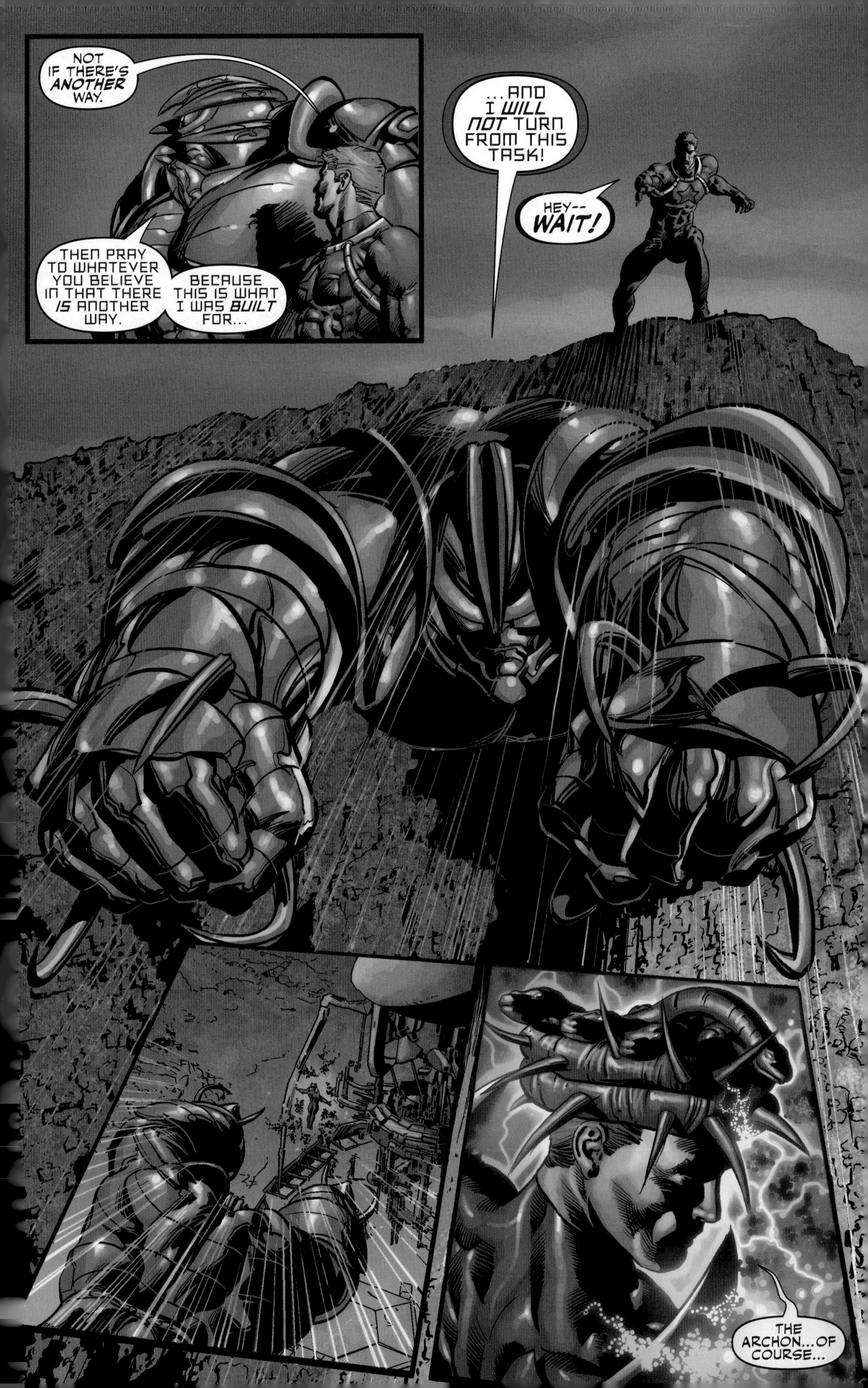
NOT IF THERE'S ANOTHER WAY.
THEN PRAY TO WHATEVER YOU BELIEVE IN THAT THERE IS ANOTHER WAY.
BECAUSE THIS IS WHAT I WAS BUILT FOR...
...AND I WILL NOT TURN FROM THIS TASK!
HEY-- WAIT!
THE ARCHON...OF COURSE...

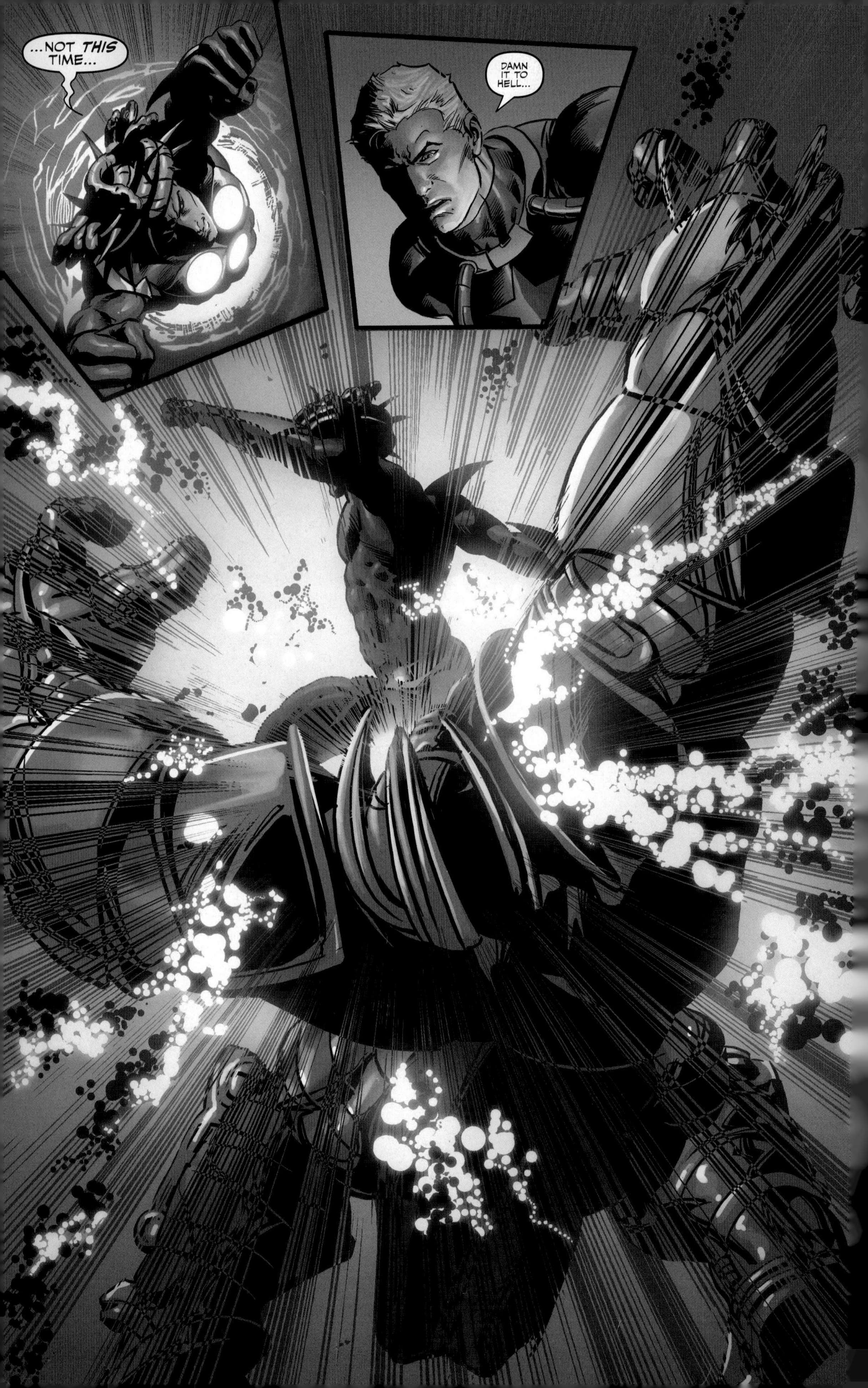
...NOT *THIS* TIME...
DAMN IT TO HELL...

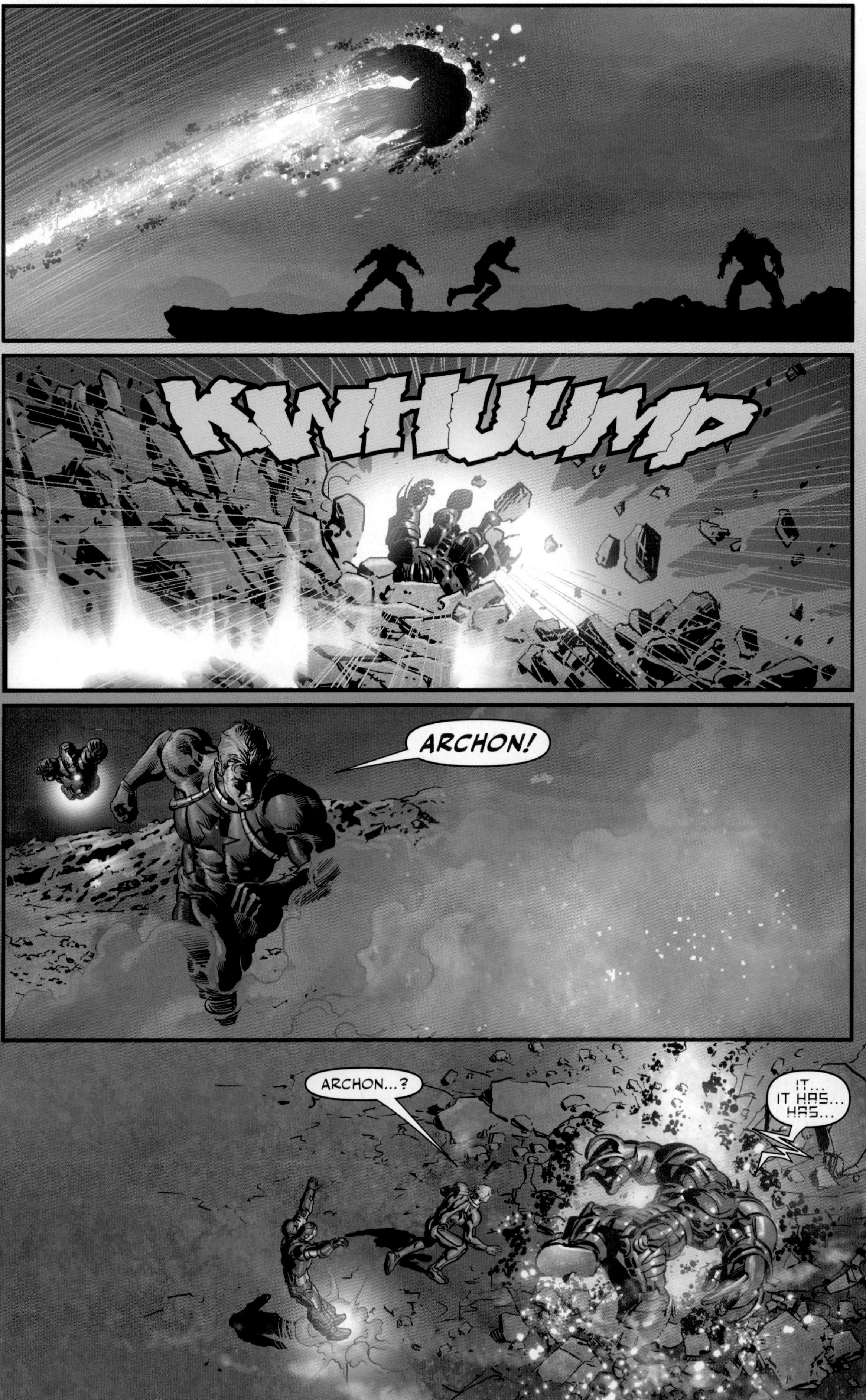
KWHUUMP
ARCHON!
ARCHON...?
IT... IT HAS... HAS...

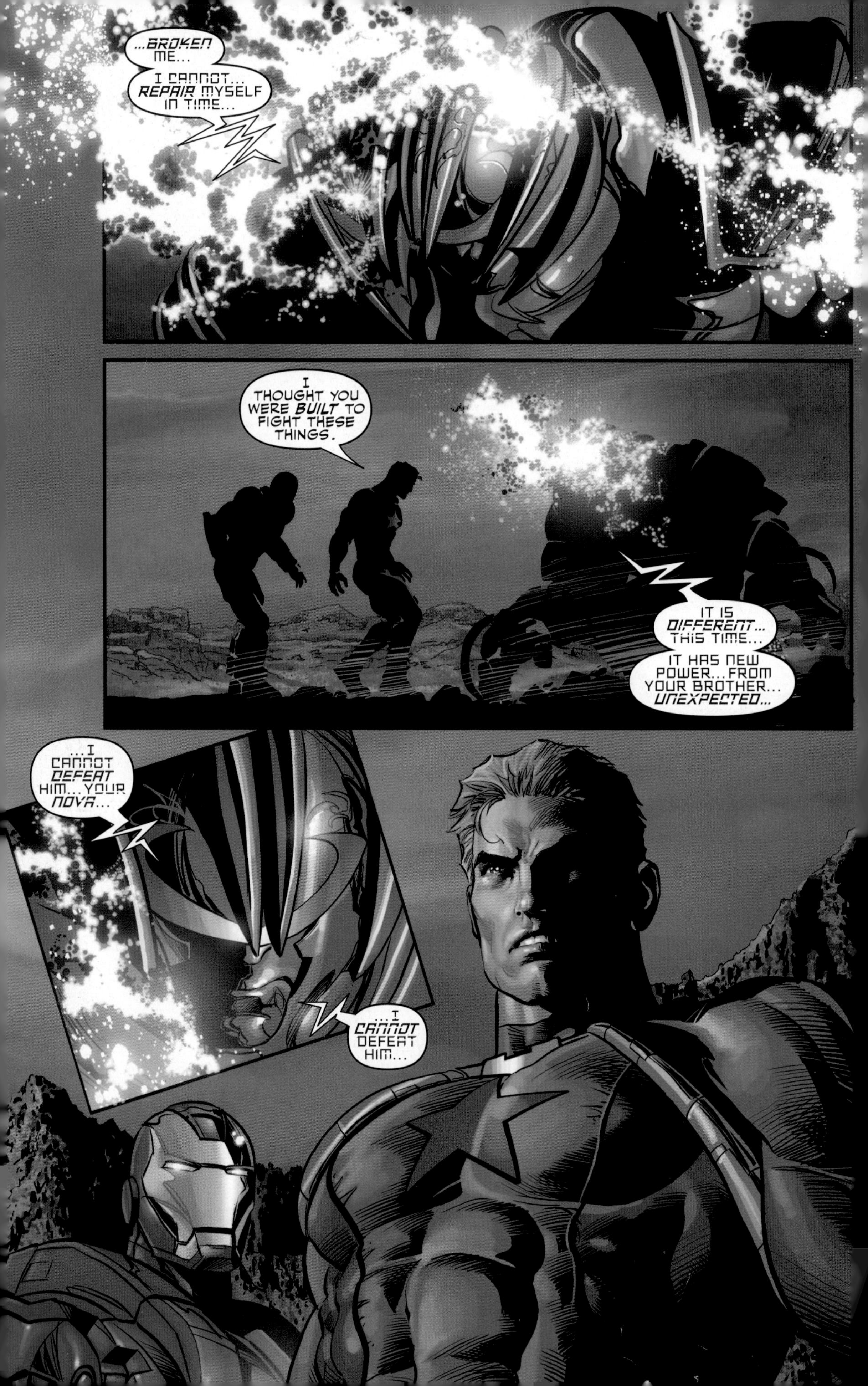
...BROKEN ME...
I CANNOT... REPAIR MYSELF IN TIME...
I THOUGHT YOU WERE BUILT TO FIGHT THESE THINGS.
IT IS DIFFERENT... THIS TIME...
IT HAS NEW POWER... FROM YOUR BROTHER... UNEXPECTED...
...I CANNOT DEFEAT HIM... YOUR NOVA...
...I CANNOT DEFEAT HIM...

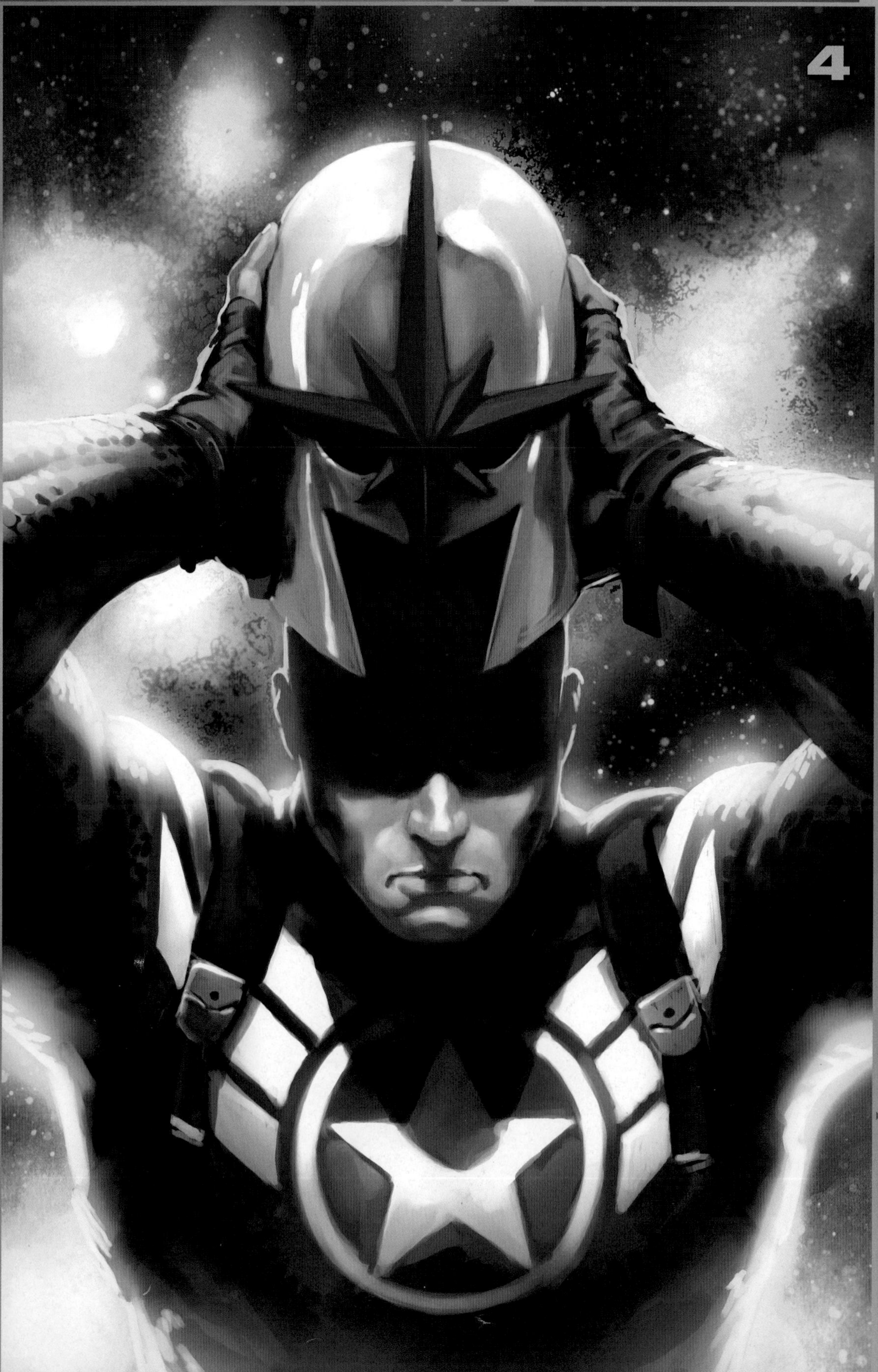
4

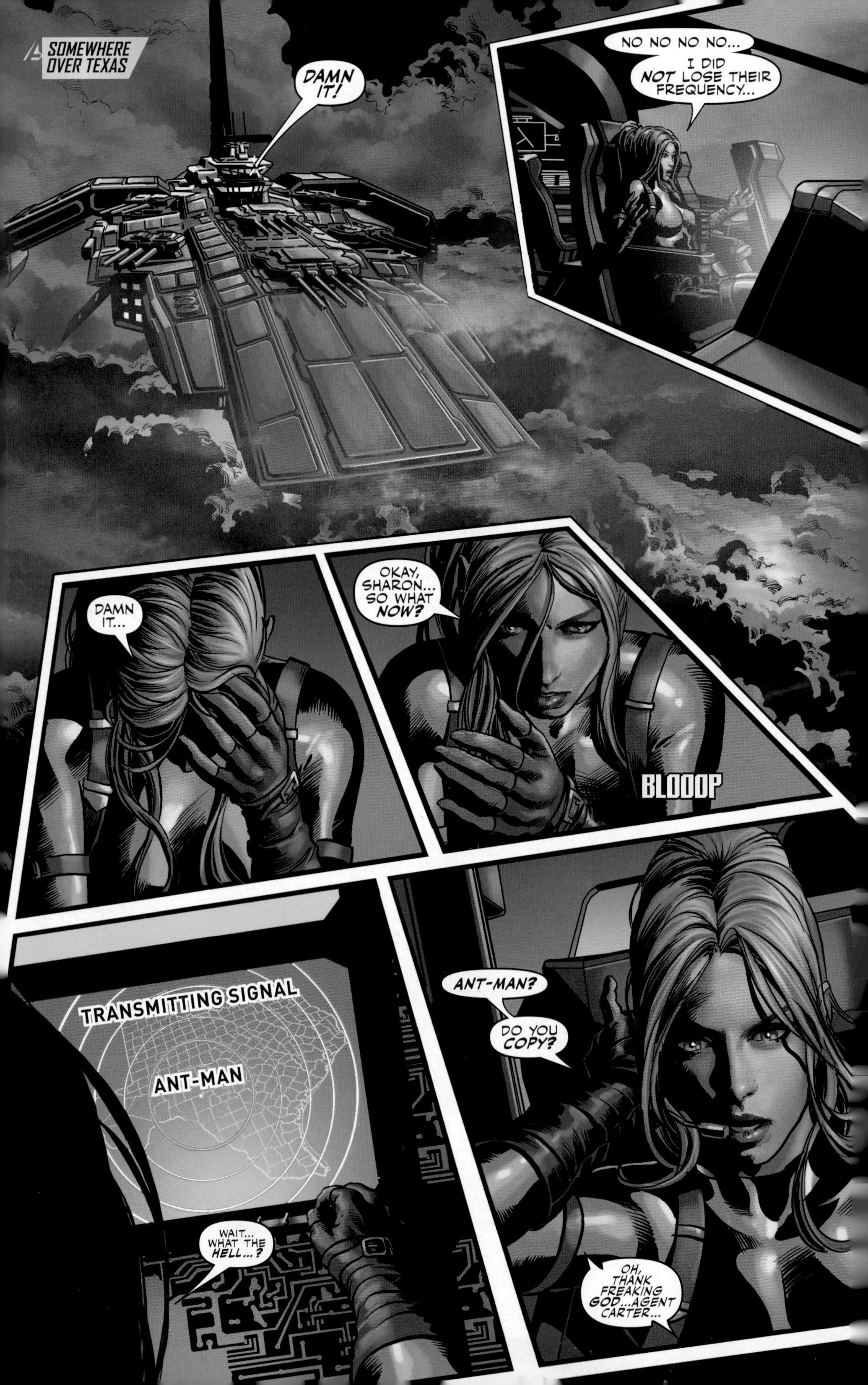
SOMEWHERE OVER TEXAS
DAMN IT!
NO NO NO NO... I DID NOT LOSE THEIR FREQUENCY...
DAMN IT...
OKAY, SHARON... SO WHAT NOW?
BLOOOP
TRANSMITTING SIGNAL
ANT-MAN
WAIT... WHAT THE HELL...?
ANT-MAN?
DO YOU COPY?
OH, THANK FREAKING GOD...AGENT CARTER...

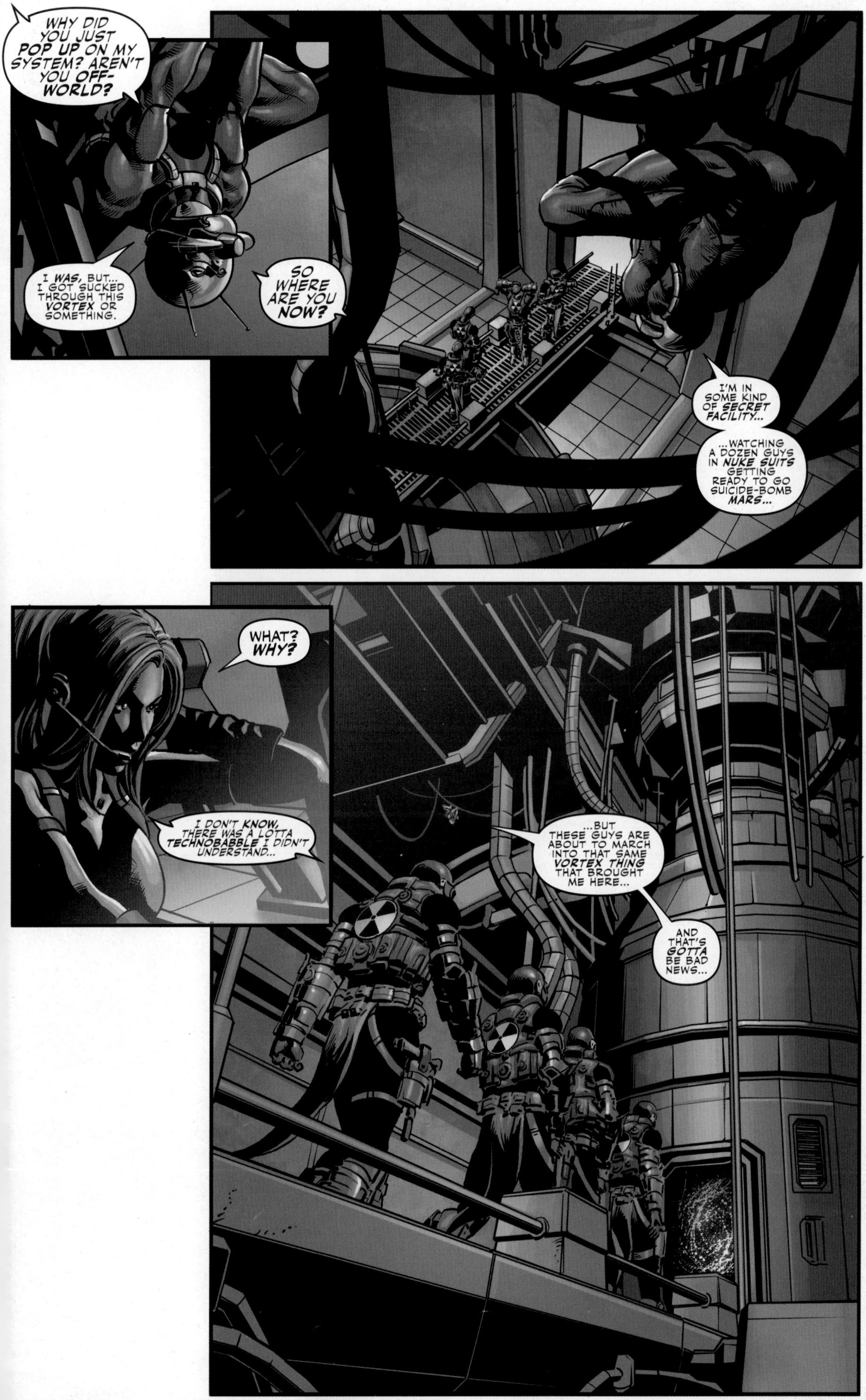
WHY DID YOU JUST POP UP ON MY SYSTEM? AREN'T YOU OFF-WORLD?
I WAS, BUT... I GOT SUCKED THROUGH THIS VORTEX OR SOMETHING.
SO WHERE ARE YOU NOW?
I'M IN SOME KIND OF SECRET FACILITY...
...WATCHING A DOZEN GUYS IN NUKE SUITS GETTING READY TO GO SUICIDE-BOMB MARS...
WHAT? WHY?
I DON'T KNOW, THERE WAS A LOTTA TECHNOBABBLE I DIDN'T UNDERSTAND...
...BUT THESE GUYS ARE ABOUT TO MARCH INTO THAT SAME VORTEX THING THAT BROUGHT ME HERE...
AND THAT'S GOTTA BE BAD NEWS...

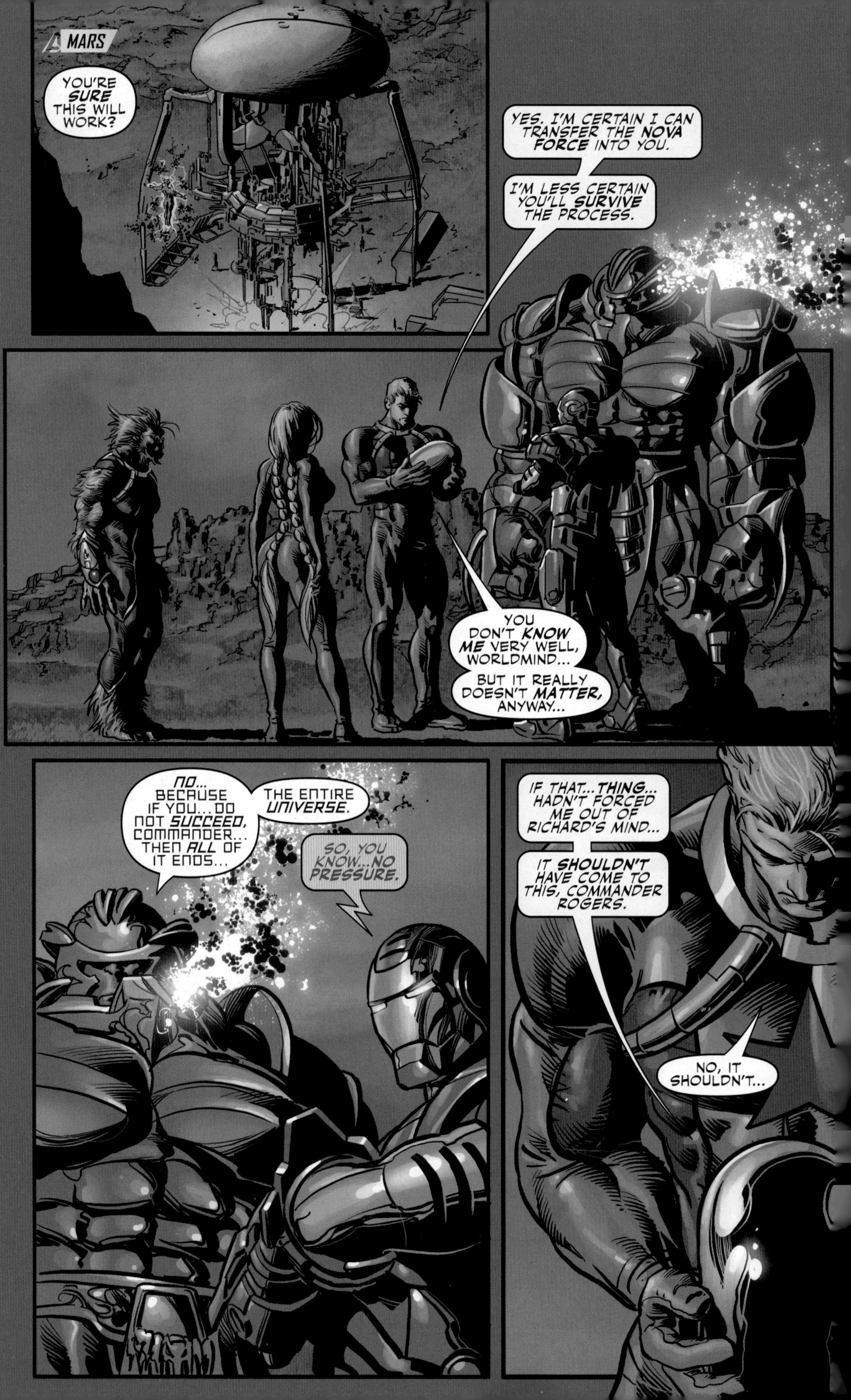
MARS
YOU'RE SURE THIS WILL WORK?
YES. I'M CERTAIN I CAN TRANSFER THE NOVA FORCE INTO YOU.
I'M LESS CERTAIN YOU'LL SURVIVE THE PROCESS.
YOU DON'T KNOW ME VERY WELL, WORLDMIND...
BUT IT REALLY DOESN'T MATTER, ANYWAY...
NO... BECAUSE IF YOU... DO NOT SUCCEED, COMMANDER... THEN ALL OF IT ENDS...
THE ENTIRE UNIVERSE.
SO, YOU KNOW...NO PRESSURE.
IF THAT...THING... HADN'T FORCED ME OUT OF RICHARD'S MIND...
IT SHOULDN'T HAVE COME TO THIS, COMMANDER ROGERS.
NO, IT SHOULDN'T...

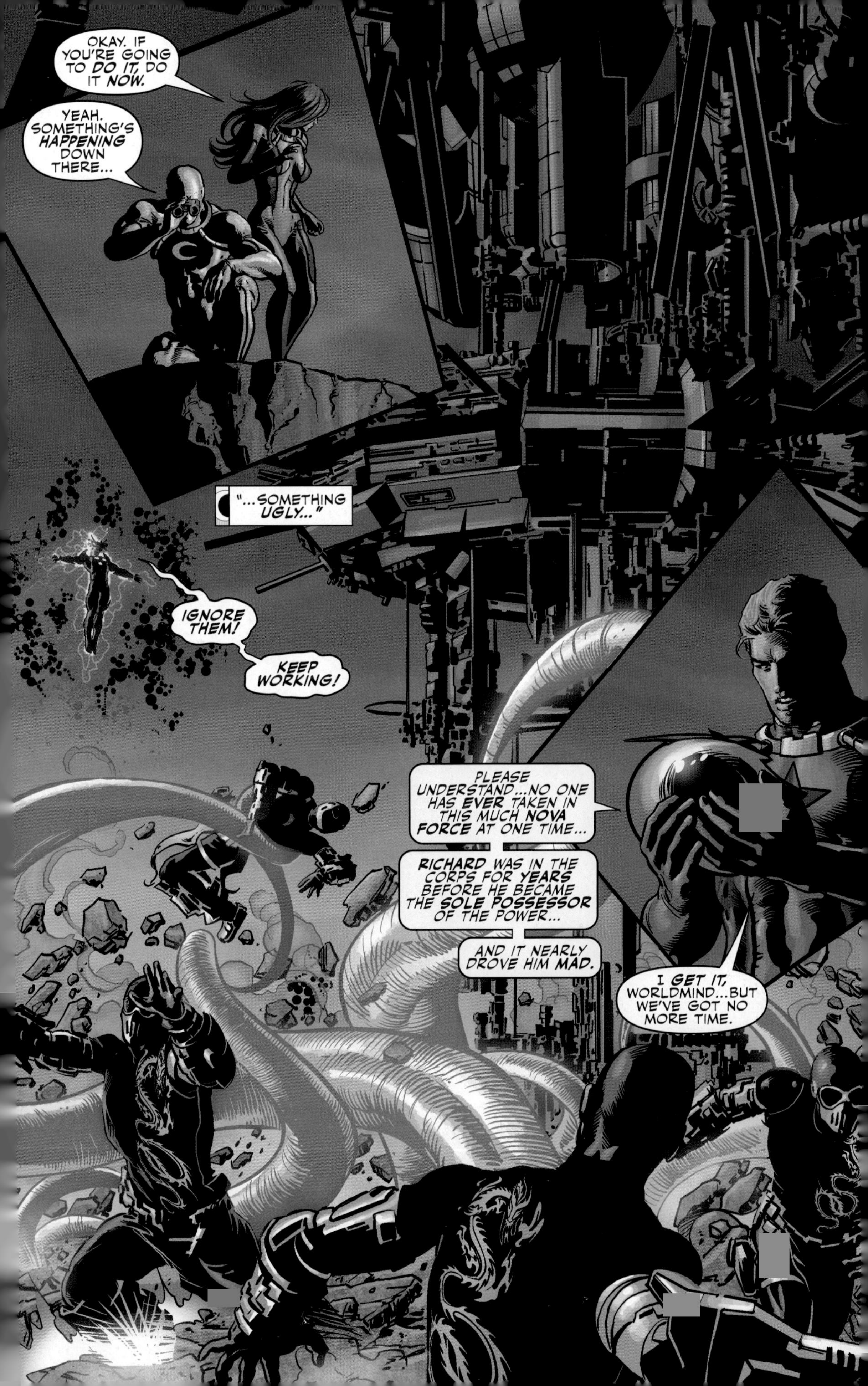

OKAY. IF YOU'RE GOING TO DO IT, DO IT NOW.
YEAH. SOMETHING'S HAPPENING DOWN THERE...
"...SOMETHING UGLY..."
IGNORE THEM!
KEEP WORKING!
PLEASE UNDERSTAND...NO ONE HAS EVER TAKEN IN THIS MUCH NOVA FORCE AT ONE TIME...
RICHARD WAS IN THE CORPS FOR YEARS BEFORE HE BECAME THE SOLE POSSESSOR OF THE POWER...
AND IT NEARLY DROVE HIM MAD.
I GET IT, WORLDMIND...BUT WE'VE GOT NO MORE TIME.

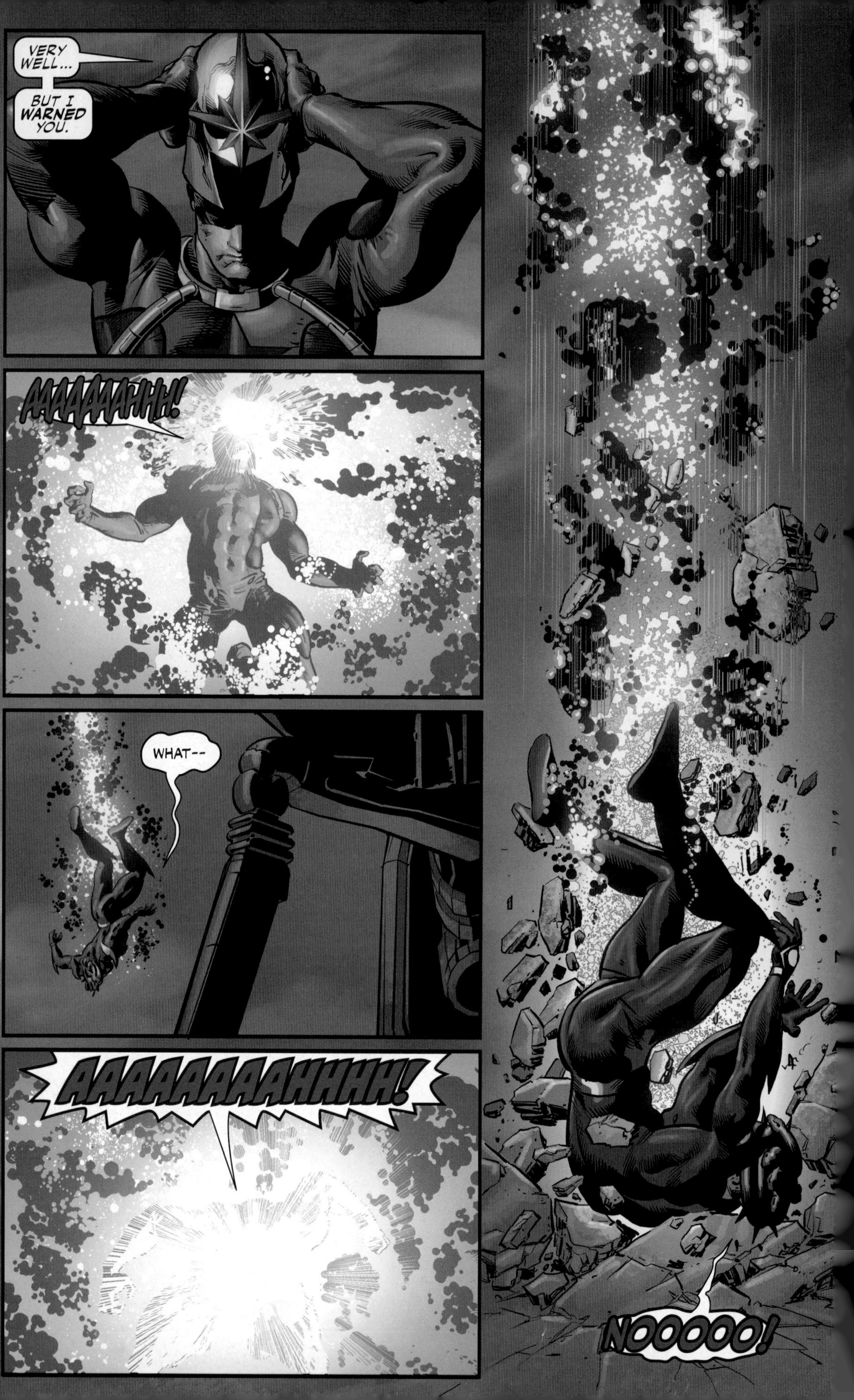

VERY WELL...
BUT I WARNED YOU.
AAAAAAAHHH!
WHAT--
AAAAAAAAHHHH!
NOOOOO!

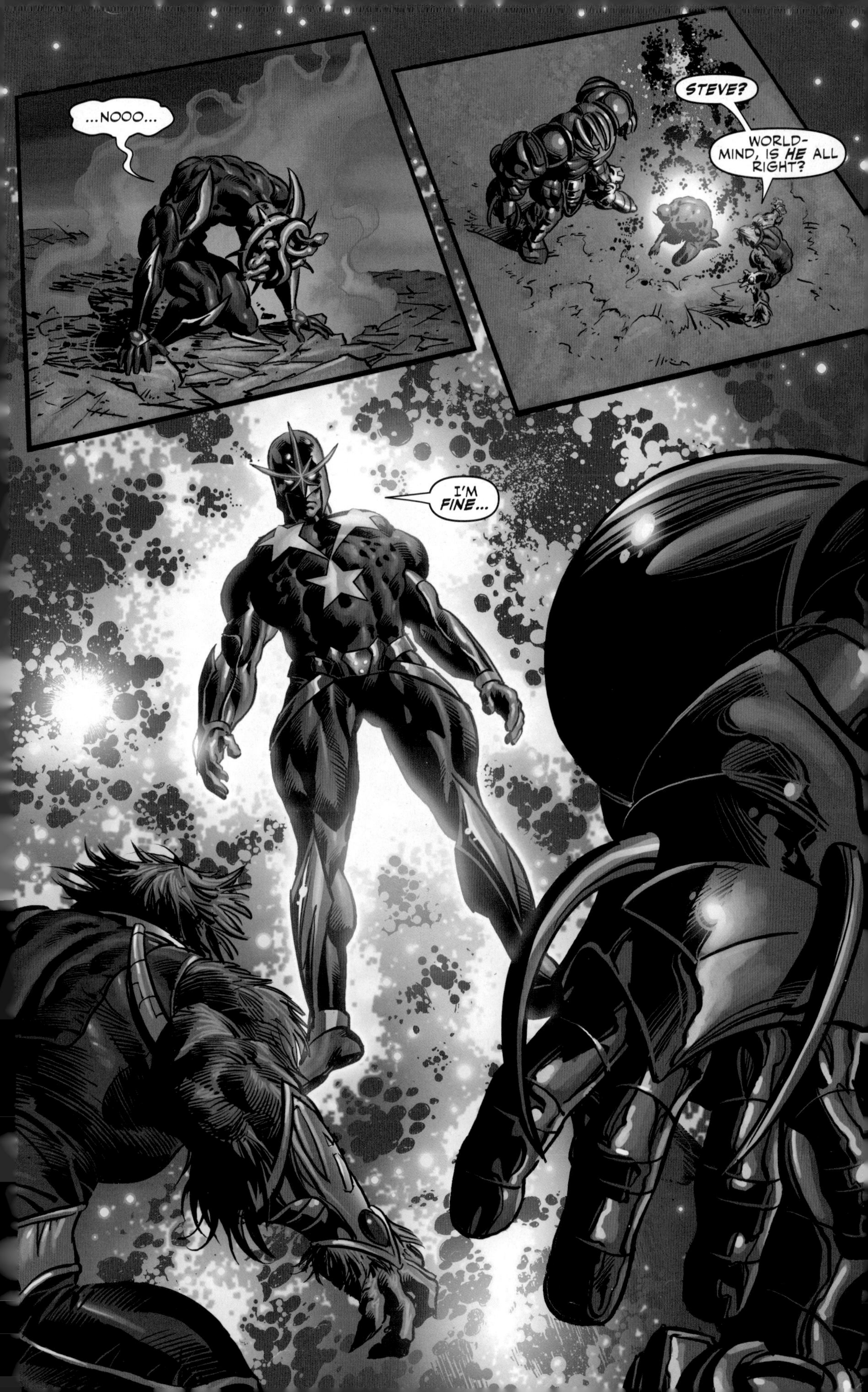
...NOOO...
STEVE?
WORLD-MIND, IS HE ALL RIGHT?
I'M FINE...

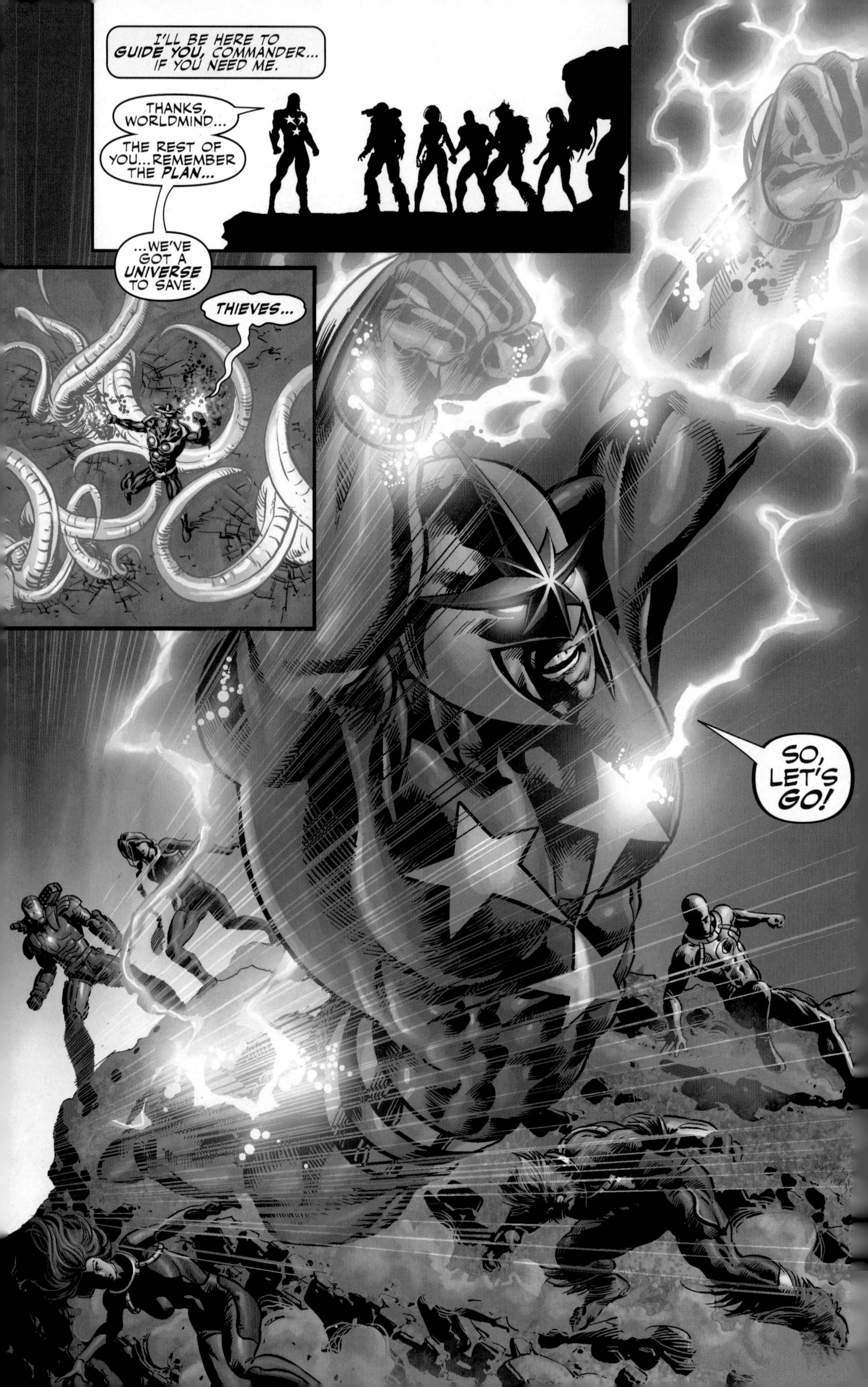
I'LL BE HERE TO GUIDE YOU, COMMANDER... IF YOU NEED ME.
THANKS, WORLDMIND...
THE REST OF YOU...REMEMBER THE PLAN...
...WE'VE GOT A UNIVERSE TO SAVE.
THIEVES...
SO, LET'S GO!

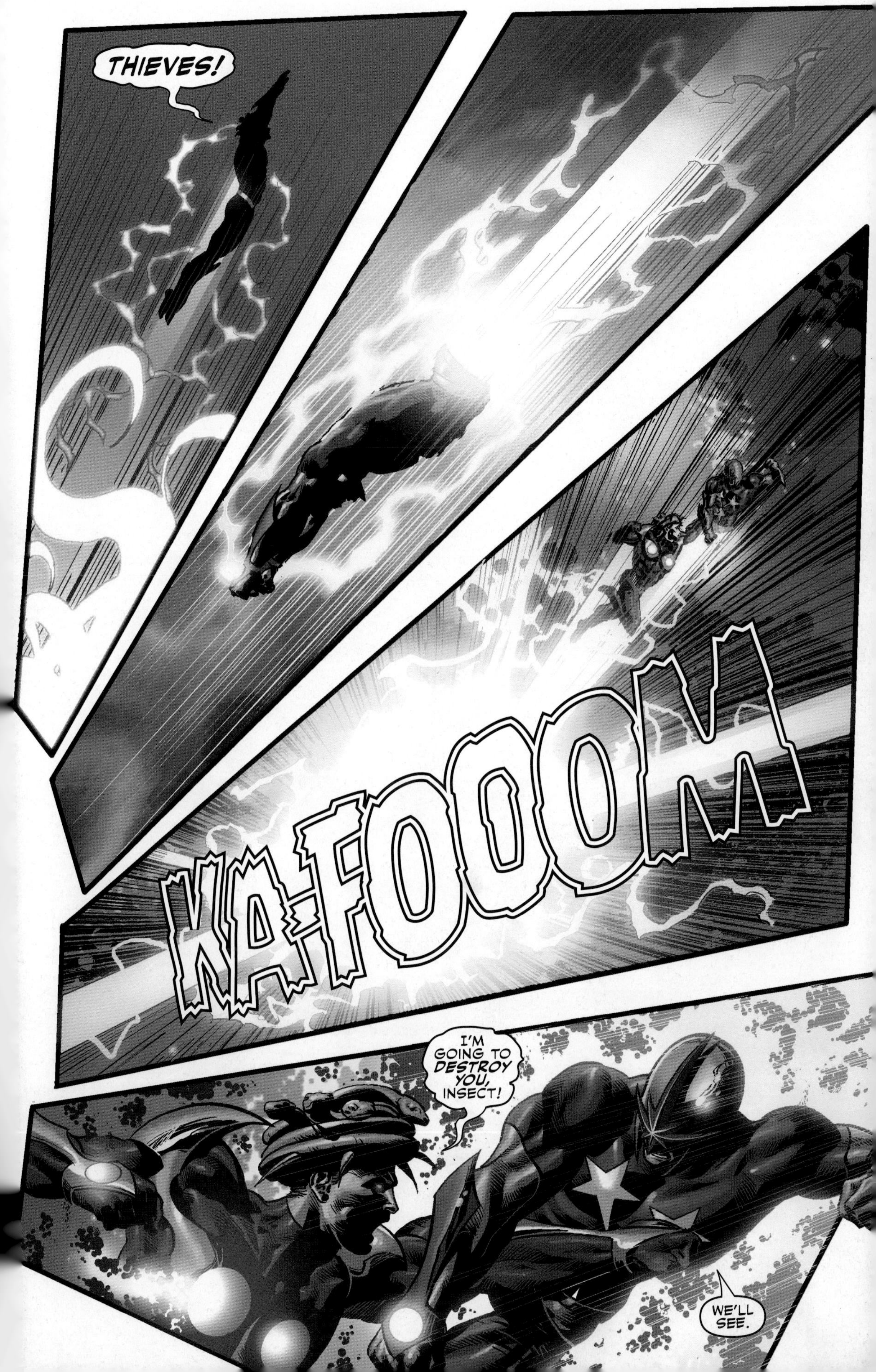
THIEVES!
KA-FOOOM
I'M GOING TO DESTROY YOU, INSECT!
WE'LL SEE.

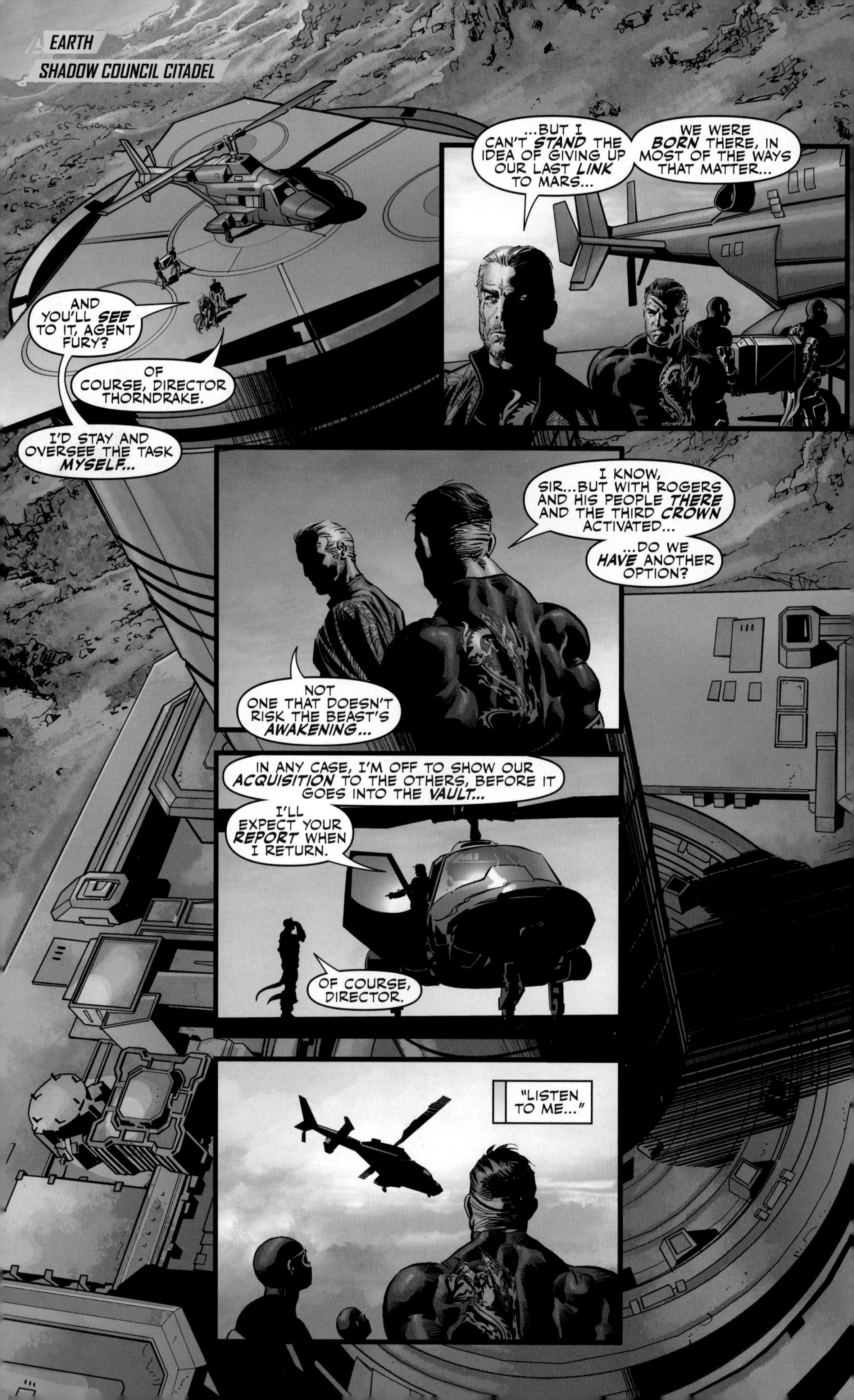
EARTH
SHADOW COUNCIL CITADEL
...BUT I CAN'T STAND THE IDEA OF GIVING UP OUR LAST LINK TO MARS...
WE WERE BORN THERE, IN MOST OF THE WAYS THAT MATTER...
AND YOU'LL SEE TO IT, AGENT FURY?
OF COURSE, DIRECTOR THORNDRAKE.
I'D STAY AND OVERSEE THE TASK MYSELF...
I KNOW, SIR...BUT WITH ROGERS AND HIS PEOPLE THERE AND THE THIRD CROWN ACTIVATED...
...DO WE HAVE ANOTHER OPTION?
NOT ONE THAT DOESN'T RISK THE BEAST'S AWAKENING...
IN ANY CASE, I'M OFF TO SHOW OUR ACQUISITION TO THE OTHERS, BEFORE IT GOES INTO THE VAULT...
I'LL EXPECT YOUR REPORT WHEN I RETURN.
OF COURSE, DIRECTOR.
"LISTEN TO ME..."

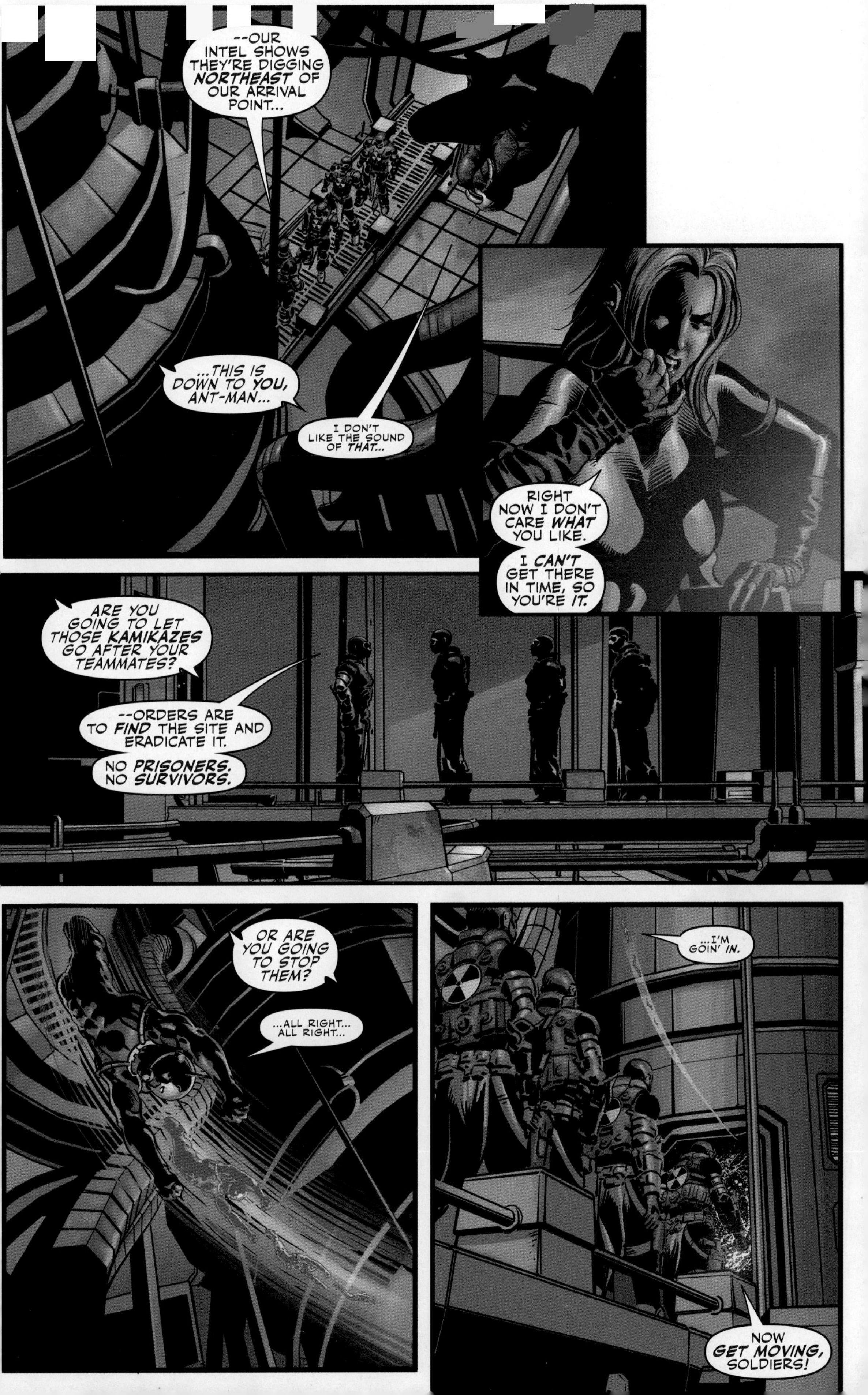
--OUR INTEL SHOWS THEY'RE DIGGING NORTHEAST OF OUR ARRIVAL POINT...
...THIS IS DOWN TO YOU, ANT-MAN...
I DON'T LIKE THE SOUND OF THAT...
RIGHT NOW I DON'T CARE WHAT YOU LIKE.
I CAN'T GET THERE IN TIME, SO YOU'RE IT.
ARE YOU GOING TO LET THOSE KAMIKAZES GO AFTER YOUR TEAMMATES?
--ORDERS ARE TO FIND THE SITE AND ERADICATE IT.
NO PRISONERS. NO SURVIVORS.
OR ARE YOU GOING TO STOP THEM?
...ALL RIGHT... ALL RIGHT...
...I'M GOIN' IN.
NOW GET MOVING, SOLDIERS!

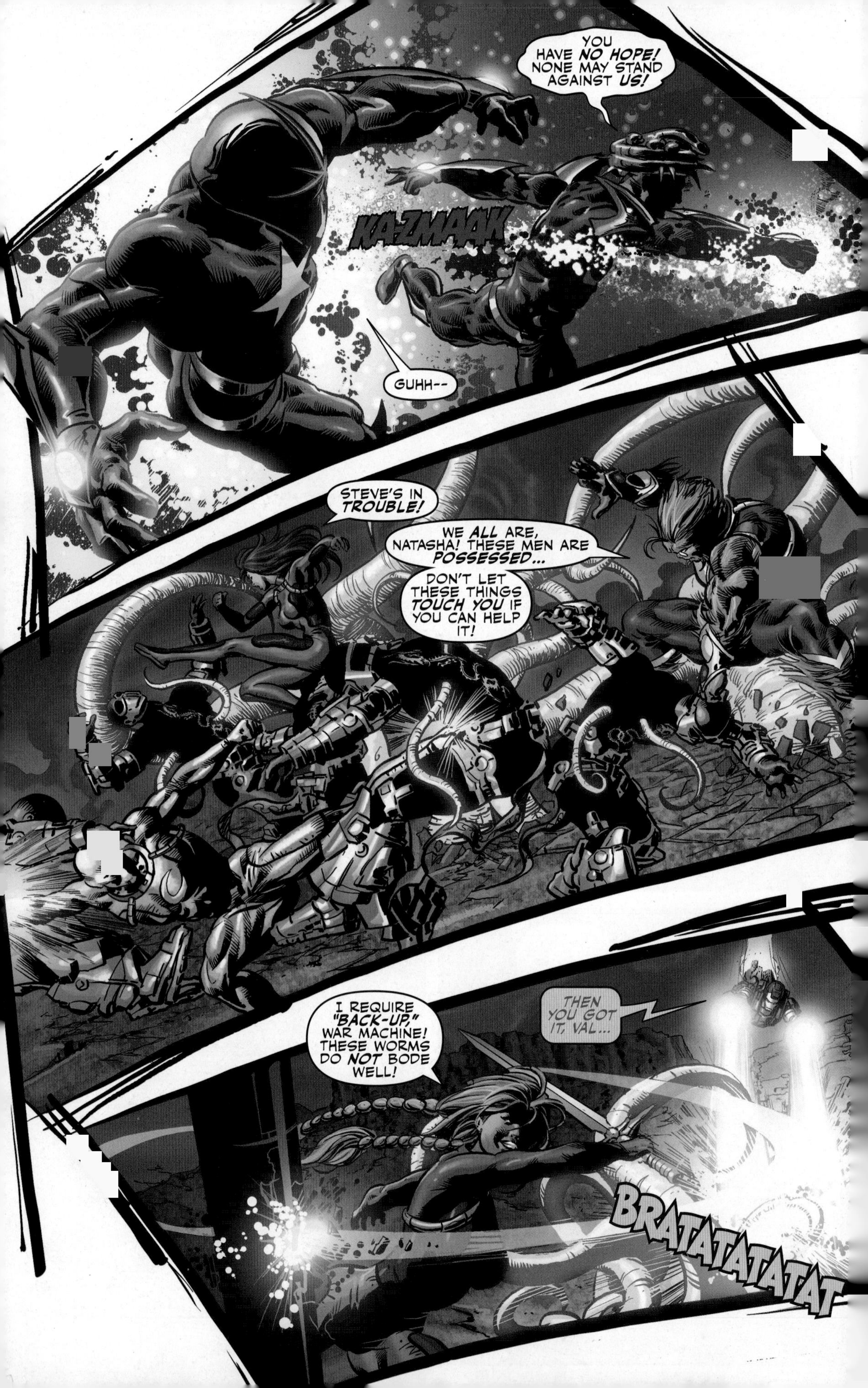
YOU HAVE NO HOPE! NONE MAY STAND AGAINST US!
KA-ZMAAK
GUHH--
STEVE'S IN TROUBLE!
WE ALL ARE, NATASHA! THESE MEN ARE POSSESSED...
DON'T LET THESE THINGS TOUCH YOU IF YOU CAN HELP IT!
I REQUIRE "BACK-UP," WAR MACHINE! THESE WORMS DO NOT BODE WELL!
THEN YOU GOT IT, VAL...
BRATATATATAT

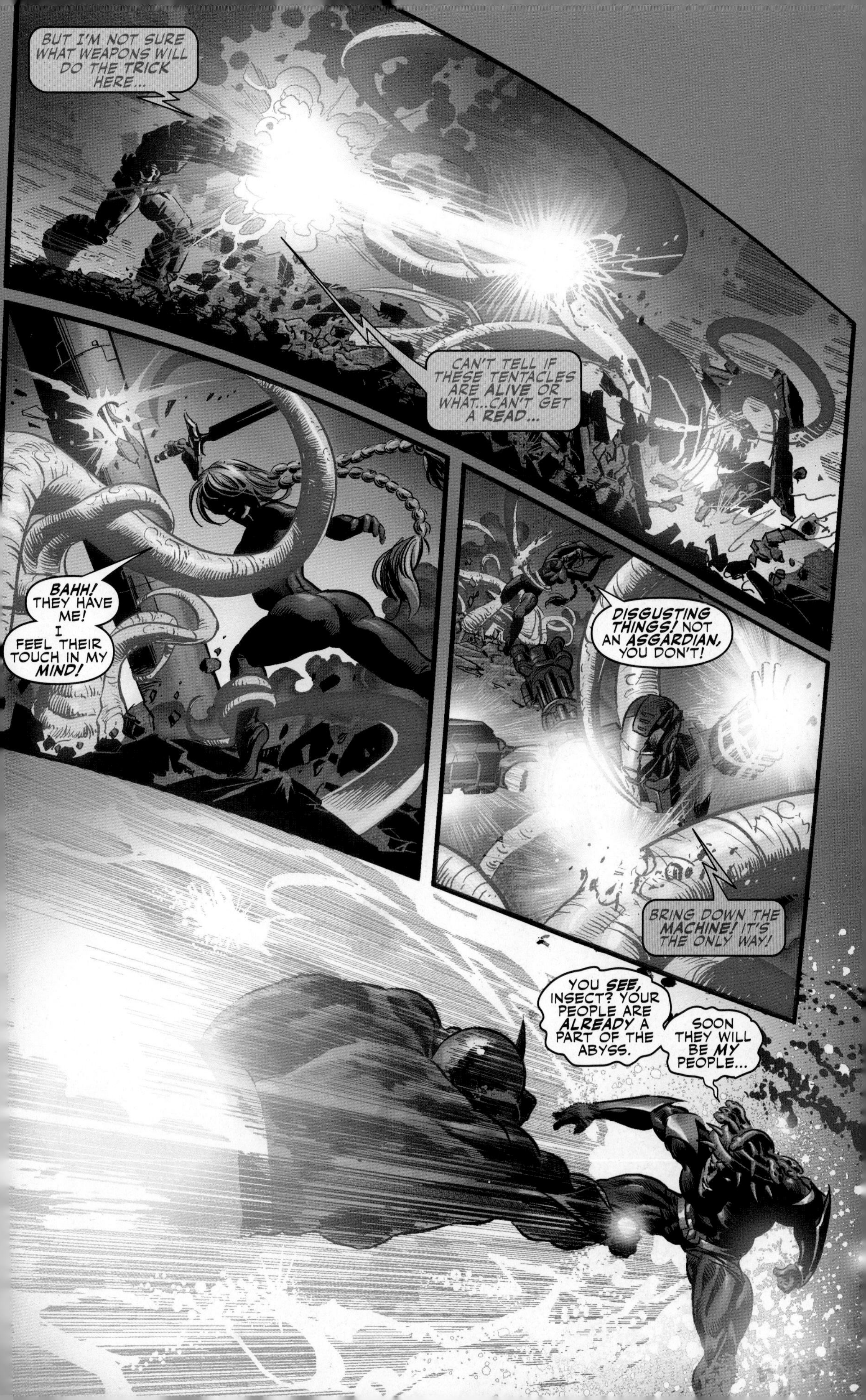
BUT I'M NOT SURE WHAT WEAPONS WILL DO THE TRICK HERE...
CAN'T TELL IF THESE TENTACLES ARE ALIVE OR WHAT...CAN'T GET A READ...
BAHH! THEY HAVE ME! I FEEL THEIR TOUCH IN MY MIND!
DISGUSTING THINGS! NOT AN ASGARDIAN, YOU DON'T!
BRING DOWN THE MACHINE! IT'S THE ONLY WAY!
YOU SEE, INSECT? YOUR PEOPLE ARE ALREADY A PART OF THE ABYSS.
SOON THEY WILL BE MY PEOPLE...

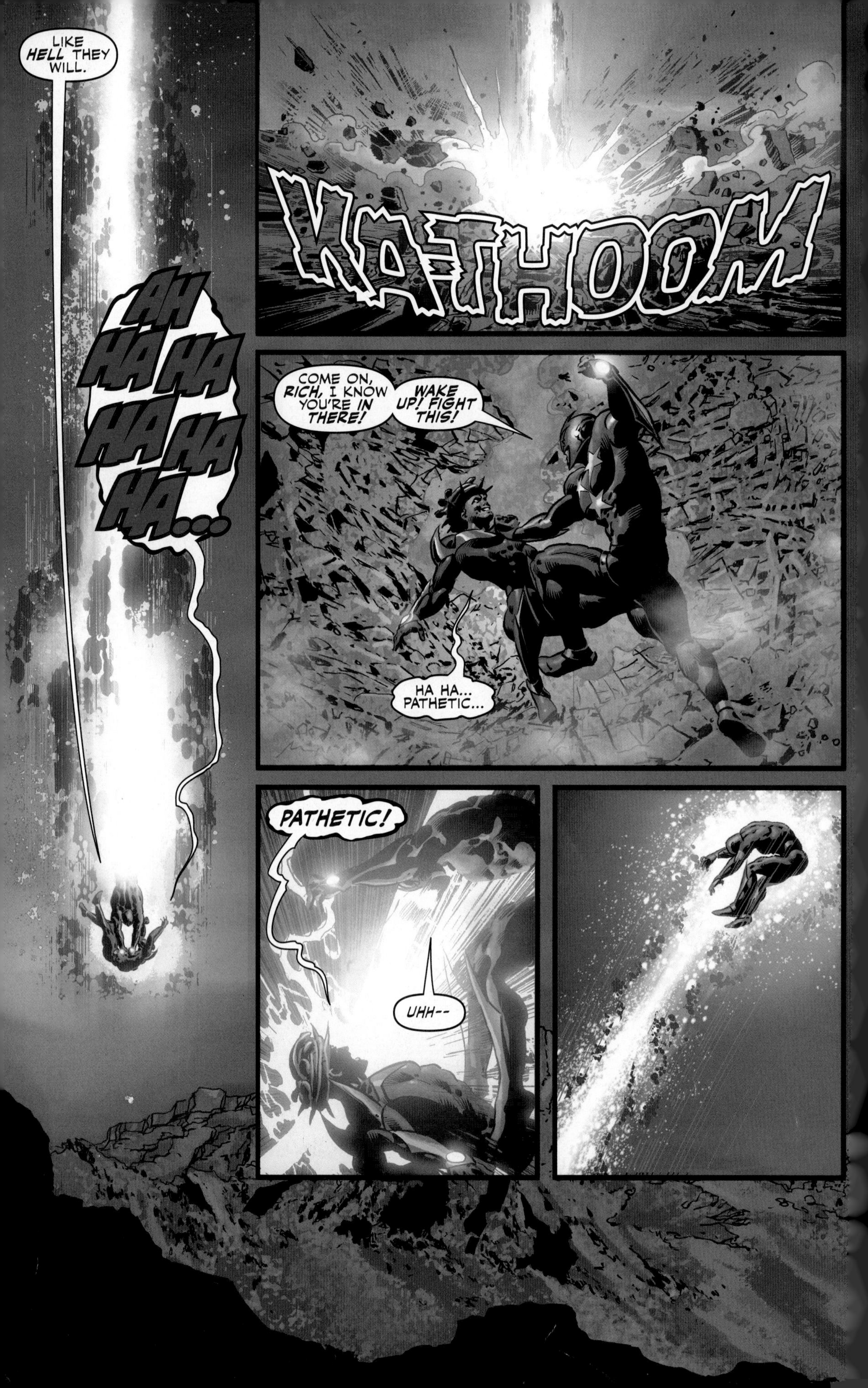

LIKE HELL THEY WILL.
AH HA HA HA HA HA...
KATHOOM
COME ON, RICH, I KNOW YOU'RE IN THERE!
WAKE UP! FIGHT THIS!
HA HA... PATHETIC...
PATHETIC!
UHH--

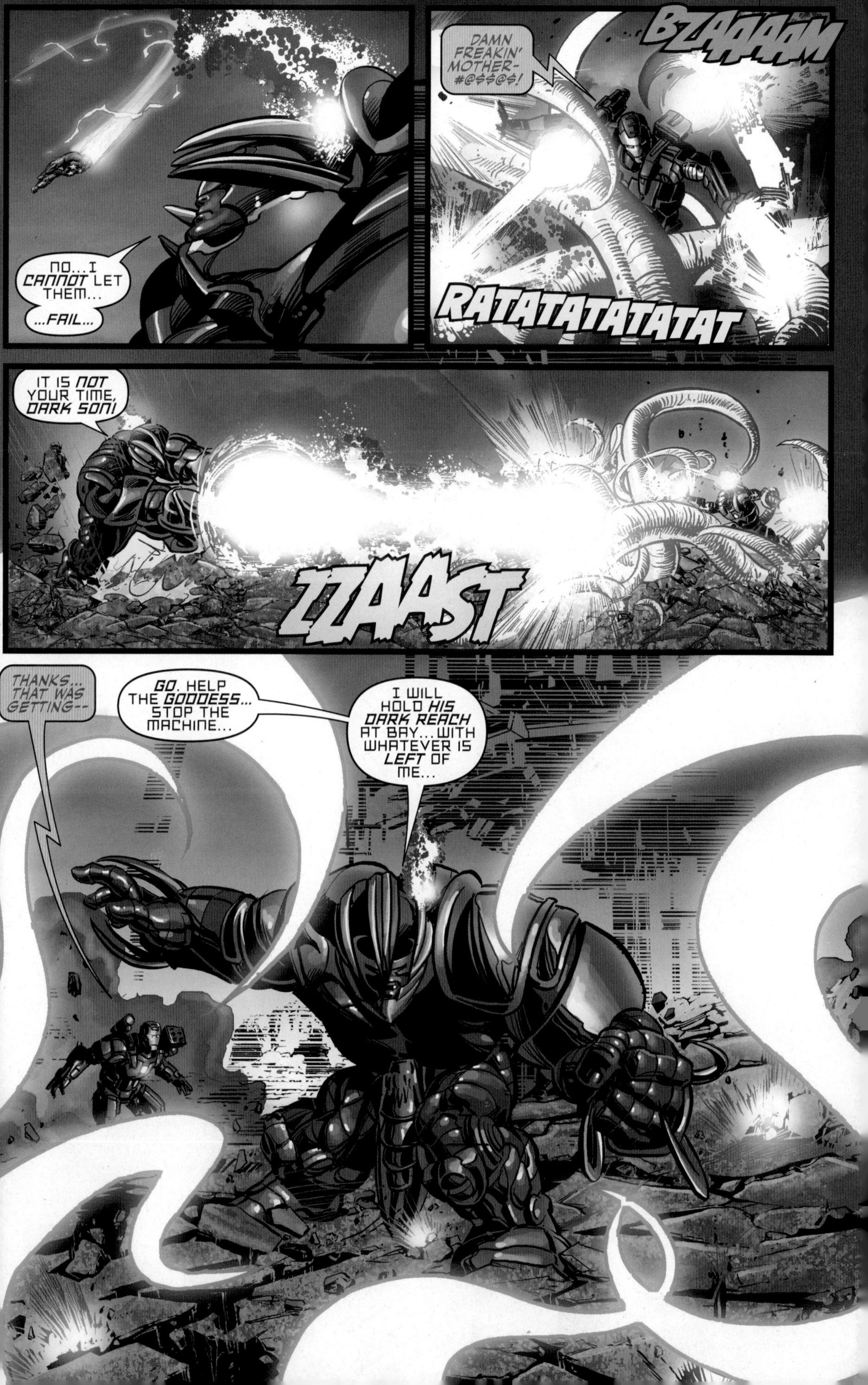
NO... I CANNOT LET THEM...
...FAIL...
DAMN FREAKIN' MOTHER-#@$$@$!
BZAAAAM
RATATATATATATAT
IT IS NOT YOUR TIME, DARK SON!
ZZAAST
THANKS... THAT WAS GETTING--
GO. HELP THE GODDESS... STOP THE MACHINE...
I WILL HOLD HIS DARK REACH AT BAY... WITH WHATEVER IS LEFT OF ME...

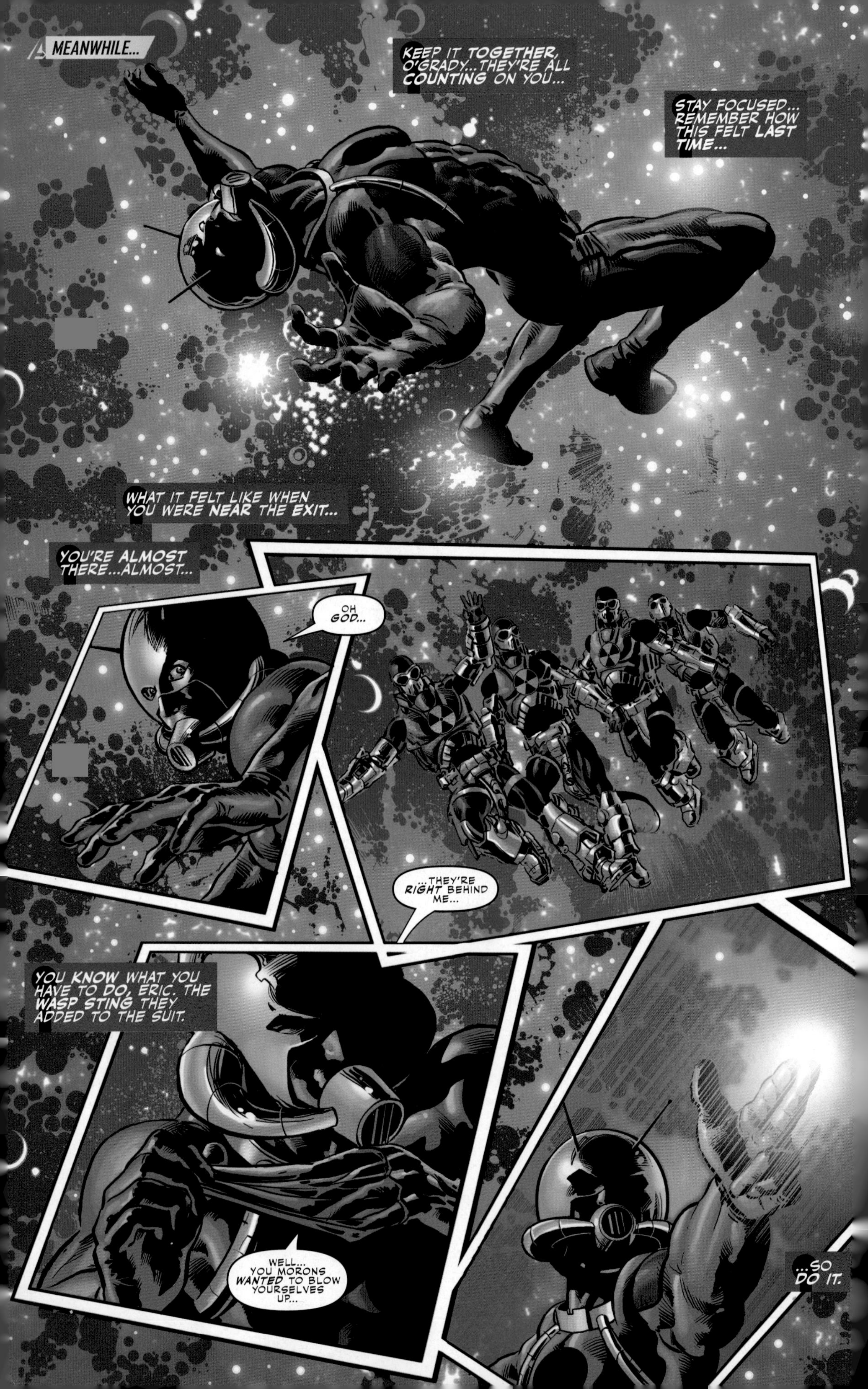
MEANWHILE...
KEEP IT TOGETHER, O'GRADY...THEY'RE ALL COUNTING ON YOU...
STAY FOCUSED... REMEMBER HOW THIS FELT LAST TIME...
WHAT IT FELT LIKE WHEN YOU WERE NEAR THE EXIT...
YOU'RE ALMOST THERE...ALMOST...
OH GOD...
...THEY'RE RIGHT BEHIND ME...
YOU KNOW WHAT YOU HAVE TO DO, ERIC. THE WASP STING THEY ADDED TO THE SUIT.
WELL... YOU MORONS WANTED TO BLOW YOURSELVES UP...
...SO DO IT.

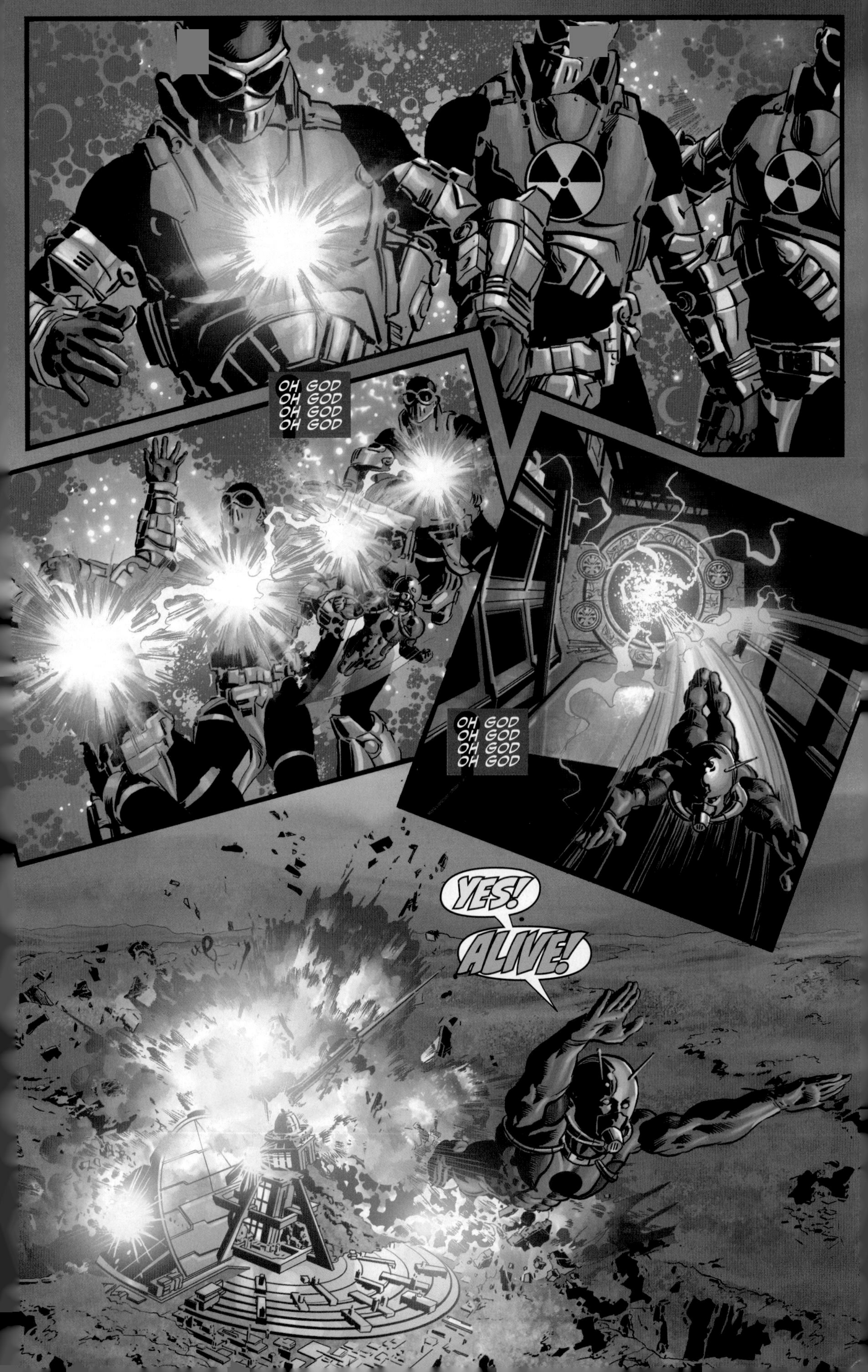
OH GOD
OH GOD
OH GOD
OH GOD
OH GOD
OH GOD
OH GOD
OH GOD
YES!
ALIVE!

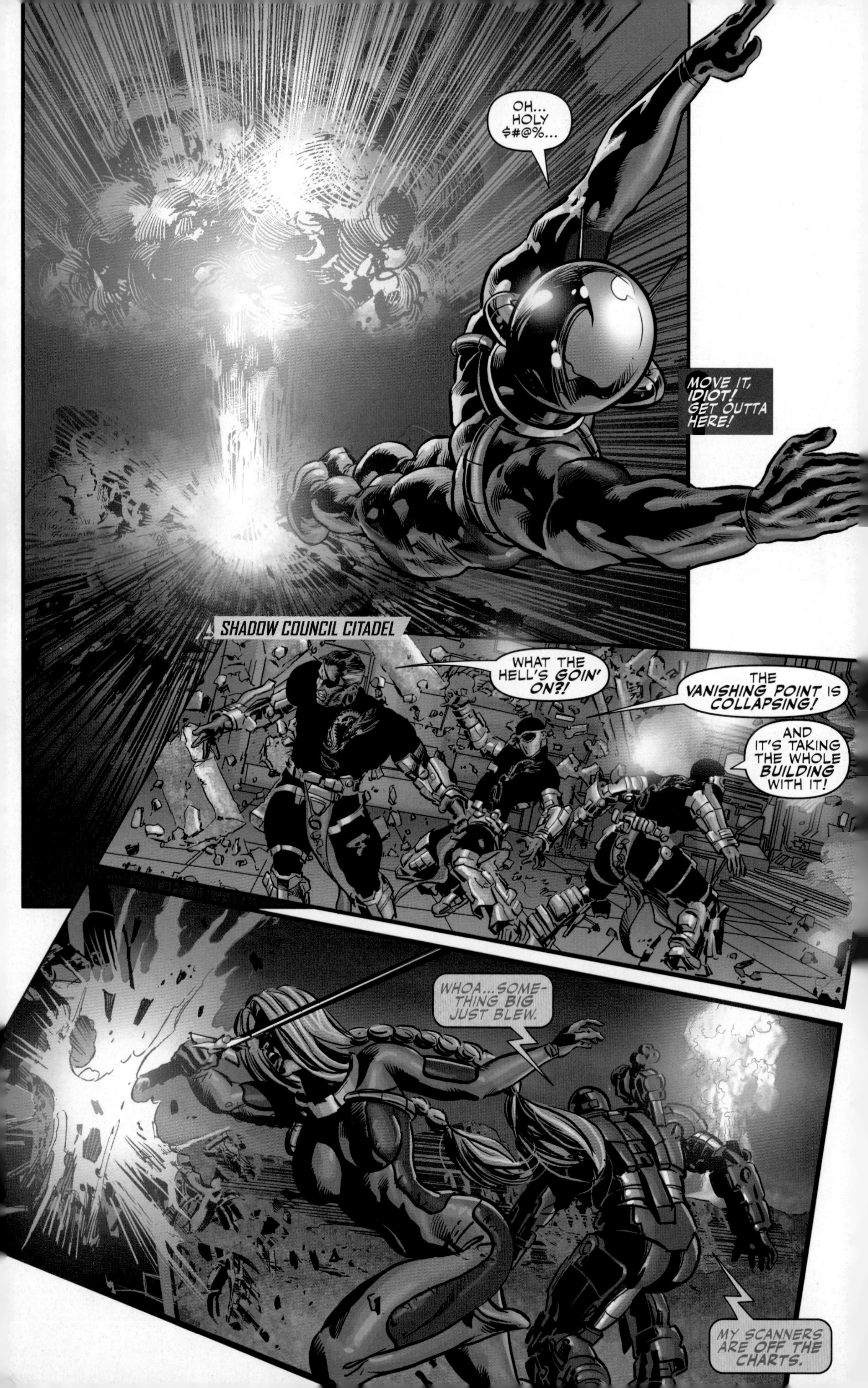
OH... HOLY $#@%...
MOVE IT, IDIOT! GET OUTTA HERE!
SHADOW COUNCIL CITADEL
WHAT THE HELL'S GOIN' ON?!
THE VANISHING POINT IS COLLAPSING!
AND IT'S TAKING THE WHOLE BUILDING WITH IT!
WHOA...SOME-THING BIG JUST BLEW.
MY SCANNERS ARE OFF THE CHARTS.

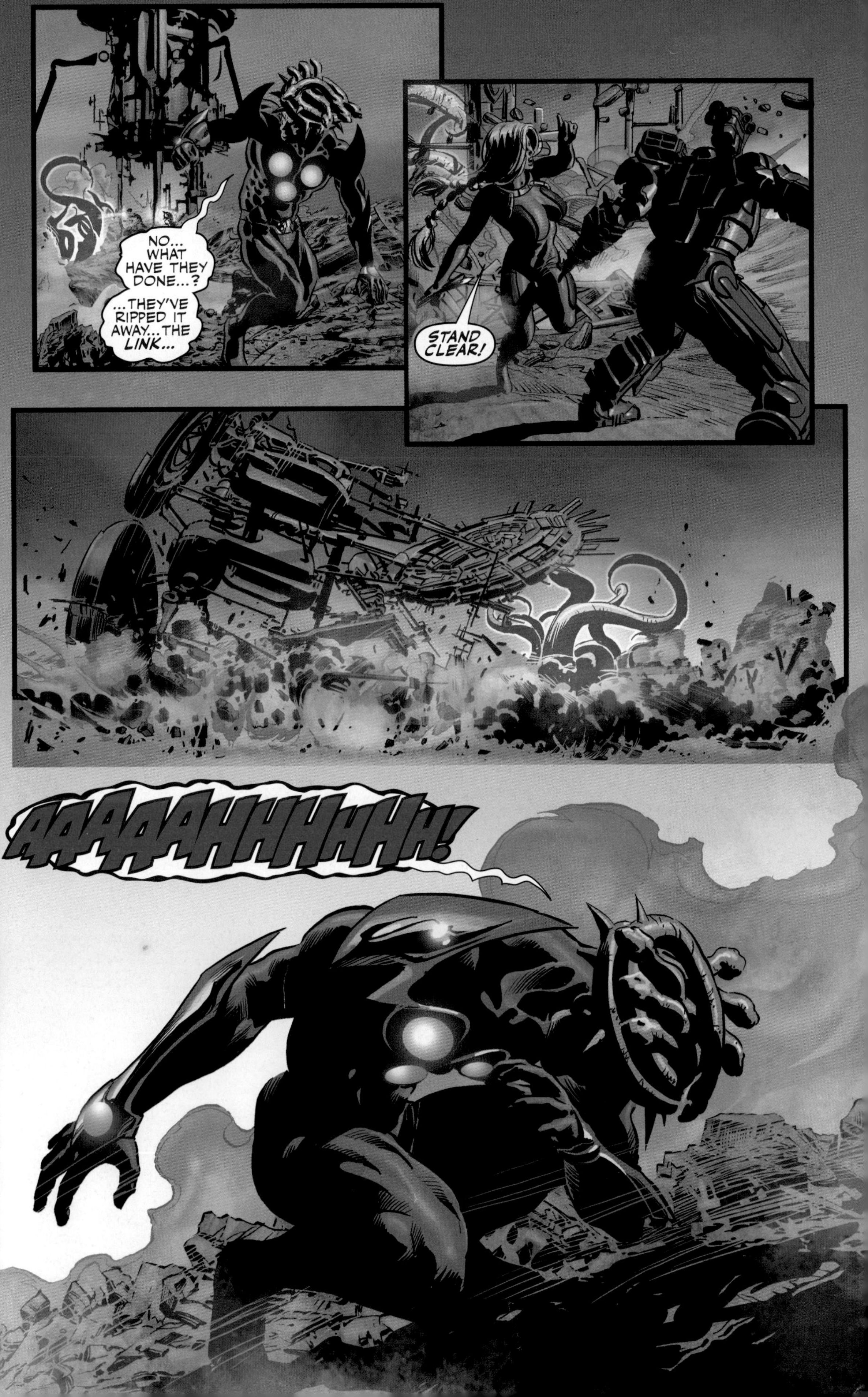
NO... WHAT HAVE THEY DONE...? ...THEY'VE RIPPED IT AWAY...THE LINK...
STAND CLEAR!
AAAAAHHHHHH!

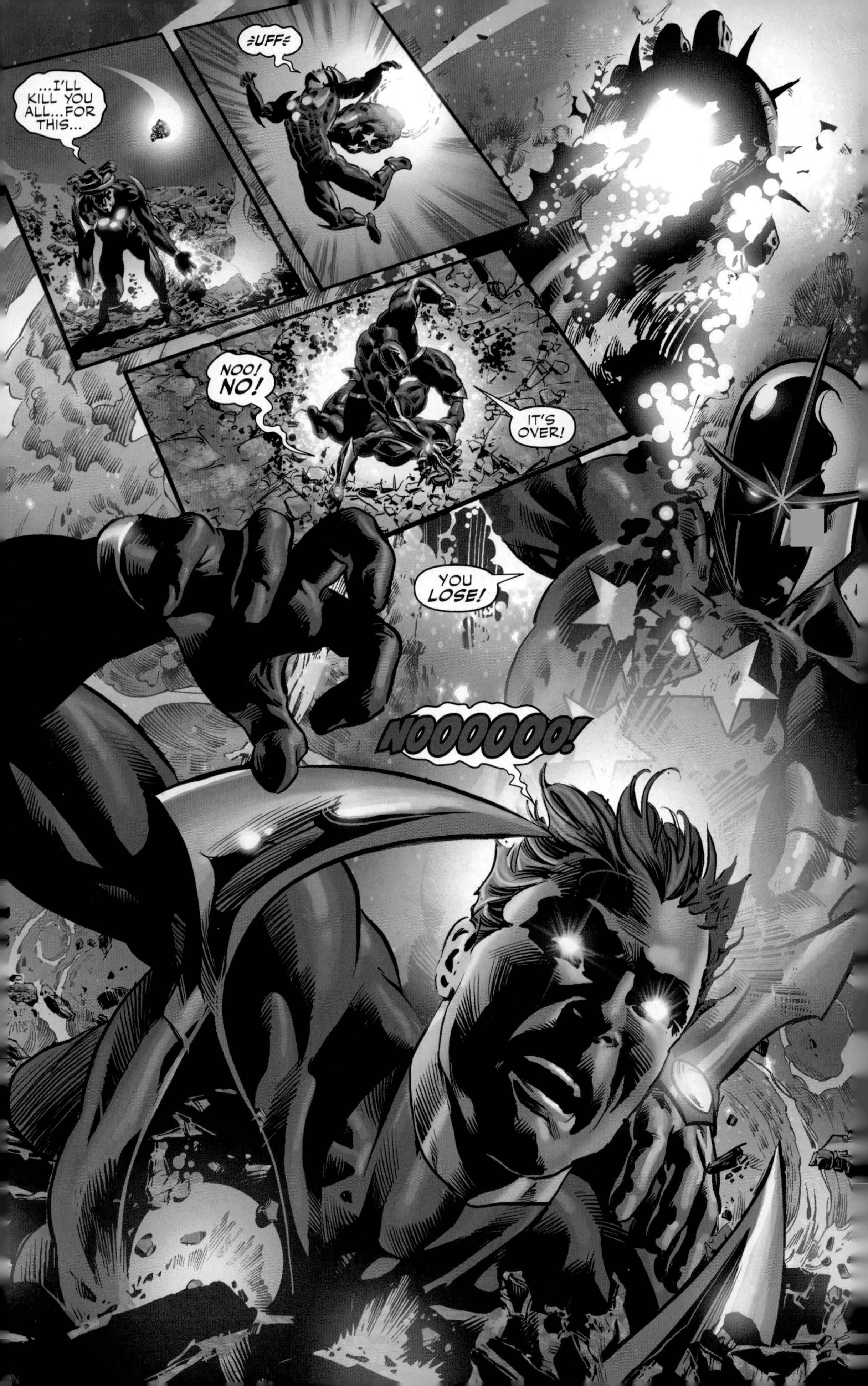
...I'LL KILL YOU ALL...FOR THIS...
UFF
NOO! NO!
IT'S OVER!
YOU LOSE!
NOOOOOO!

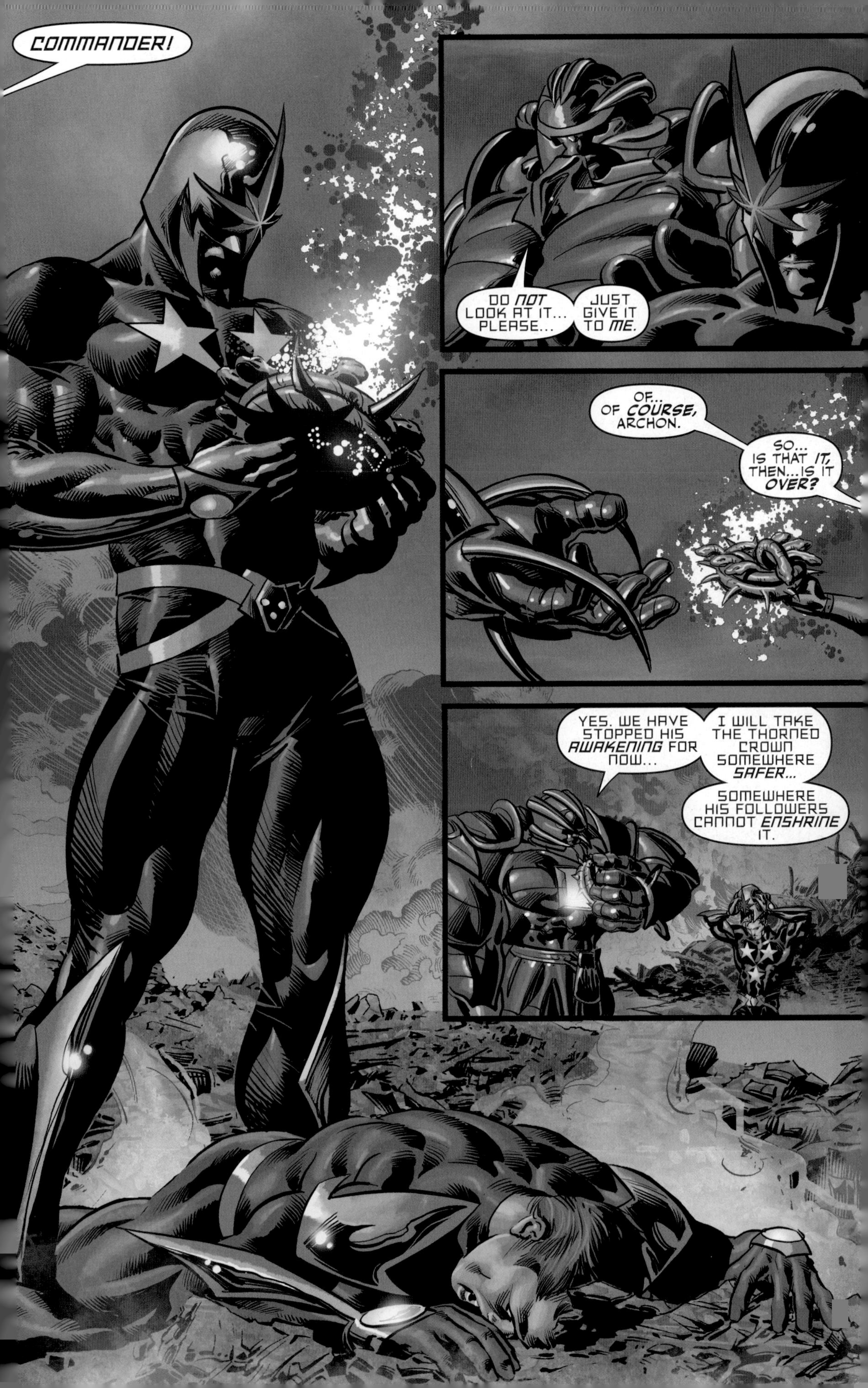
COMMANDER!
DO NOT LOOK AT IT... PLEASE...
JUST GIVE IT TO ME.
OF... OF COURSE, ARCHON.
SO... IS THAT IT, THEN... IS IT OVER?
YES. WE HAVE STOPPED HIS AWAKENING FOR NOW...
I WILL TAKE THE THORNED CROWN SOMEWHERE SAFER...
SOMEWHERE HIS FOLLOWERS CANNOT ENSHRINE IT.

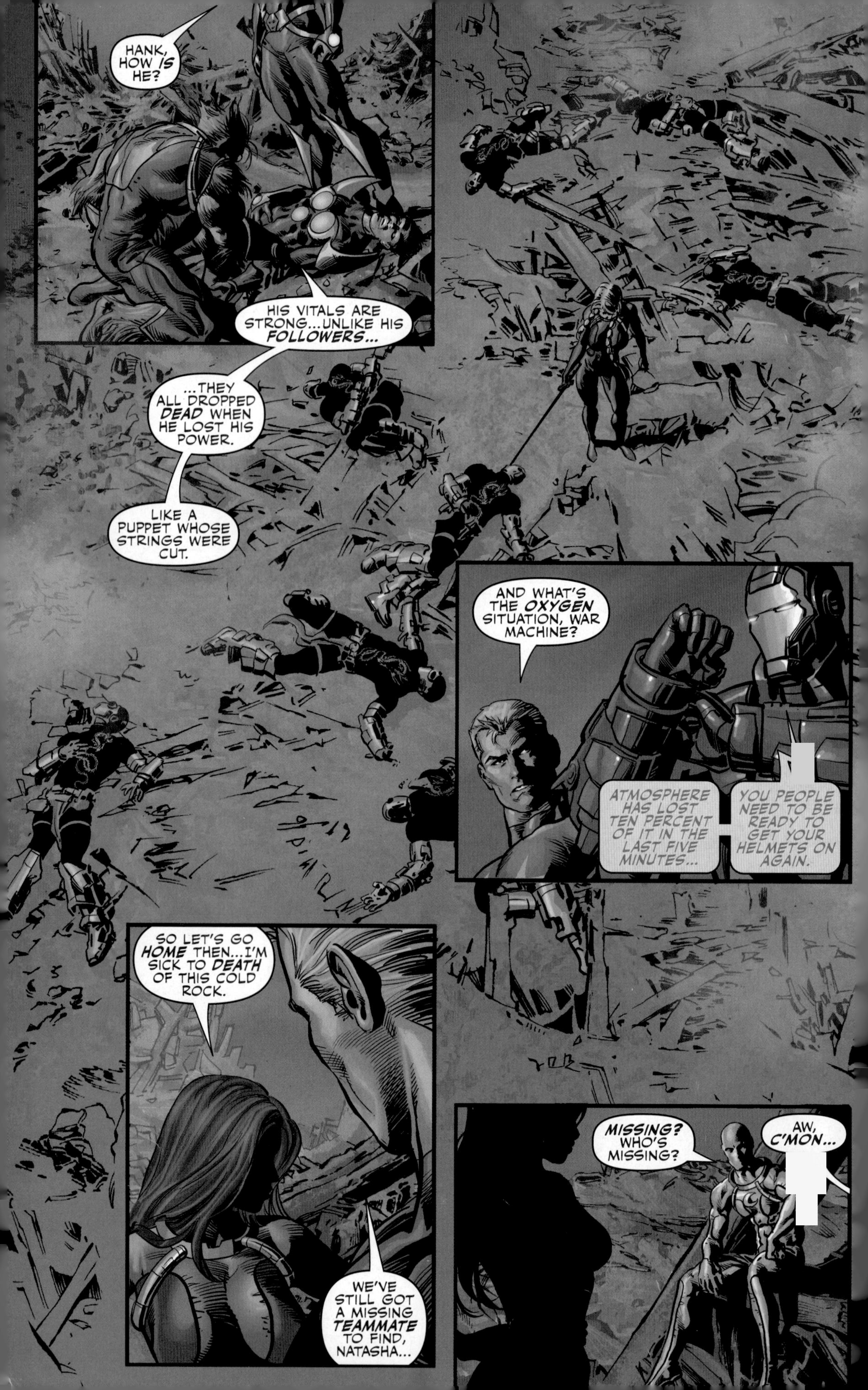
HANK, HOW *IS* HE?
HIS VITALS ARE STRONG...UNLIKE HIS ***FOLLOWERS...***
...THEY ALL DROPPED ***DEAD*** WHEN HE LOST HIS POWER.
LIKE A PUPPET WHOSE STRINGS WERE CUT.
AND WHAT'S THE ***OXYGEN*** SITUATION, WAR MACHINE?
ATMOSPHERE HAS LOST TEN PERCENT OF IT IN THE LAST FIVE MINUTES...
YOU PEOPLE NEED TO BE READY TO GET YOUR HELMETS ON AGAIN.
SO LET'S GO ***HOME*** THEN...I'M SICK TO ***DEATH*** OF THIS COLD ROCK.
WE'VE STILL GOT A MISSING ***TEAMMATE*** TO FIND, NATASHA...
***MISSING?*** WHO'S MISSING?
AW, ***C'MON...***

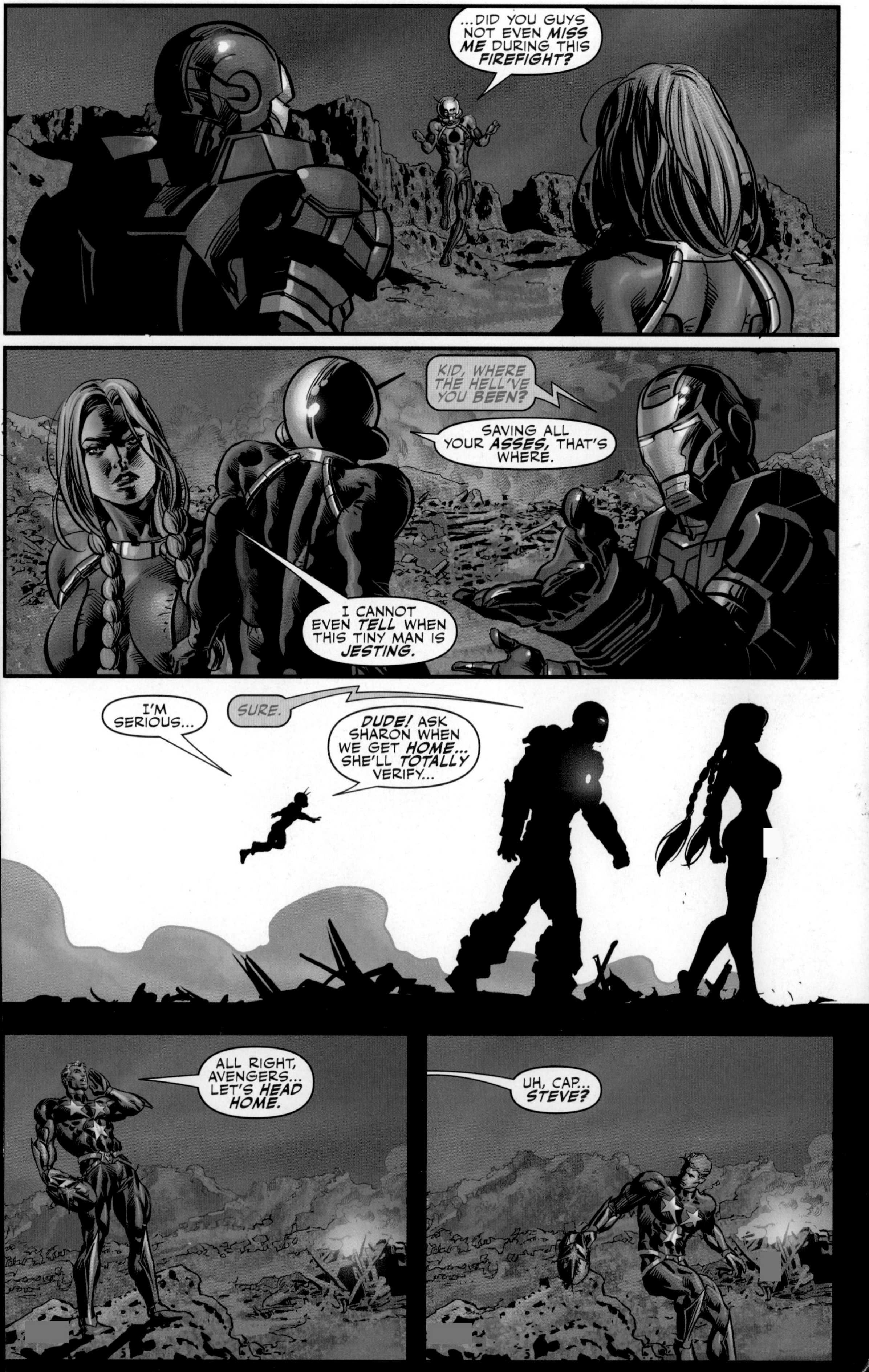
...DID YOU GUYS NOT EVEN MISS ME DURING THIS FIREFIGHT?
KID, WHERE THE HELL'VE YOU BEEN?
SAVING ALL YOUR ASSES, THAT'S WHERE.
I CANNOT EVEN TELL WHEN THIS TINY MAN IS JESTING.
I'M SERIOUS...
SURE.
DUDE! ASK SHARON WHEN WE GET HOME... SHE'LL TOTALLY VERIFY...
ALL RIGHT, AVENGERS... LET'S HEAD HOME.
UH, CAP... STEVE?

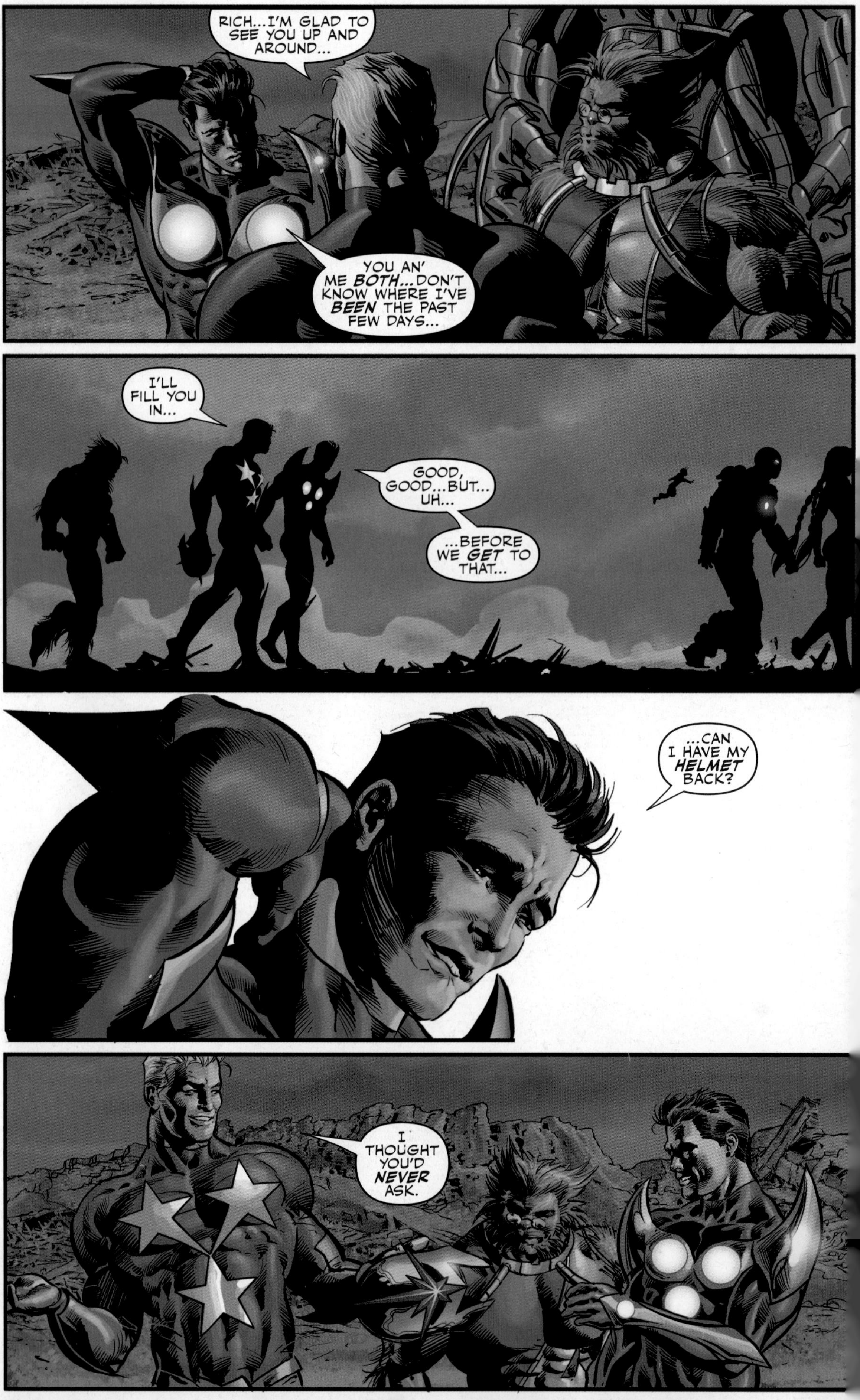
RICH...I'M GLAD TO SEE YOU UP AND AROUND...
YOU AN' ME BOTH...DON'T KNOW WHERE I'VE BEEN THE PAST FEW DAYS...
I'LL FILL YOU IN...
GOOD, GOOD...BUT... UH...
...BEFORE WE GET TO THAT...
...CAN I HAVE MY HELMET BACK?
I THOUGHT YOU'D NEVER ASK.

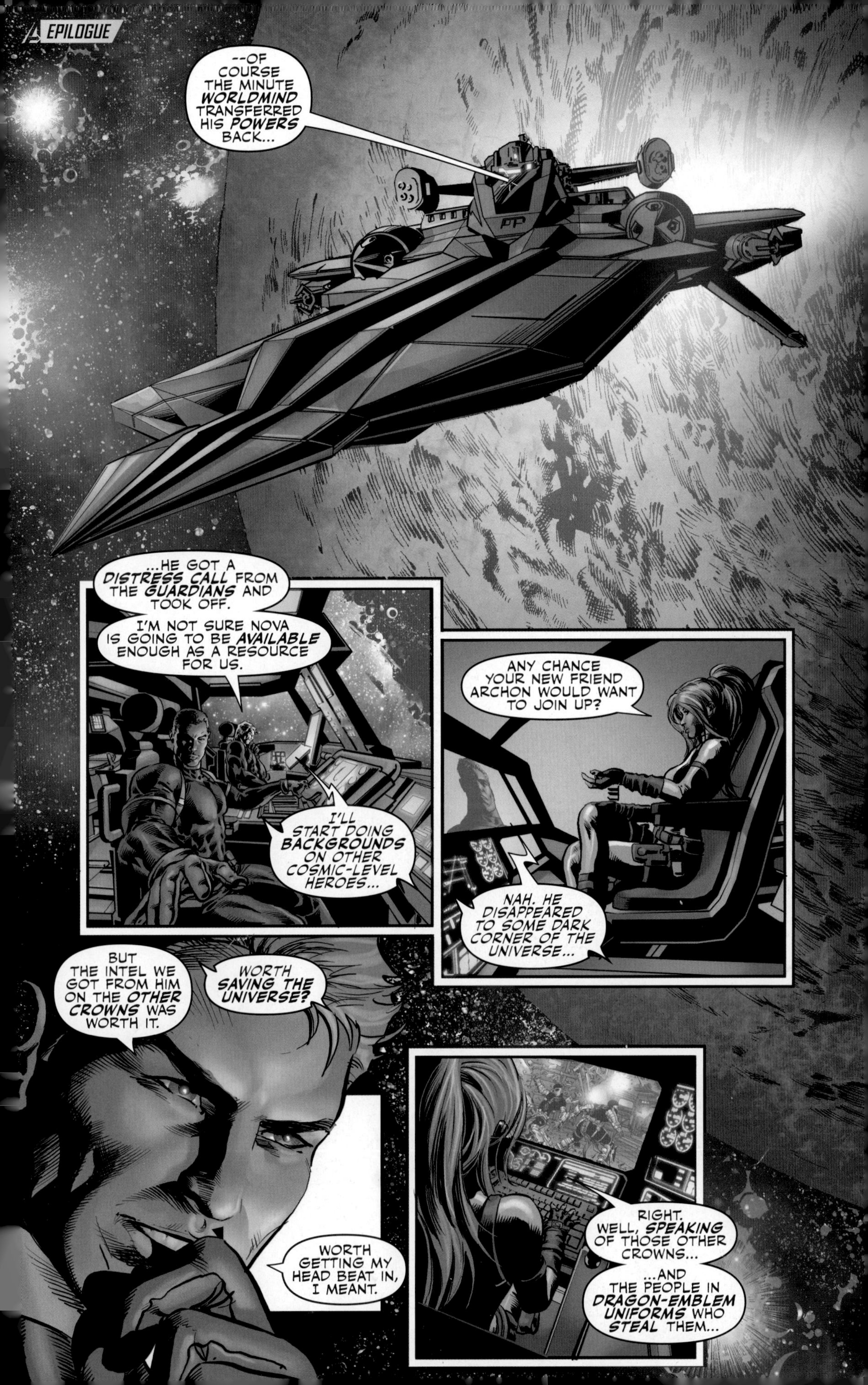
EPILOGUE
--OF COURSE THE MINUTE WORLDMIND TRANSFERRED HIS POWERS BACK...
...HE GOT A DISTRESS CALL FROM THE GUARDIANS AND TOOK OFF.
I'M NOT SURE NOVA IS GOING TO BE AVAILABLE ENOUGH AS A RESOURCE FOR US.
I'LL START DOING BACKGROUNDS ON OTHER COSMIC-LEVEL HEROES...
ANY CHANCE YOUR NEW FRIEND ARCHON WOULD WANT TO JOIN UP?
NAH. HE DISAPPEARED TO SOME DARK CORNER OF THE UNIVERSE...
BUT THE INTEL WE GOT FROM HIM ON THE OTHER CROWNS WAS WORTH IT.
WORTH SAVING THE UNIVERSE?
WORTH GETTING MY HEAD BEAT IN, I MEANT.
RIGHT. WELL, SPEAKING OF THOSE OTHER CROWNS...
...AND THE PEOPLE IN DRAGON-EMBLEM UNIFORMS WHO STEAL THEM...

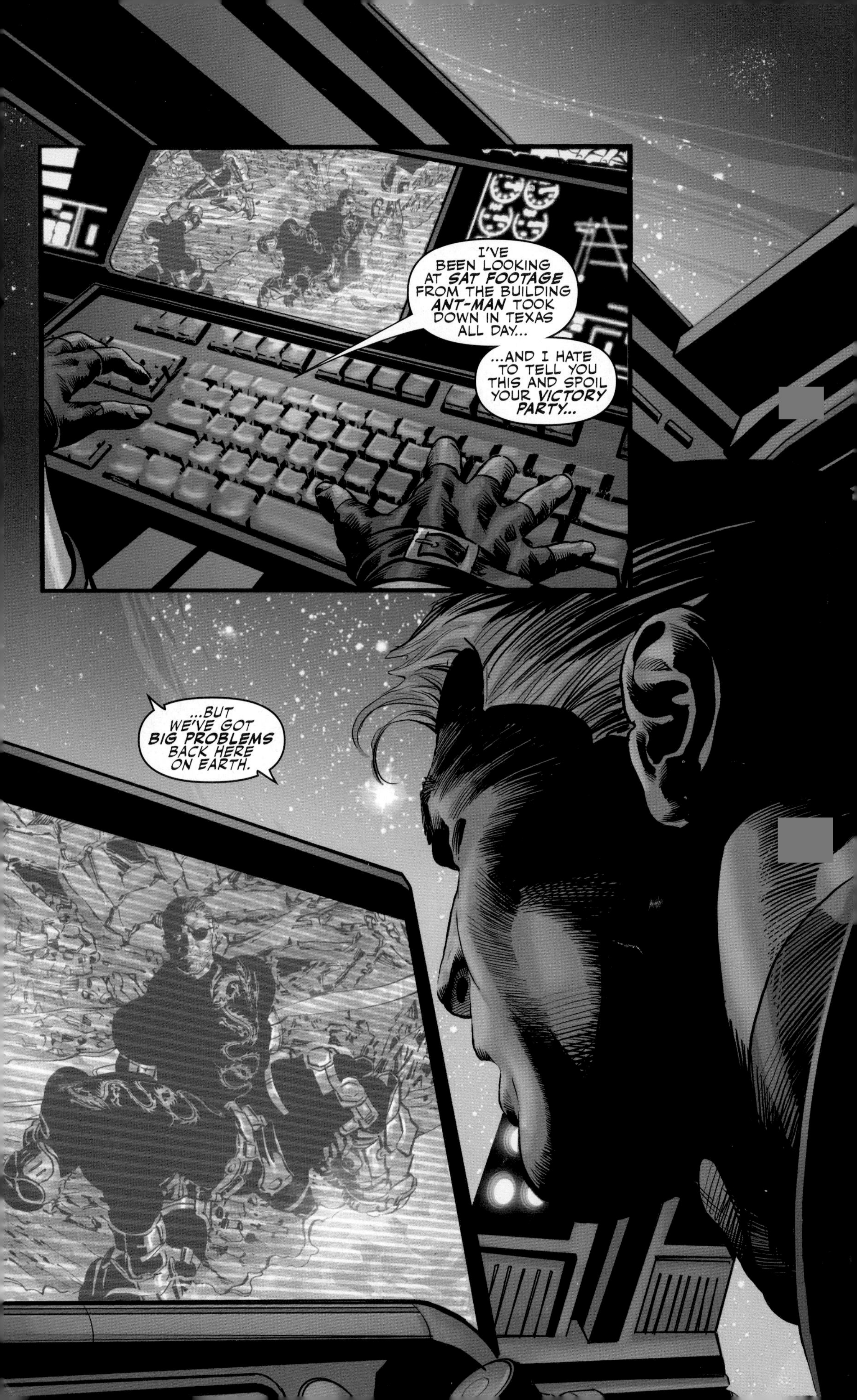
I'VE BEEN LOOKING AT SAT FOOTAGE FROM THE BUILDING ANT-MAN TOOK DOWN IN TEXAS ALL DAY...
...AND I HATE TO TELL YOU THIS AND SPOIL YOUR VICTORY PARTY...
...BUT WE'VE GOT BIG PROBLEMS BACK HERE ON EARTH.

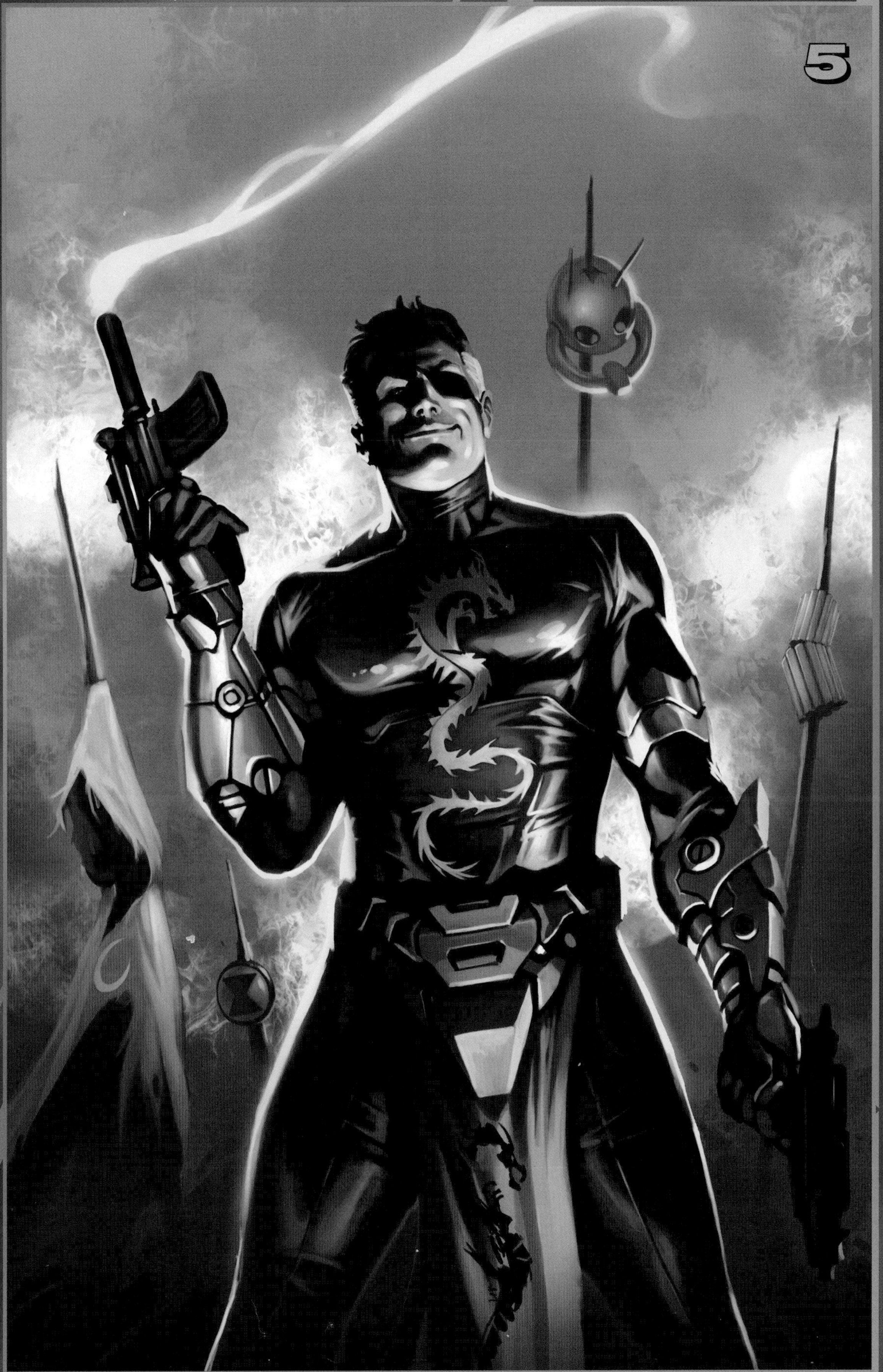
5

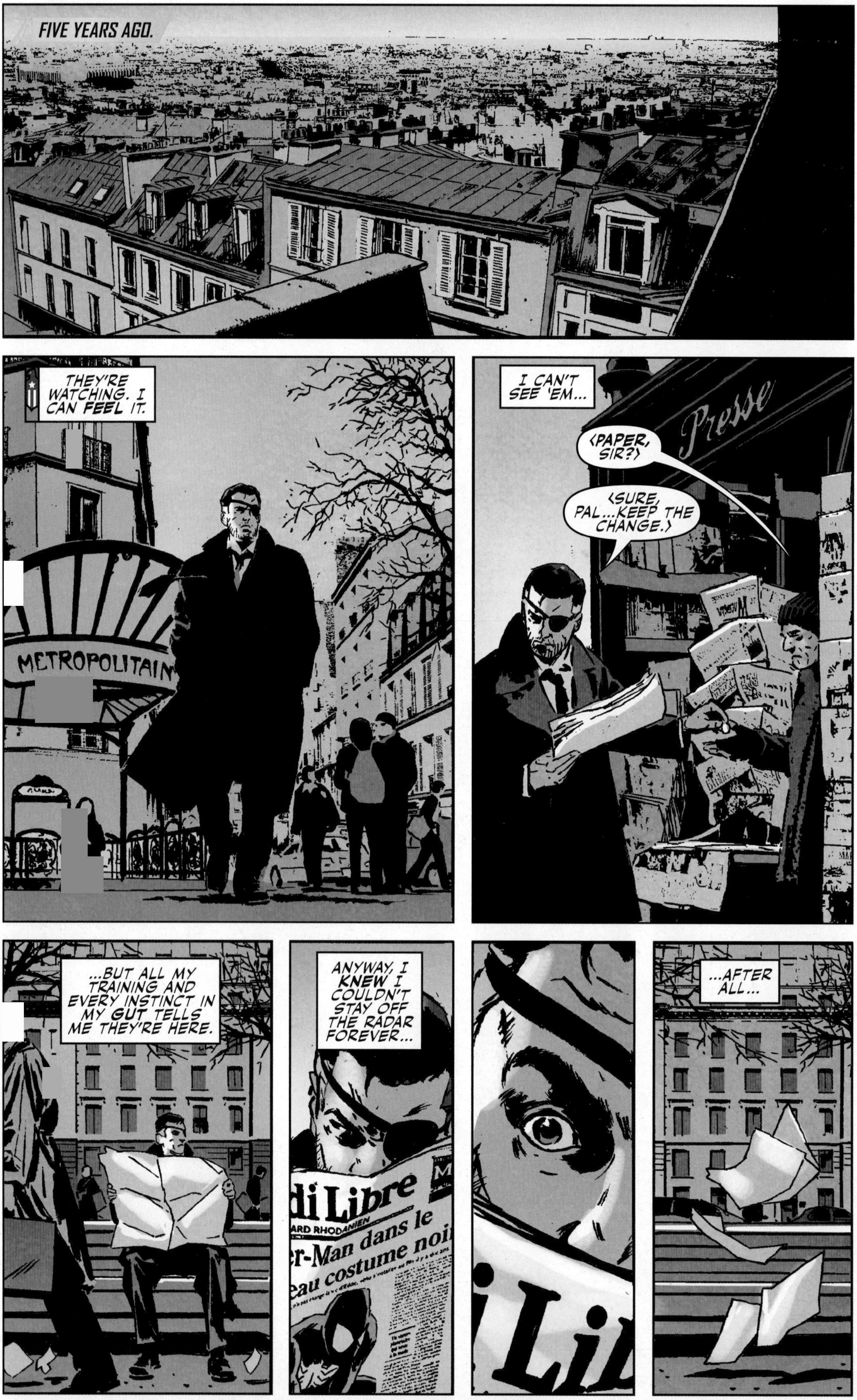
FIVE YEARS AGO.
THEY'RE WATCHING. I CAN FEEL IT.
METROPOLITAIN
I CAN'T SEE 'EM...
Presse
‹PAPER, SIR?›
‹SURE, PAL...KEEP THE CHANGE.›
...BUT ALL MY TRAINING AND EVERY INSTINCT IN MY GUT TELLS ME THEY'RE HERE.
ANYWAY, I KNEW I COULDN'T STAY OFF THE RADAR FOREVER...
di Libre
ARD RHODANIEN
er-Man dans le
eau costume noi
...AFTER ALL...

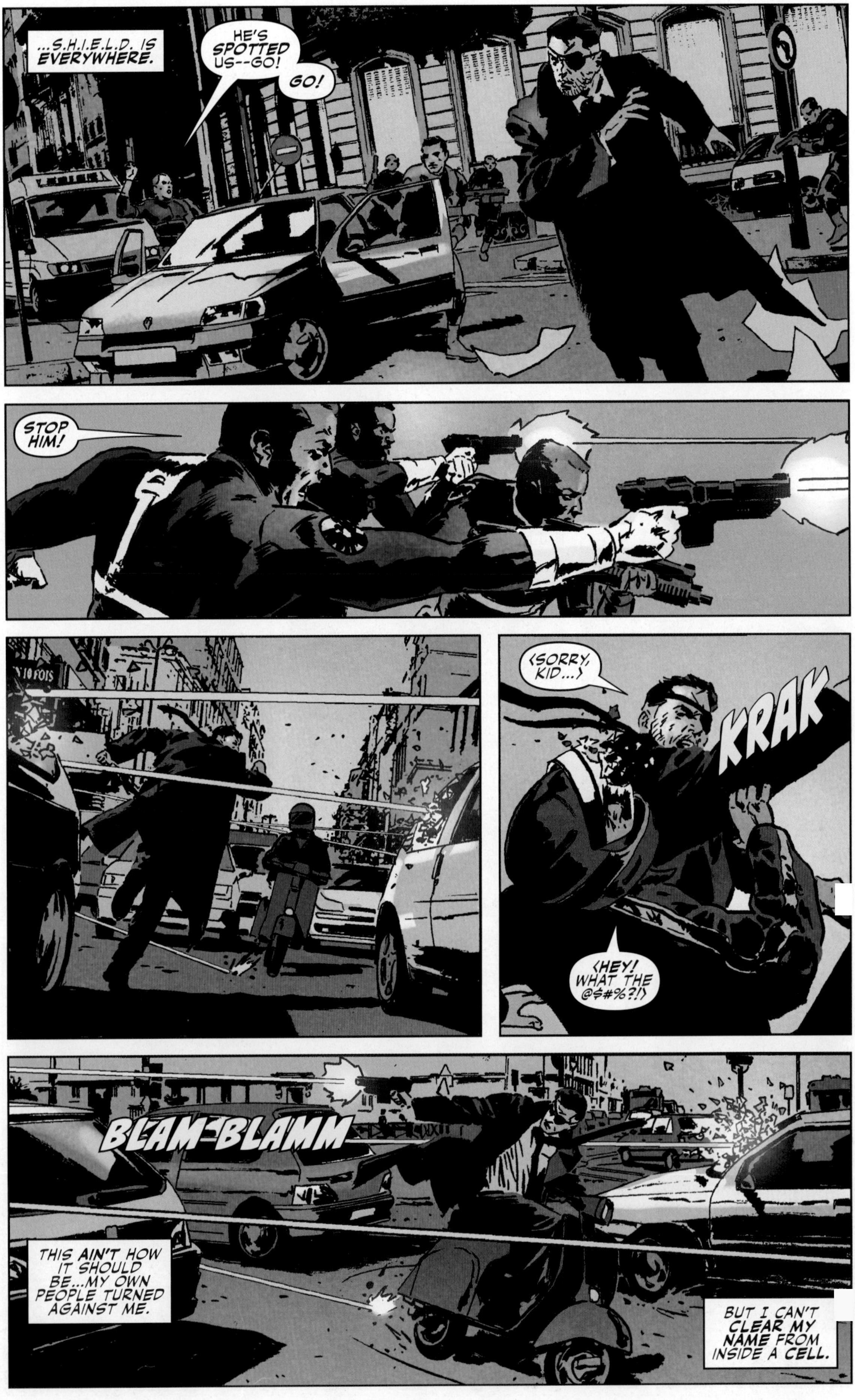
...S.H.I.E.L.D. IS EVERYWHERE.
HE'S SPOTTED US--GO!
GO!
STOP HIM!
<SORRY, KID...>
KRAK
<HEY! WHAT THE @$#%?!>
BLAM-BLAMM
THIS AIN'T HOW IT SHOULD BE...MY OWN PEOPLE TURNED AGAINST ME.
BUT I CAN'T CLEAR MY NAME FROM INSIDE A CELL.

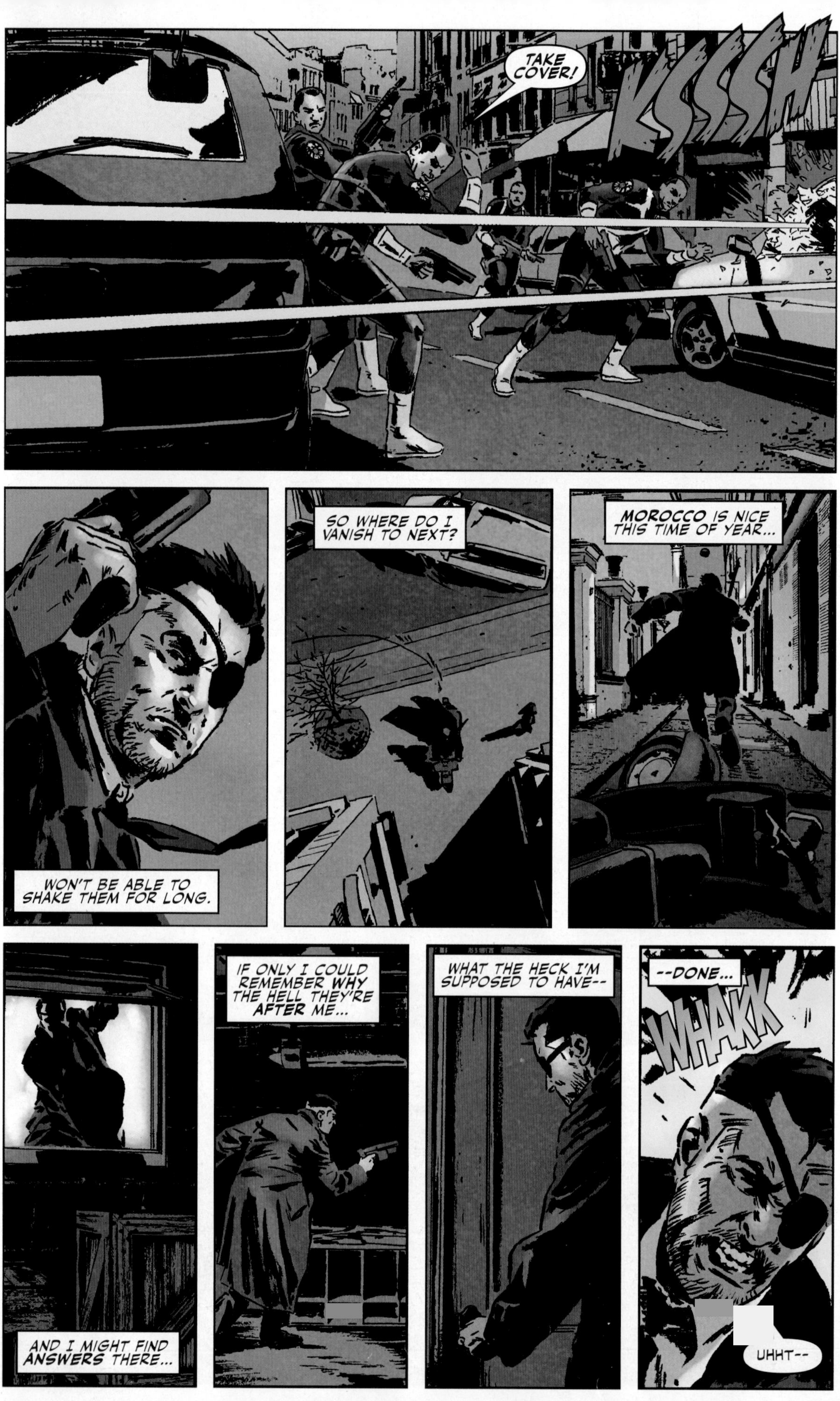

TAKE COVER!
KSSSH
WON'T BE ABLE TO SHAKE THEM FOR LONG.
SO WHERE DO I VANISH TO NEXT?
MOROCCO IS NICE THIS TIME OF YEAR...
AND I MIGHT FIND ANSWERS THERE...
IF ONLY I COULD REMEMBER WHY THE HELL THEY'RE AFTER ME...
WHAT THE HECK I'M SUPPOSED TO HAVE--
--DONE...
WHAKK
UHHT--

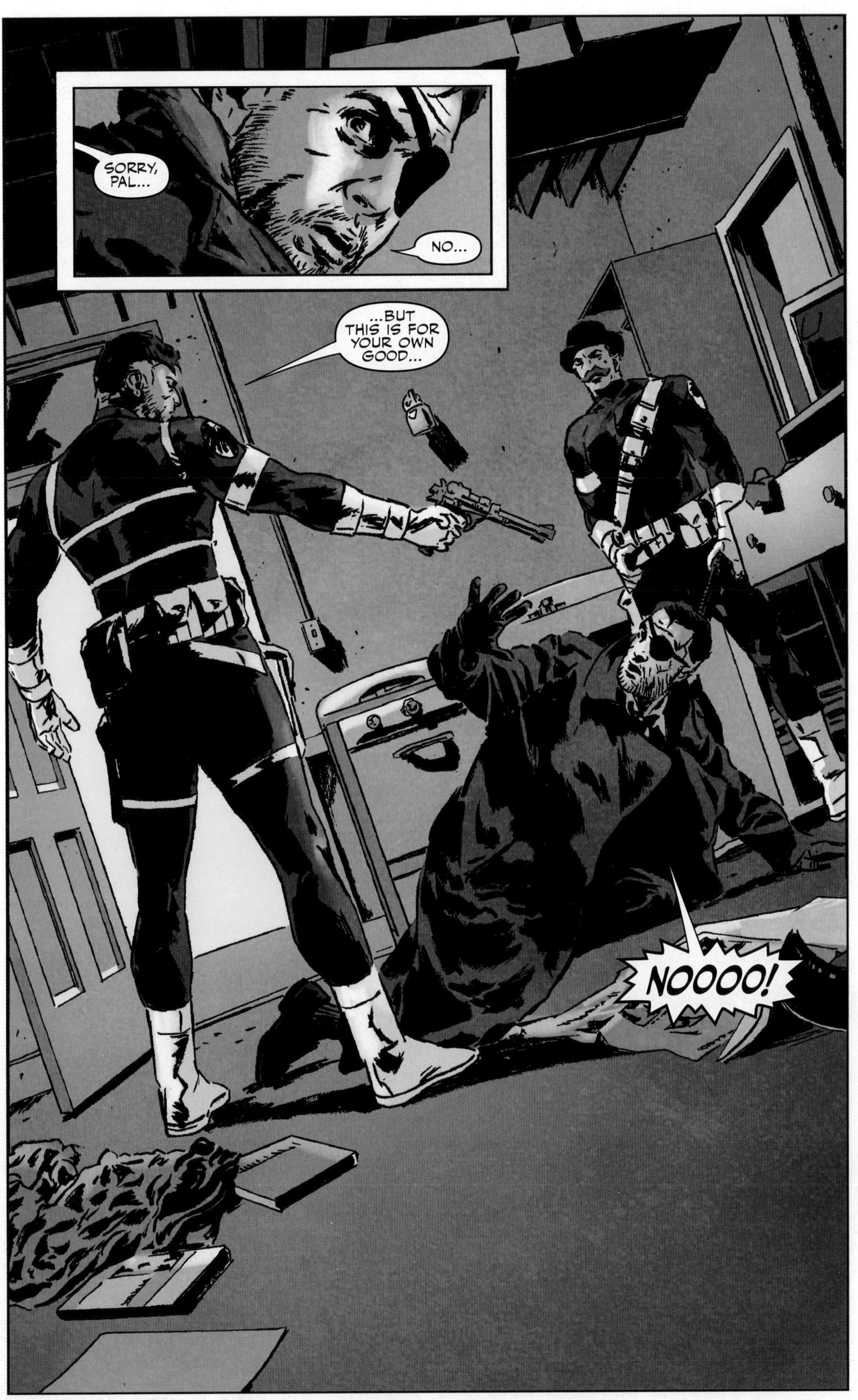
SORRY, PAL...
NO...
...BUT THIS IS FOR YOUR OWN GOOD...
NOOOO!

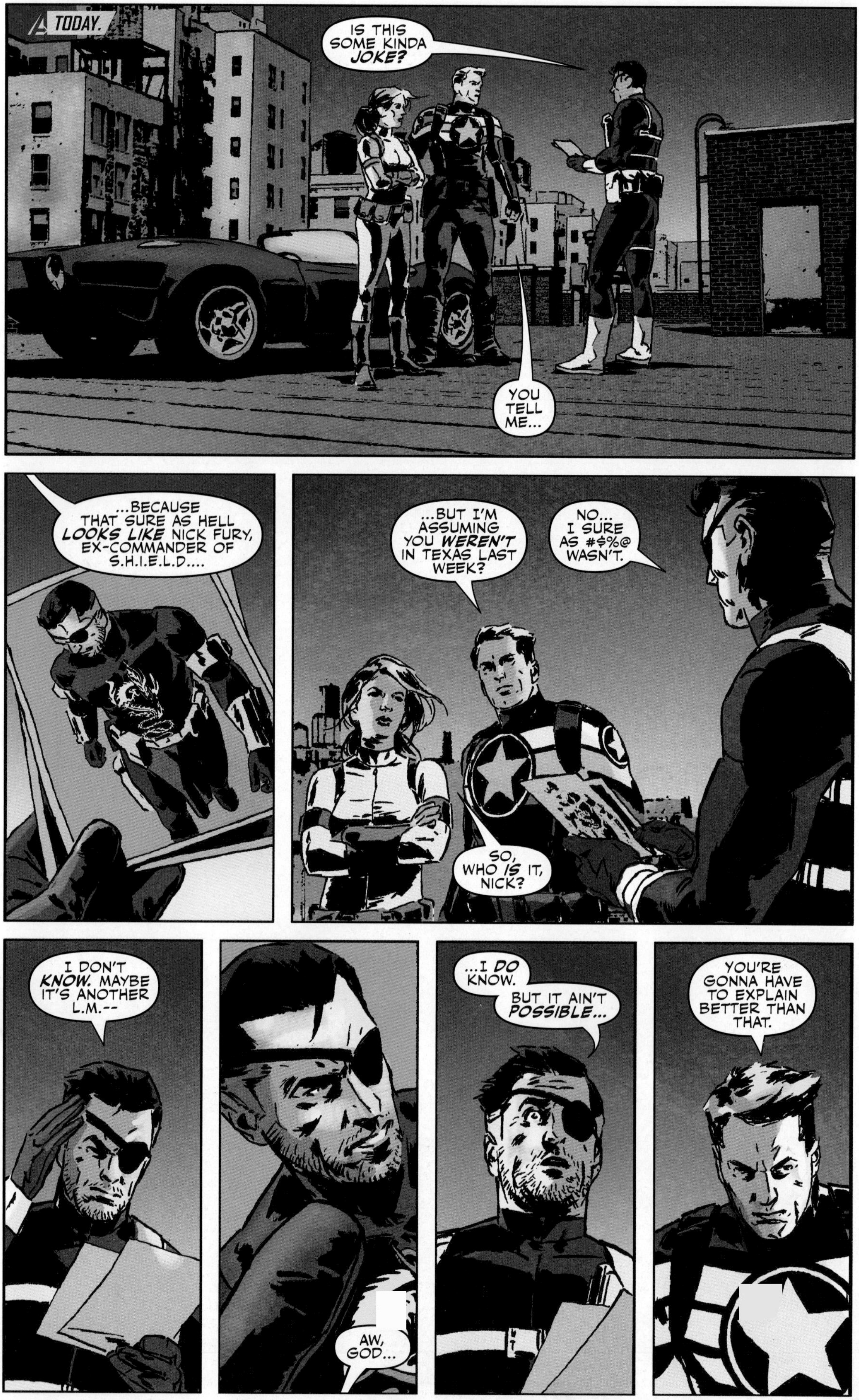
TODAY.
IS THIS SOME KINDA JOKE?
YOU TELL ME...
...BECAUSE THAT SURE AS HELL LOOKS LIKE NICK FURY, EX-COMMANDER OF S.H.I.E.L.D....
...BUT I'M ASSUMING YOU WEREN'T IN TEXAS LAST WEEK?
NO... I SURE AS #$%@ WASN'T.
SO, WHO IS IT, NICK?
I DON'T KNOW. MAYBE IT'S ANOTHER L.M.--
AW, GOD...
...I DO KNOW.
BUT IT AIN'T POSSIBLE...
YOU'RE GONNA HAVE TO EXPLAIN BETTER THAN THAT.

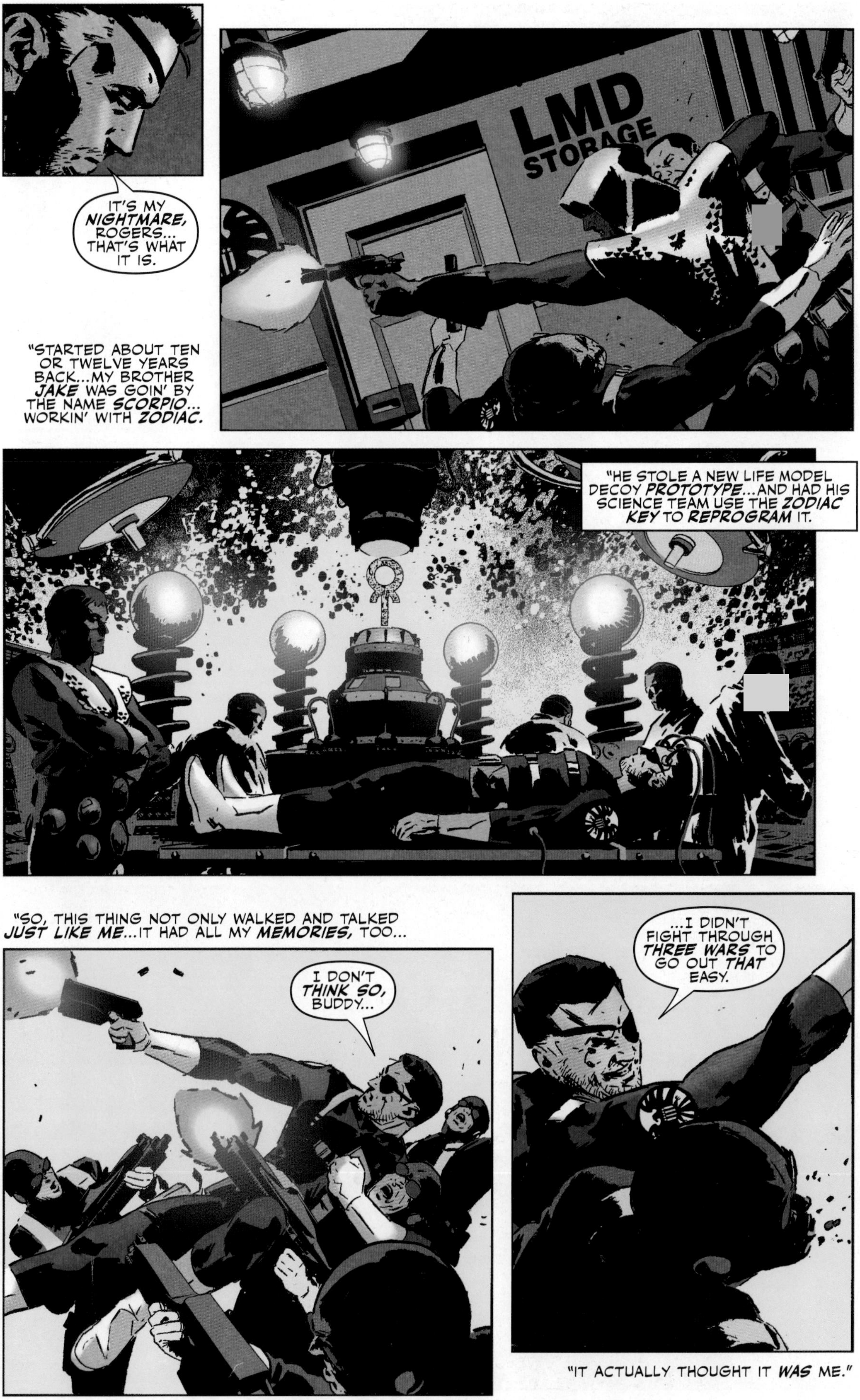
IT'S MY NIGHTMARE, ROGERS... THAT'S WHAT IT IS.
"STARTED ABOUT TEN OR TWELVE YEARS BACK...MY BROTHER JAKE WAS GOIN' BY THE NAME SCORPIO... WORKIN' WITH ZODIAC.
LMD STORAGE
"HE STOLE A NEW LIFE MODEL DECOY PROTOTYPE...AND HAD HIS SCIENCE TEAM USE THE ZODIAC KEY TO REPROGRAM IT.
"SO, THIS THING NOT ONLY WALKED AND TALKED JUST LIKE ME...IT HAD ALL MY MEMORIES, TOO...
I DON'T THINK SO, BUDDY...
...I DIDN'T FIGHT THROUGH THREE WARS TO GO OUT THAT EASY.
"IT ACTUALLY THOUGHT IT WAS ME."

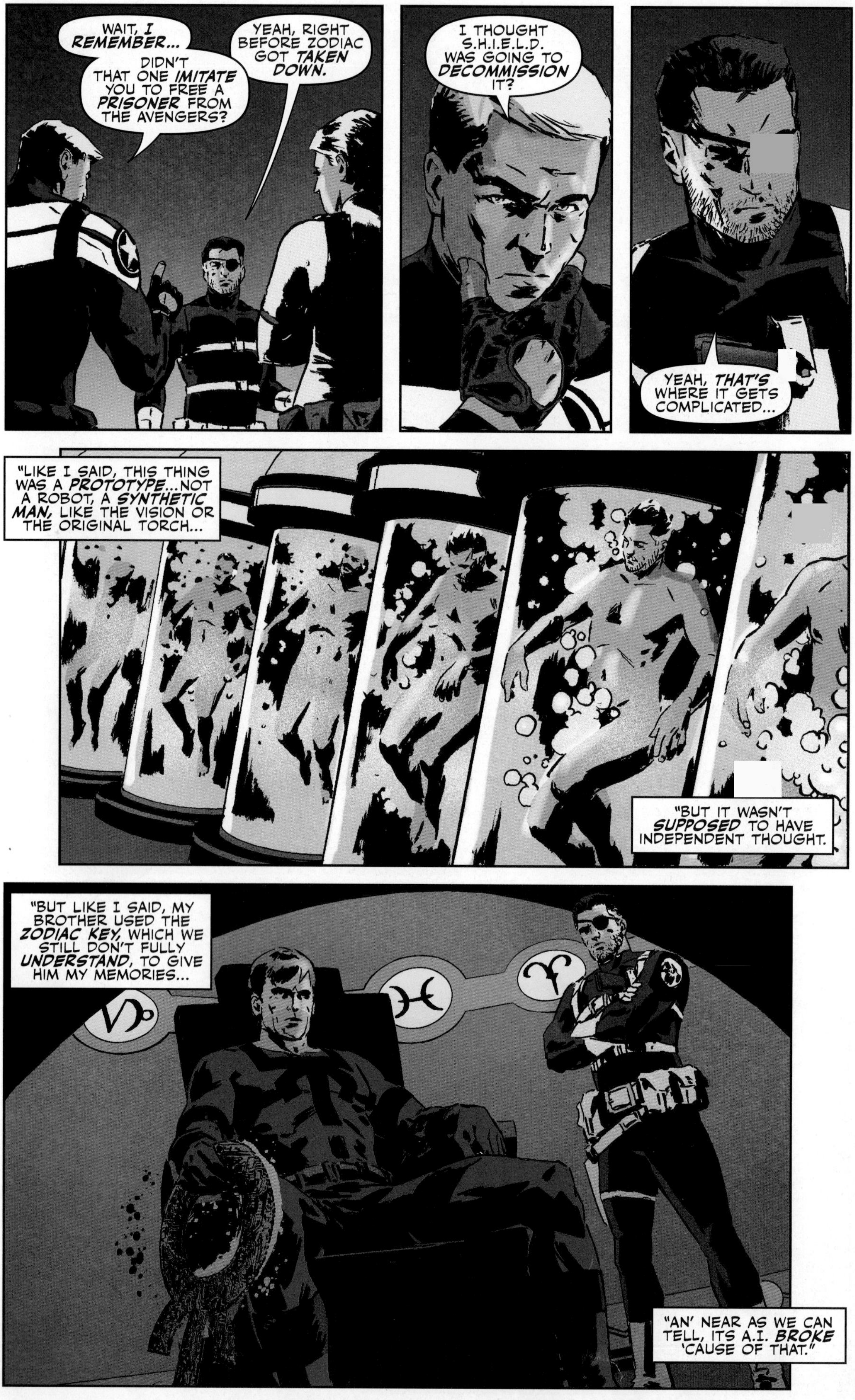
WAIT, I REMEMBER... DIDN'T THAT ONE IMITATE YOU TO FREE A PRISONER FROM THE AVENGERS?
YEAH, RIGHT BEFORE ZODIAC GOT TAKEN DOWN.
I THOUGHT S.H.I.E.L.D. WAS GOING TO DECOMMISSION IT?
YEAH, THAT'S WHERE IT GETS COMPLICATED...
"LIKE I SAID, THIS THING WAS A PROTOTYPE...NOT A ROBOT, A SYNTHETIC MAN, LIKE THE VISION OR THE ORIGINAL TORCH...
"BUT IT WASN'T SUPPOSED TO HAVE INDEPENDENT THOUGHT.
"BUT LIKE I SAID, MY BROTHER USED THE ZODIAC KEY, WHICH WE STILL DON'T FULLY UNDERSTAND, TO GIVE HIM MY MEMORIES...
"AN' NEAR AS WE CAN TELL, ITS A.I. BROKE 'CAUSE OF THAT."

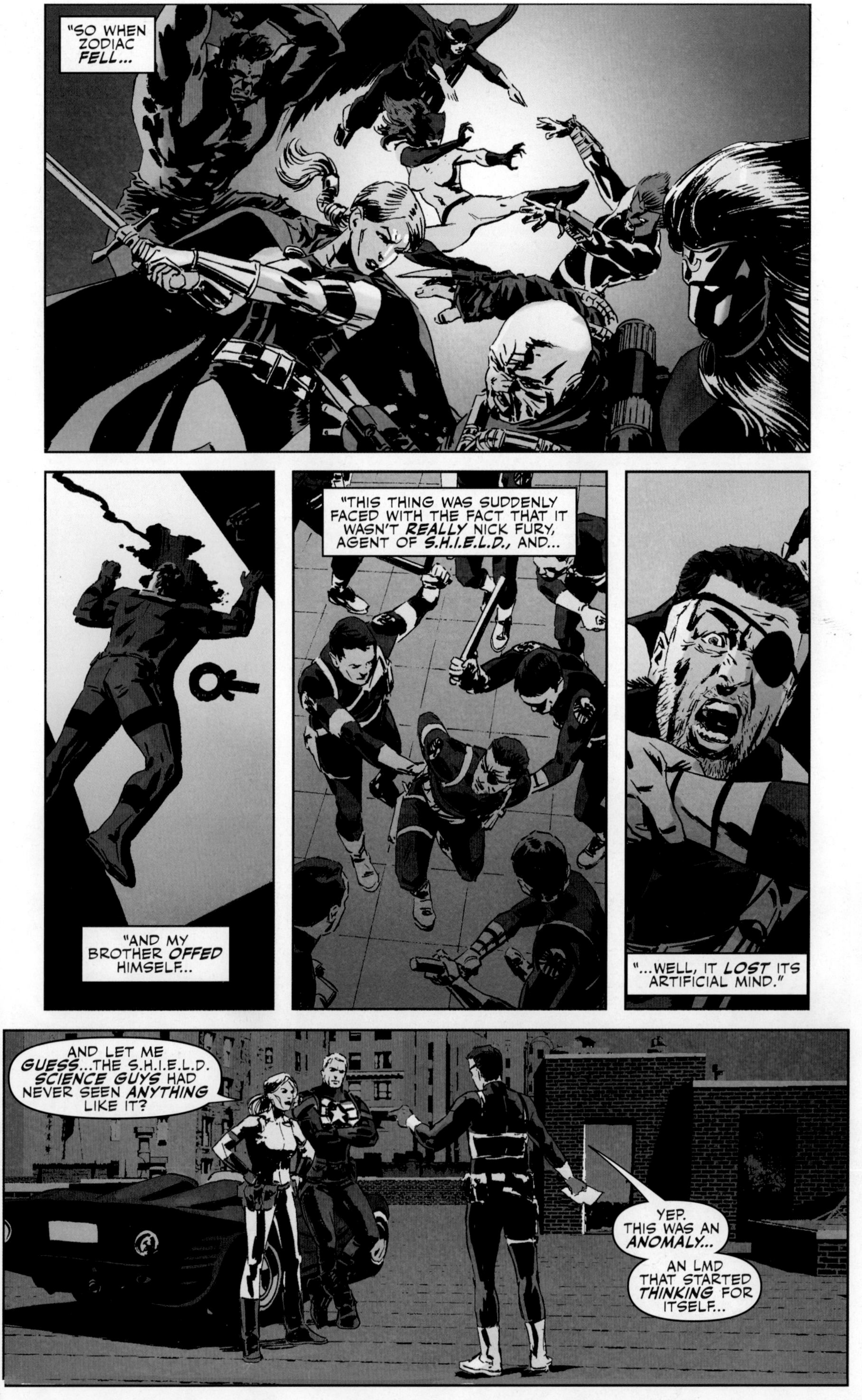
"SO WHEN ZODIAC FELL...
"AND MY BROTHER OFFED HIMSELF...
"THIS THING WAS SUDDENLY FACED WITH THE FACT THAT IT WASN'T REALLY NICK FURY, AGENT OF S.H.I.E.L.D., AND...
"...WELL, IT LOST ITS ARTIFICIAL MIND."
AND LET ME GUESS...THE S.H.I.E.L.D. SCIENCE GUYS HAD NEVER SEEN ANYTHING LIKE IT?
YEP. THIS WAS AN ANOMALY...
AN LMD THAT STARTED THINKING FOR ITSELF...

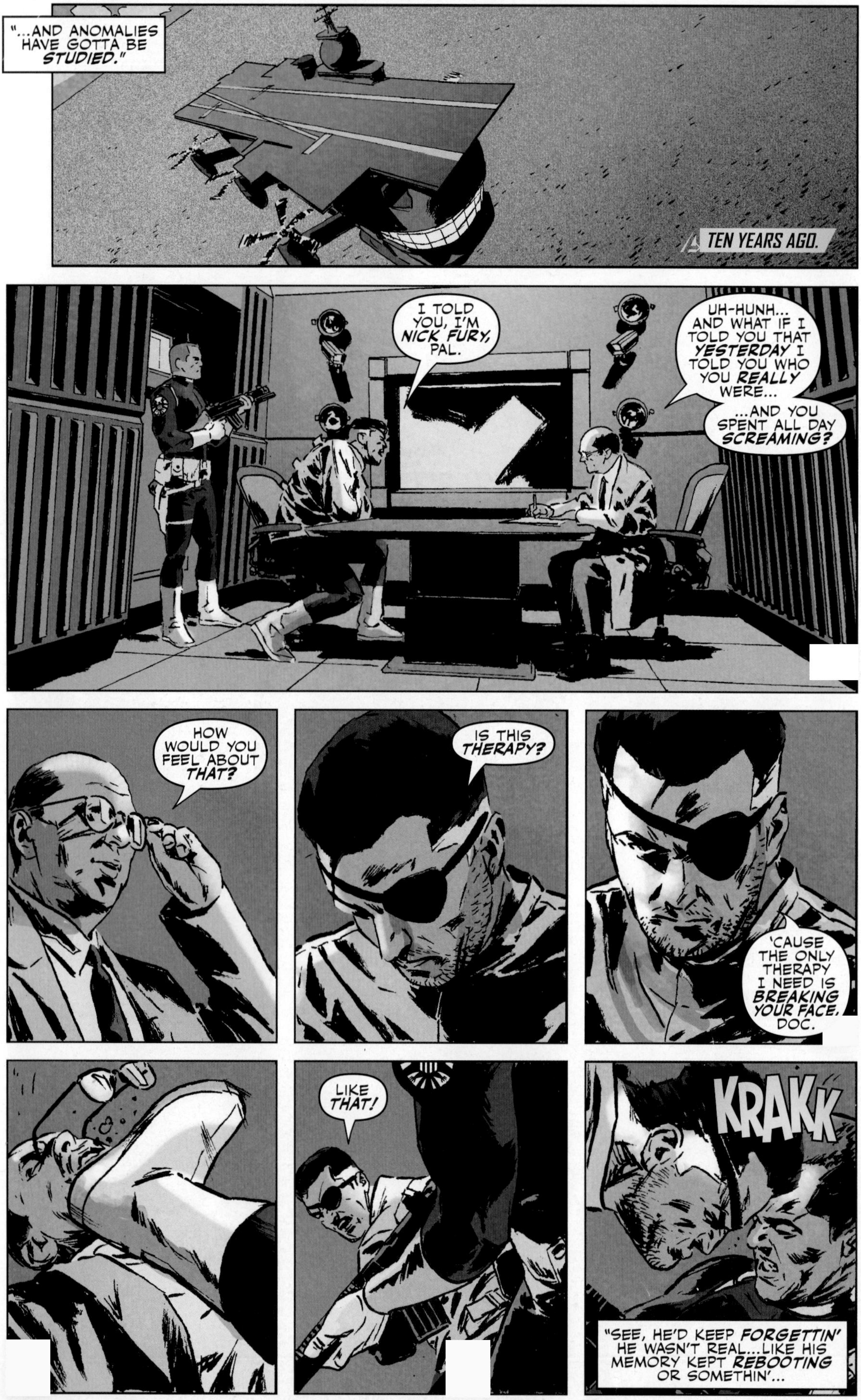
"...AND ANOMALIES HAVE GOTTA BE STUDIED."
TEN YEARS AGO.
I TOLD YOU, I'M NICK FURY, PAL.
UH-HUNH... AND WHAT IF I TOLD YOU THAT YESTERDAY I TOLD YOU WHO YOU REALLY WERE...
...AND YOU SPENT ALL DAY SCREAMING?
HOW WOULD YOU FEEL ABOUT THAT?
IS THIS THERAPY?
'CAUSE THE ONLY THERAPY I NEED IS BREAKING YOUR FACE, DOC.
LIKE THAT!
KRAKK
"SEE, HE'D KEEP FORGETTIN' HE WASN'T REAL...LIKE HIS MEMORY KEPT REBOOTING OR SOMETHIN'...

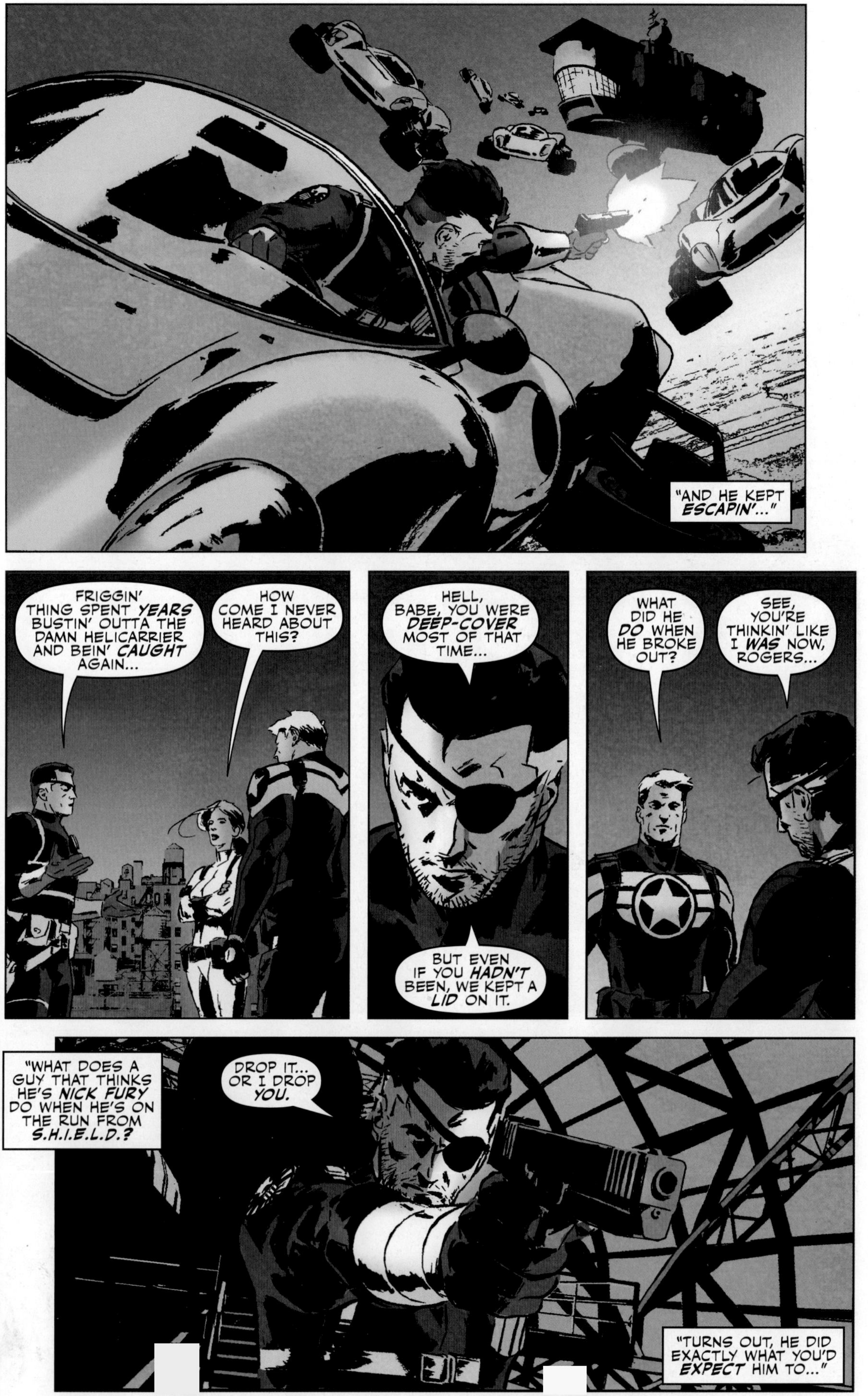
"AND HE KEPT *ESCAPIN'*..."
FRIGGIN' THING SPENT *YEARS* BUSTIN' OUTTA THE DAMN HELICARRIER AND BEIN' *CAUGHT* AGAIN...
HOW COME I NEVER HEARD ABOUT THIS?
HELL, BABE, YOU WERE *DEEP-COVER* MOST OF THAT TIME...
BUT EVEN IF YOU *HADN'T* BEEN, WE KEPT A *LID* ON IT.
WHAT DID HE *DO* WHEN HE BROKE OUT?
SEE, YOU'RE THINKIN' LIKE I *WAS* NOW, ROGERS...
"WHAT DOES A GUY THAT THINKS HE'S *NICK FURY* DO WHEN HE'S ON THE RUN FROM *S.H.I.E.L.D.?*
DROP IT... OR I DROP *YOU.*
"TURNS OUT, HE DID EXACTLY WHAT YOU'D *EXPECT* HIM TO..."

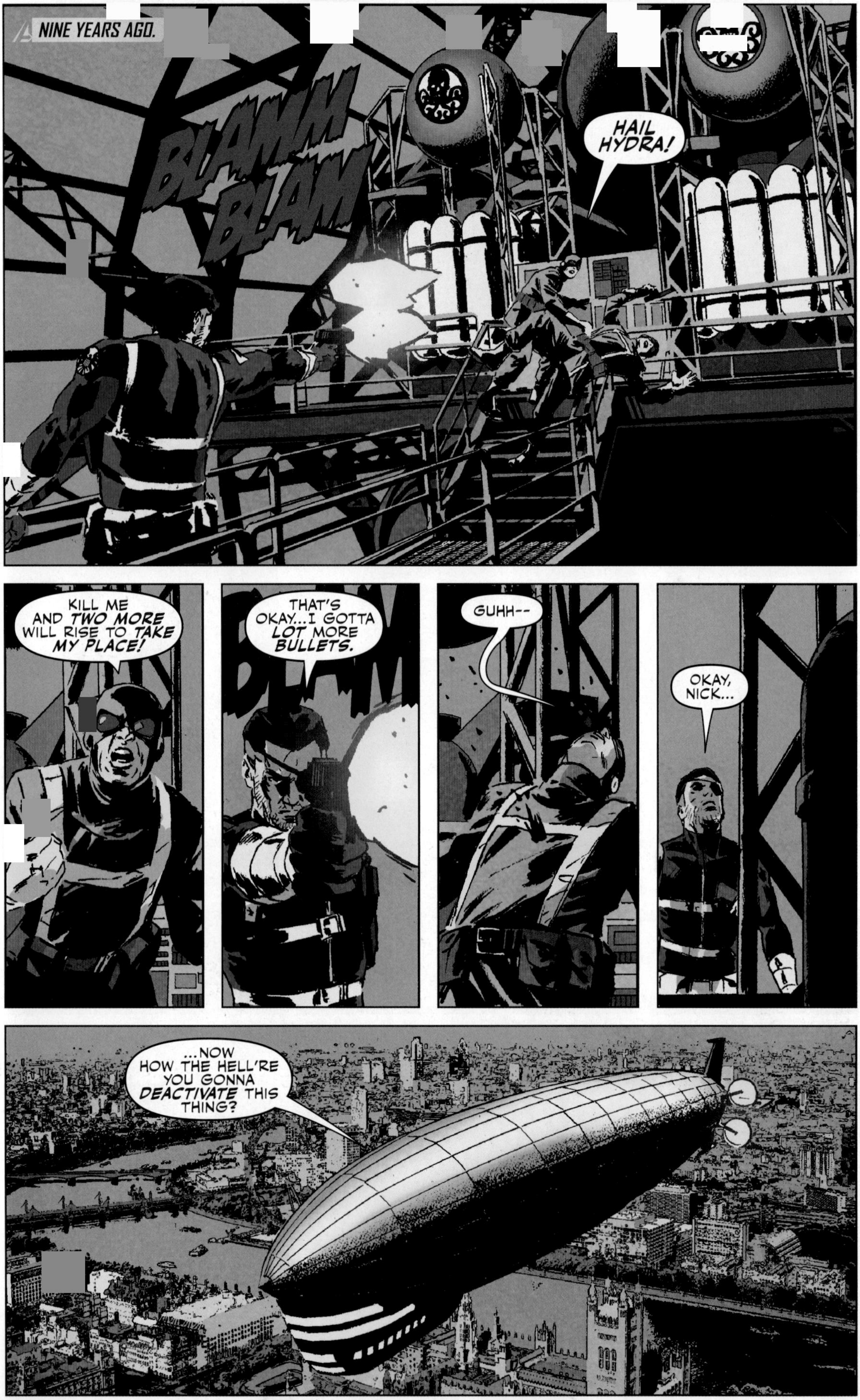
NINE YEARS AGO.
BLAMM BLAM
HAIL HYDRA!
KILL ME AND TWO MORE WILL RISE TO TAKE MY PLACE!
BLAM
THAT'S OKAY...I GOTTA LOT MORE BULLETS.
GUHH--
OKAY, NICK...
...NOW HOW THE HELL'RE YOU GONNA DEACTIVATE THIS THING?

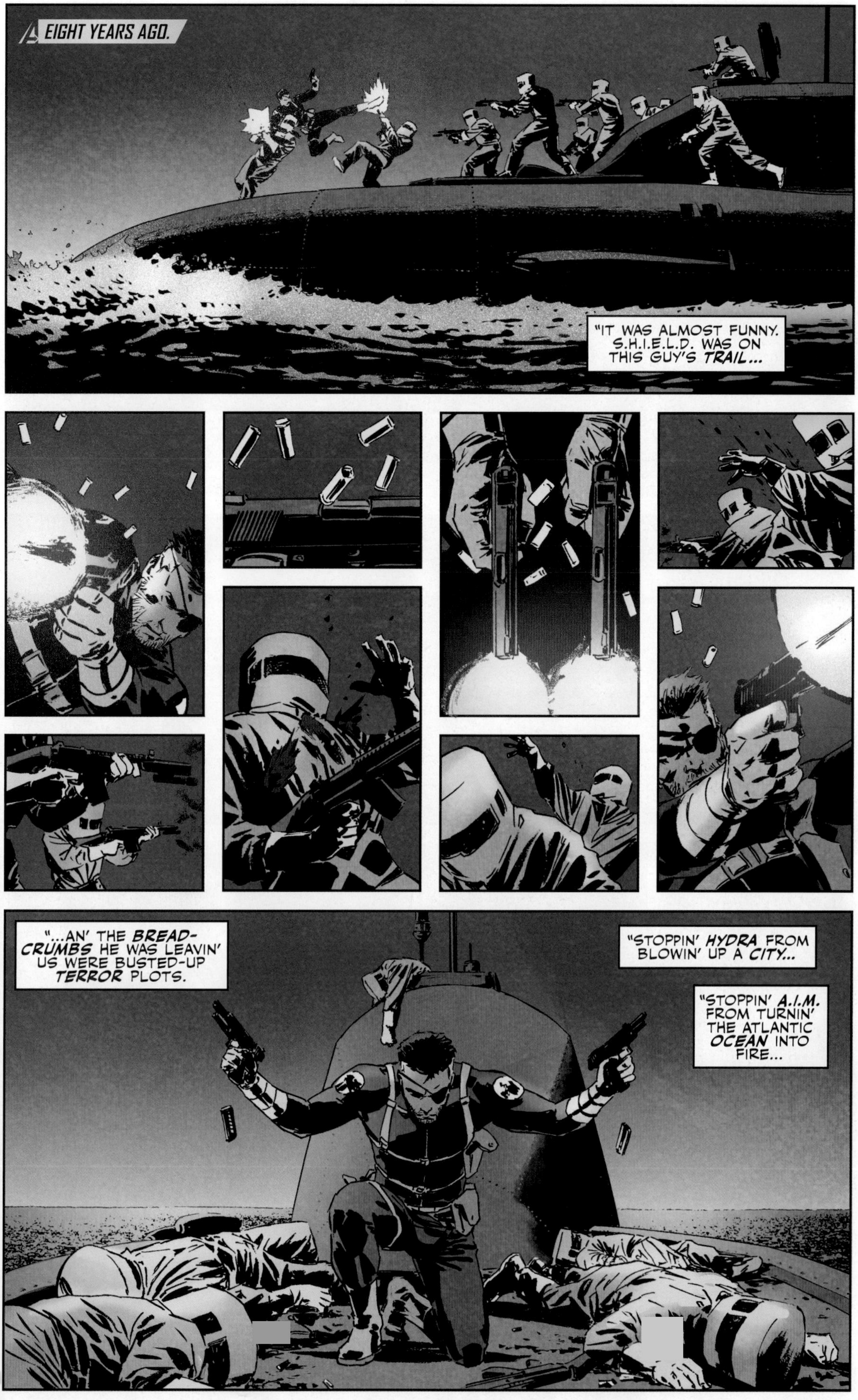
EIGHT YEARS AGO.
"IT WAS ALMOST FUNNY. S.H.I.E.L.D. WAS ON THIS GUY'S TRAIL...
"...AN' THE BREAD-CRUMBS HE WAS LEAVIN' US WERE BUSTED-UP TERROR PLOTS.
"STOPPIN' HYDRA FROM BLOWIN' UP A CITY...
"STOPPIN' A.I.M. FROM TURNIN' THE ATLANTIC OCEAN INTO FIRE...

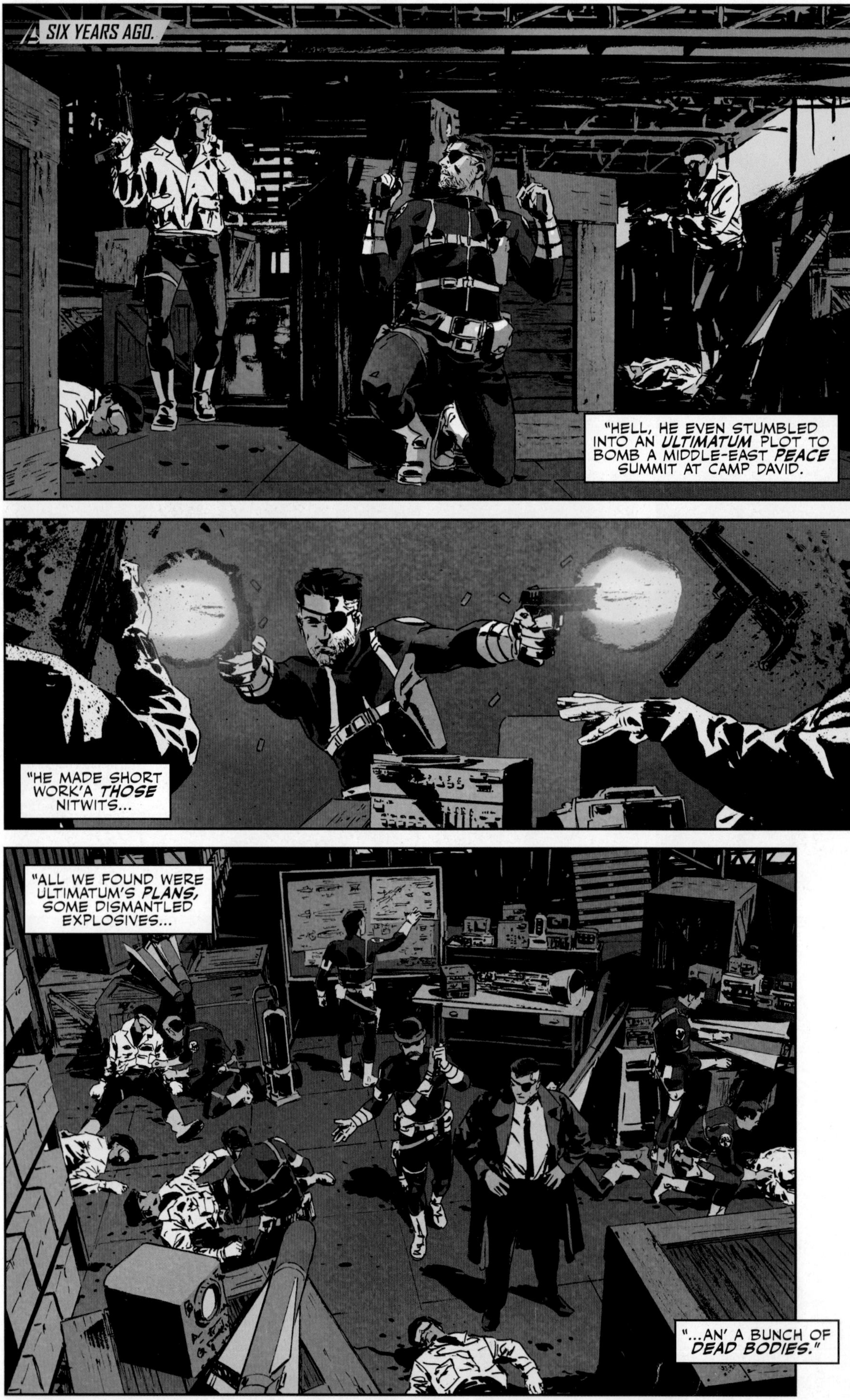
SIX YEARS AGO.
"HELL, HE EVEN STUMBLED INTO AN ULTIMATUM PLOT TO BOMB A MIDDLE-EAST PEACE SUMMIT AT CAMP DAVID.
"HE MADE SHORT WORK'A THOSE NITWITS...
"ALL WE FOUND WERE ULTIMATUM'S PLANS, SOME DISMANTLED EXPLOSIVES...
"...AN' A BUNCH OF DEAD BODIES."

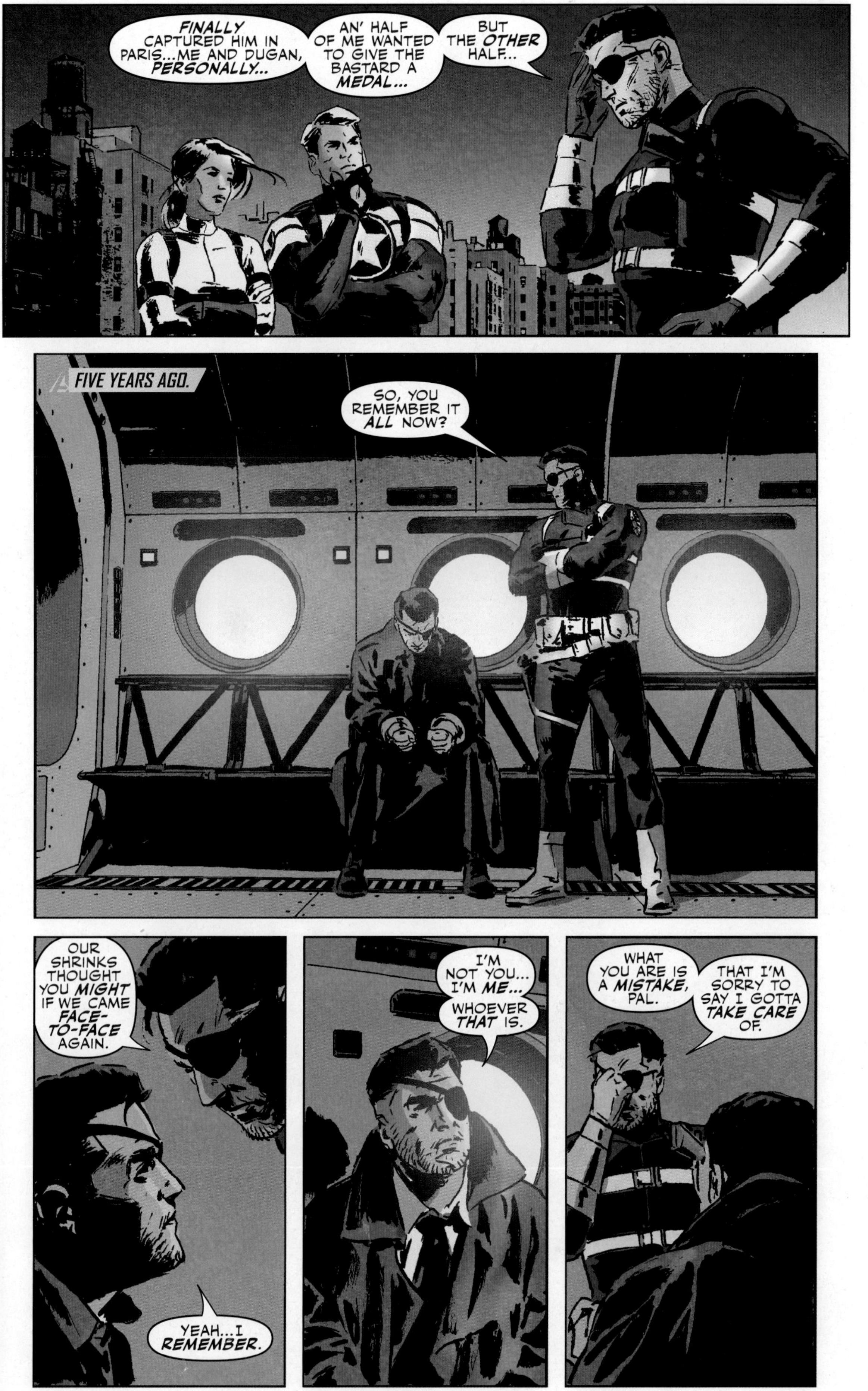
FINALLY CAPTURED HIM IN PARIS...ME AND DUGAN, PERSONALLY...
AN' HALF OF ME WANTED TO GIVE THE BASTARD A MEDAL...
BUT THE OTHER HALF...
FIVE YEARS AGO.
SO, YOU REMEMBER IT ALL NOW?
OUR SHRINKS THOUGHT YOU MIGHT IF WE CAME FACE-TO-FACE AGAIN.
YEAH...I REMEMBER.
I'M NOT YOU... I'M ME...
WHOEVER THAT IS.
WHAT YOU ARE IS A MISTAKE, PAL.
THAT I'M SORRY TO SAY I GOTTA TAKE CARE OF.

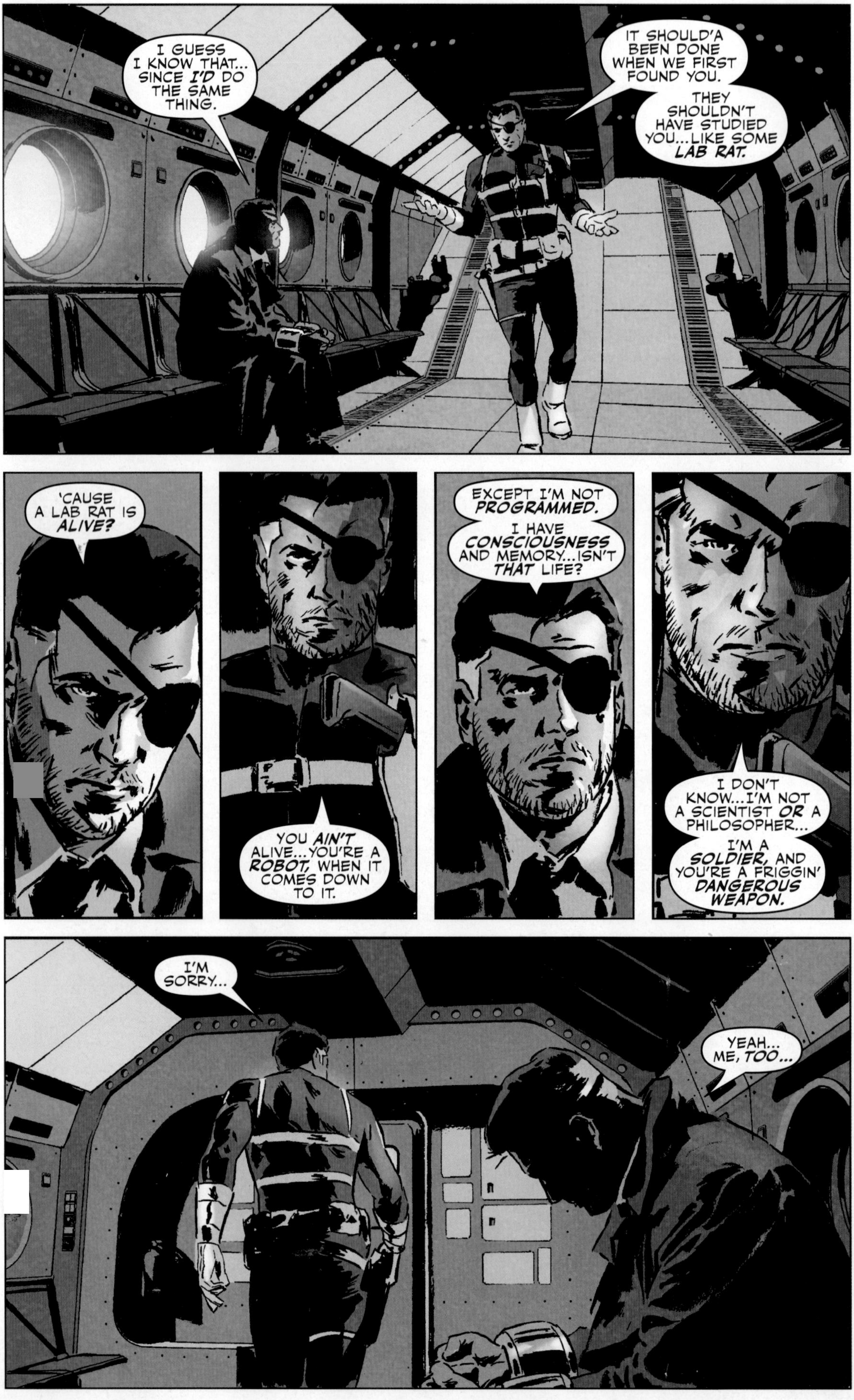

I GUESS I KNOW THAT... SINCE I'D DO THE SAME THING.
IT SHOULD'A BEEN DONE WHEN WE FIRST FOUND YOU.
THEY SHOULDN'T HAVE STUDIED YOU...LIKE SOME LAB RAT.
'CAUSE A LAB RAT IS ALIVE?
YOU AIN'T ALIVE...YOU'RE A ROBOT, WHEN IT COMES DOWN TO IT.
EXCEPT I'M NOT PROGRAMMED.
I HAVE CONSCIOUSNESS AND MEMORY...ISN'T THAT LIFE?
I DON'T KNOW...I'M NOT A SCIENTIST OR A PHILOSOPHER...
I'M A SOLDIER, AND YOU'RE A FRIGGIN' DANGEROUS WEAPON.
I'M SORRY...
YEAH... ME, TOO...

"AND THAT WAS IT...HE WAS *DEACTIVATED* WHEN WE GOT BACK TO THE HELICARRIER..."

...AND *INCINERATED* A FEW DAYS LATER.

OR SO YOU THOUGHT?

YEAH, OR SO I *THOUGHT.*

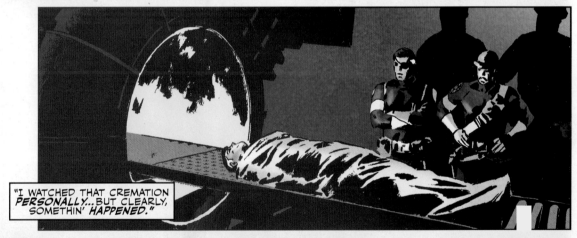

"I WATCHED THAT CREMATION *PERSONALLY*...BUT CLEARLY, SOMETHIN' *HAPPENED.*"

BECAUSE THIS IS *HIM.* IT'S GOTTA BE.

AND THIS *UNIFORM* HE'S WEARING?

NEVER *SEEN* IT BEFORE...

GREAT...

WHAT?

YOU'RE *PISSED* AT ME?

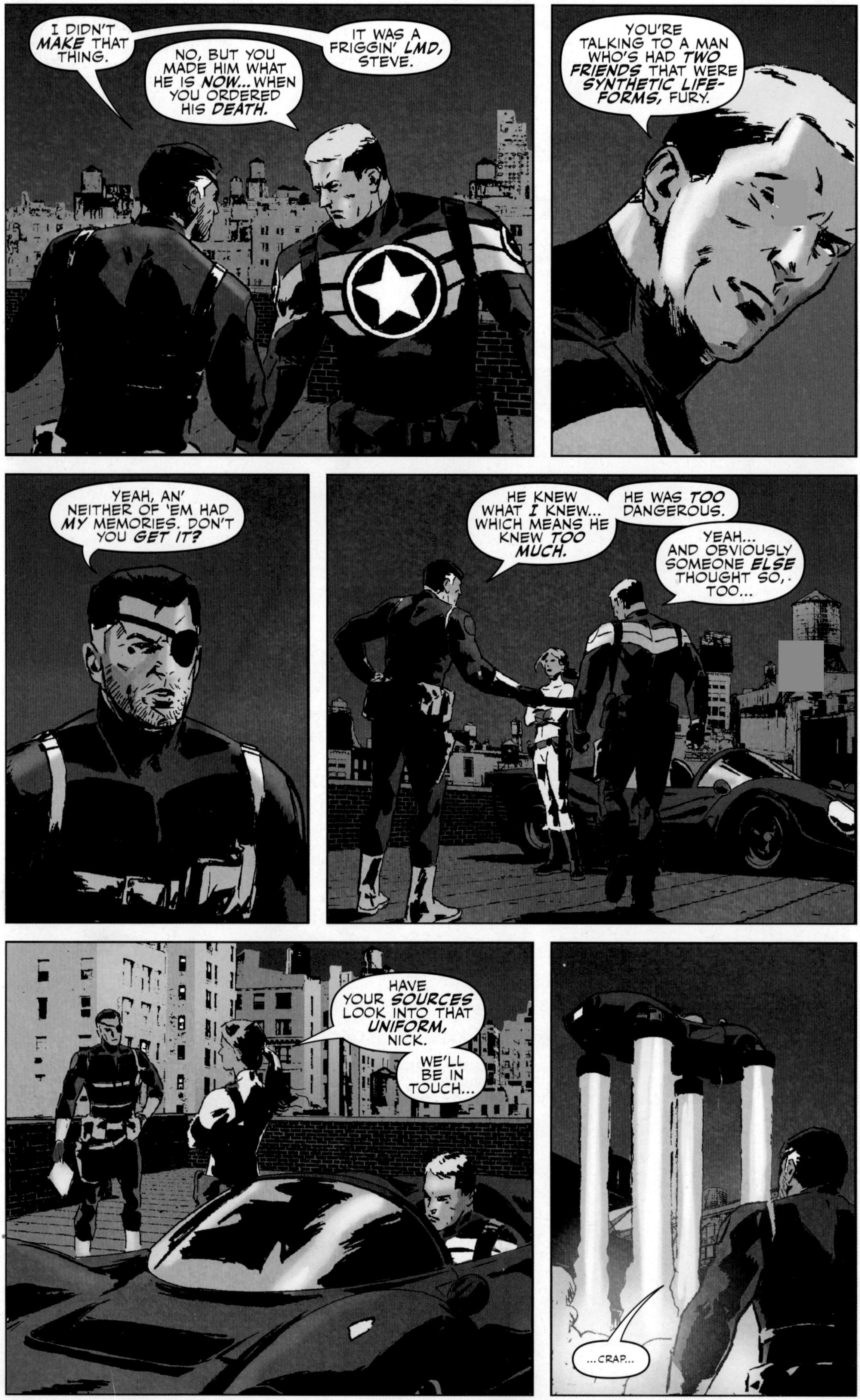

I DIDN'T *MAKE* THAT THING.
IT WAS A FRIGGIN' *LMD,* STEVE.
NO, BUT YOU MADE HIM WHAT HE IS *NOW...* WHEN YOU ORDERED HIS *DEATH.*
YOU'RE TALKING TO A MAN WHO'S HAD *TWO FRIENDS* THAT WERE *SYNTHETIC LIFE-FORMS,* FURY.
YEAH, AN' NEITHER OF 'EM HAD *MY* MEMORIES. DON'T YOU *GET IT?*
HE KNEW WHAT *I* KNEW... WHICH MEANS HE KNEW *TOO MUCH.*
HE WAS *TOO* DANGEROUS.
YEAH... AND OBVIOUSLY SOMEONE *ELSE* THOUGHT SO,. TOO...
HAVE YOUR *SOURCES* LOOK INTO THAT *UNIFORM,* NICK.
WE'LL BE IN TOUCH...
...CRAP...

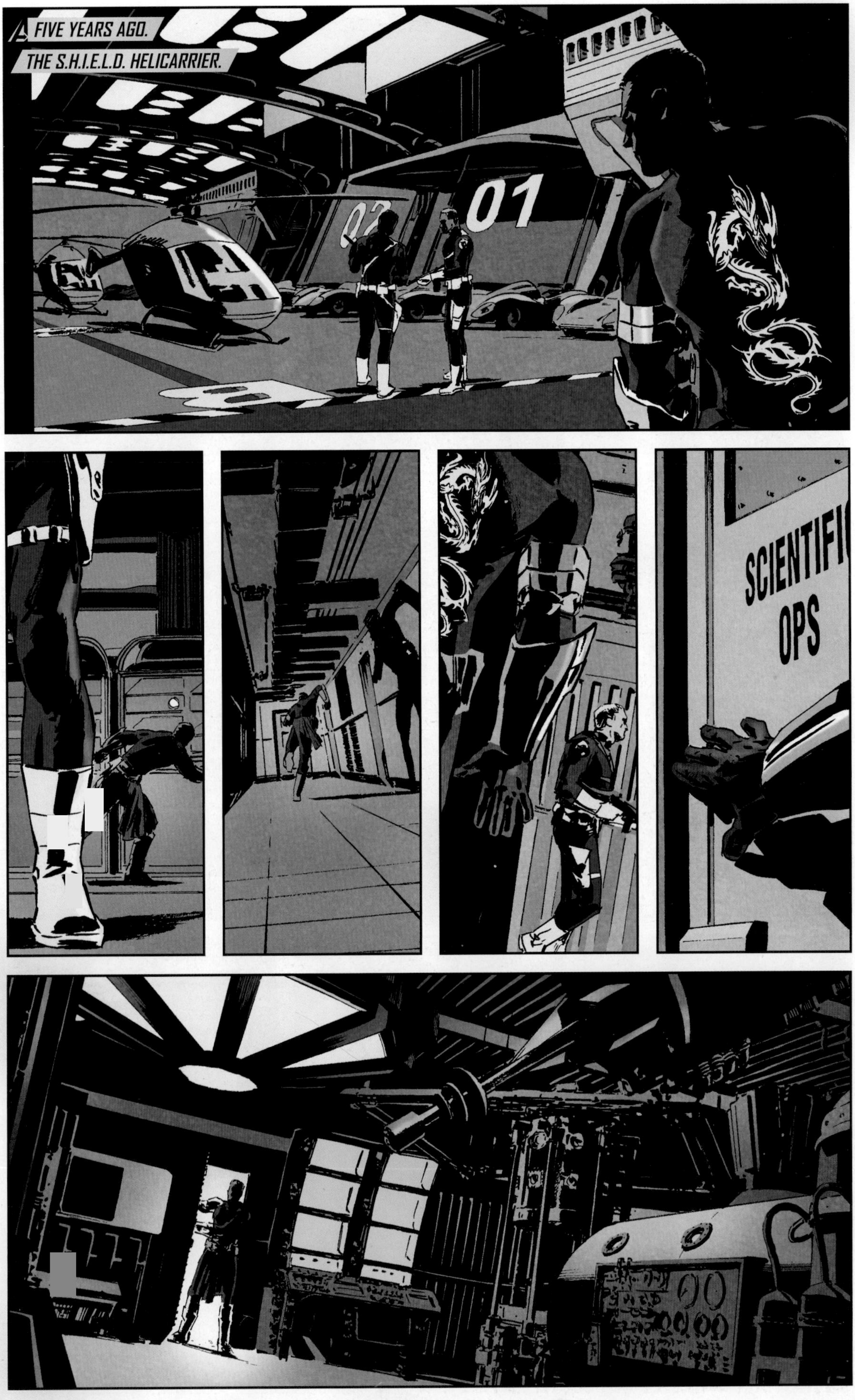
FIVE YEARS AGO.
THE S.H.I.E.L.D. HELICARRIER.
02
01
SCIENTIFIC
OPS

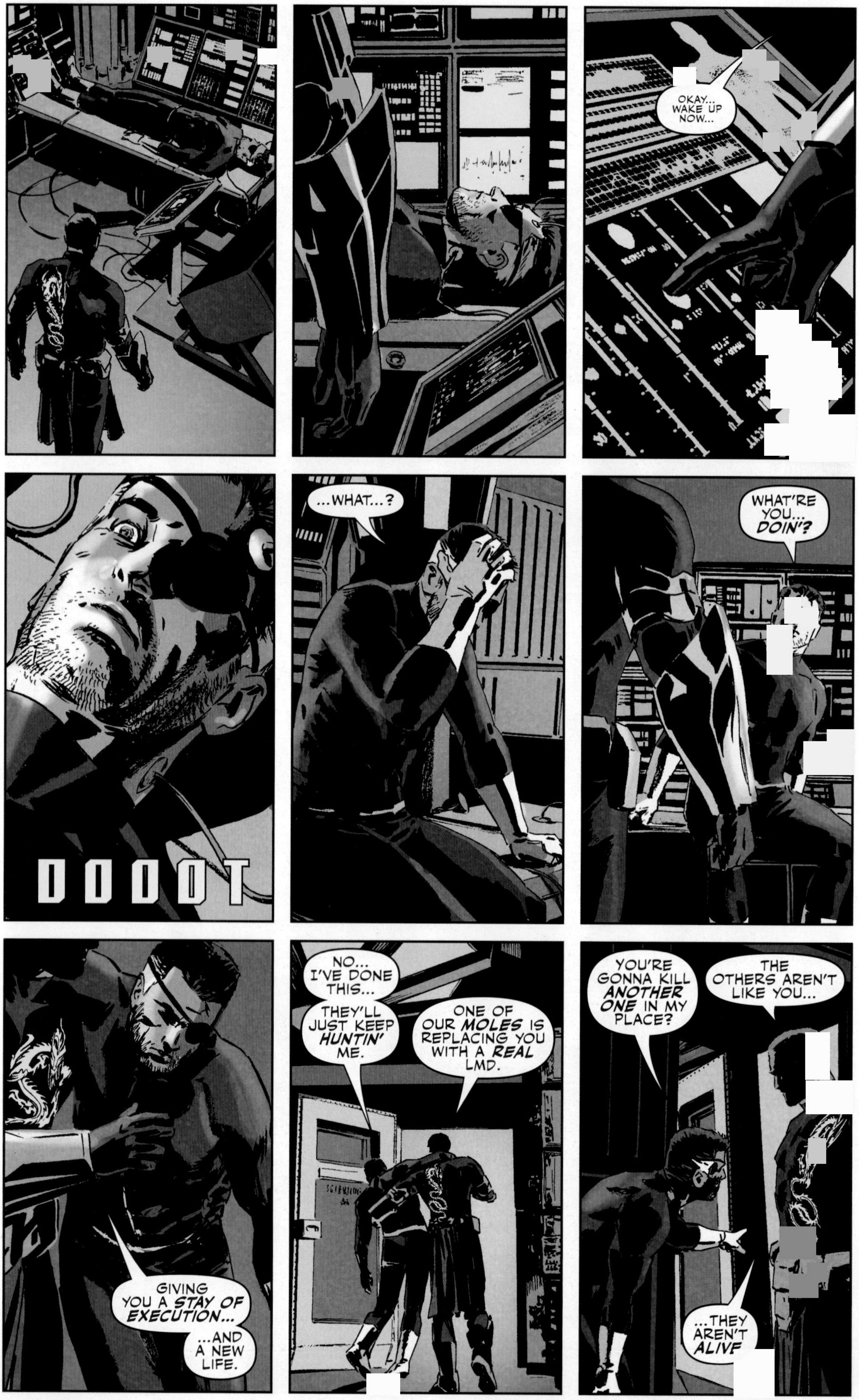
OKAY... WAKE UP NOW...
DOOOT
...WHAT...?
WHAT'RE YOU... DOIN'?
GIVING YOU A STAY OF EXECUTION...
...AND A NEW LIFE.
NO... I'VE DONE THIS...
THEY'LL JUST KEEP HUNTIN' ME.
ONE OF OUR MOLES IS REPLACING YOU WITH A REAL LMD.
YOU'RE GONNA KILL ANOTHER ONE IN MY PLACE?
THE OTHERS AREN'T LIKE YOU...
...THEY AREN'T ALIVE

WAIT. I RECOGNIZE YOU...FROM THE WAR...

GOOD. THEN YOU WERE WORTH THE RISK...

NOW LET'S MOVE.

WHO SENT YOU?

WHATTA THEY WANT FROM ME?

MY PEOPLE WANT YOU TO HELP US SAVE THE WORLD...

AND TO GIVE YOU A REAL LIFE... STARTING WITH YOUR OWN NAME.

A NAME?

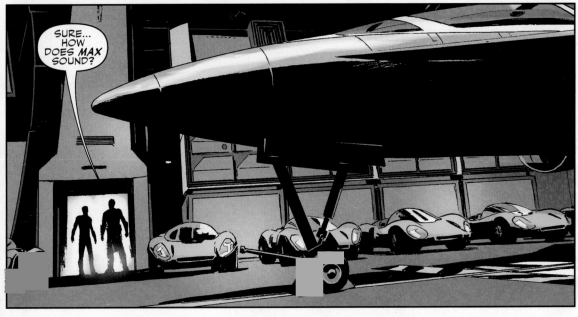

SURE... HOW DOES MAX SOUND?

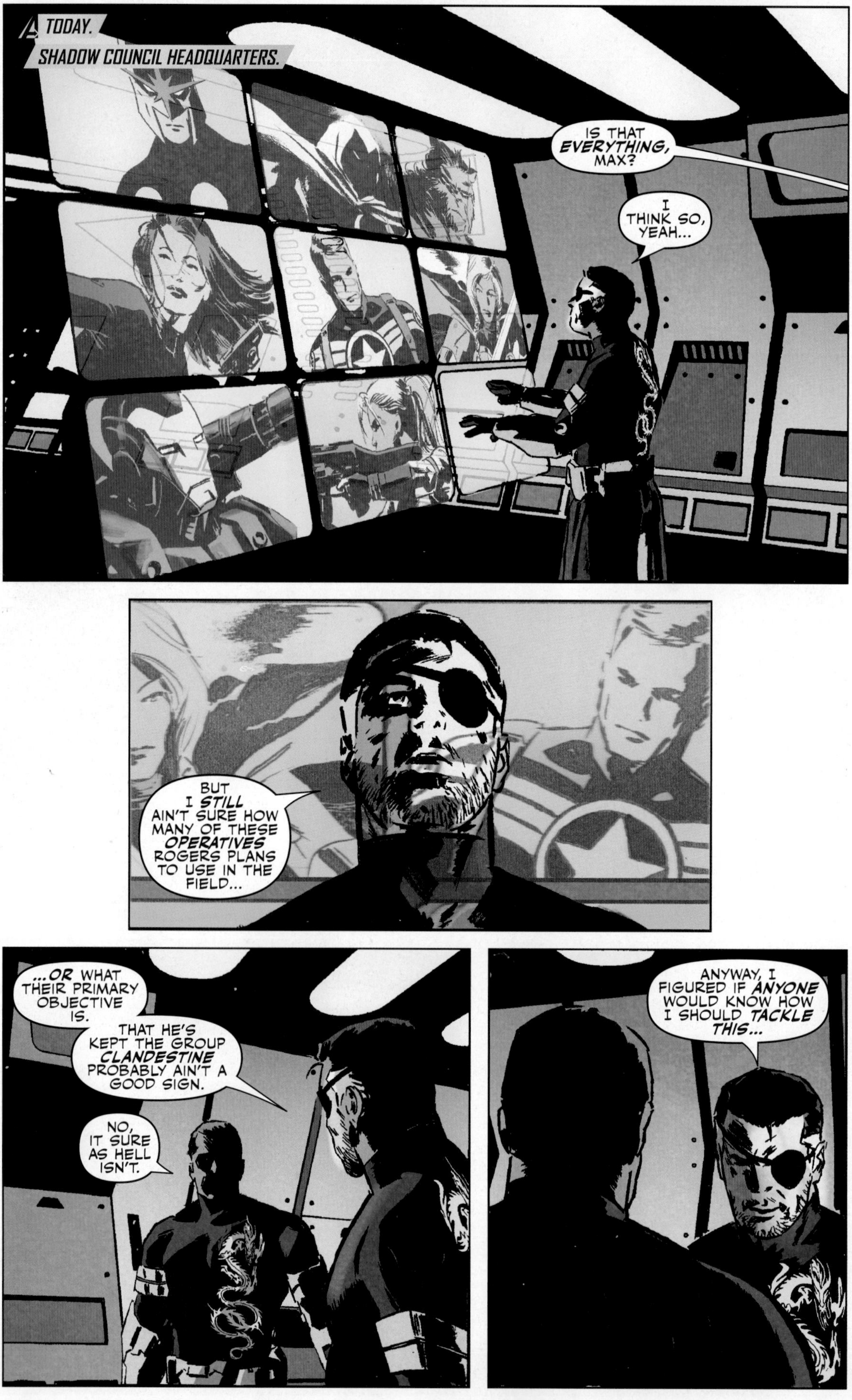
TODAY.
SHADOW COUNCIL HEADQUARTERS.
IS THAT EVERYTHING, MAX?
I THINK SO, YEAH...
BUT I STILL AIN'T SURE HOW MANY OF THESE OPERATIVES ROGERS PLANS TO USE IN THE FIELD...
...OR WHAT THEIR PRIMARY OBJECTIVE IS.
THAT HE'S KEPT THE GROUP CLANDESTINE PROBABLY AIN'T A GOOD SIGN.
NO, IT SURE AS HELL ISN'T.
ANYWAY, I FIGURED IF ANYONE WOULD KNOW HOW I SHOULD TACKLE THIS...

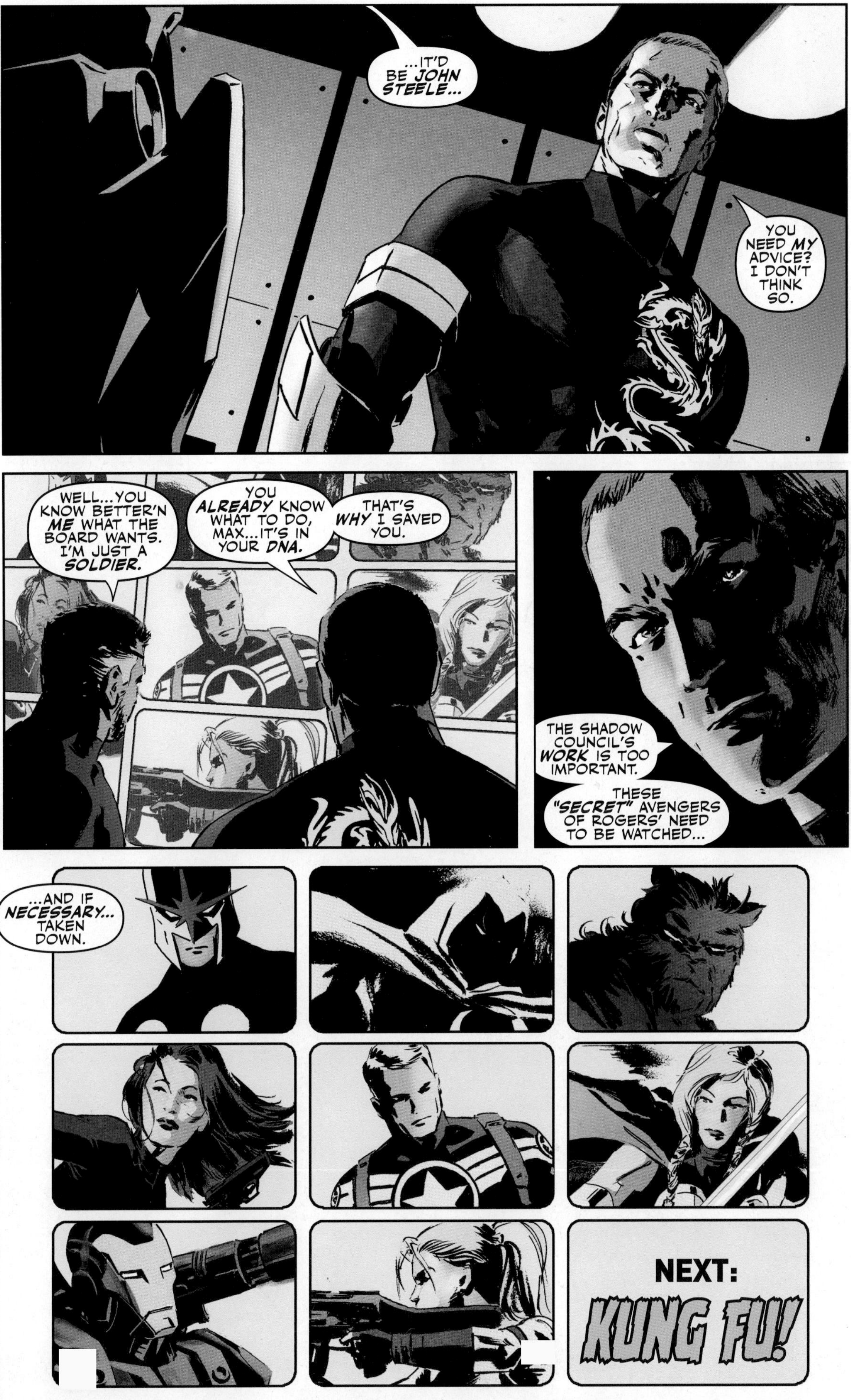
...IT'D BE JOHN STEELE...
YOU NEED MY ADVICE? I DON'T THINK SO.
WELL...YOU KNOW BETTER'N ME WHAT THE BOARD WANTS. I'M JUST A SOLDIER.
YOU ALREADY KNOW WHAT TO DO, MAX...IT'S IN YOUR DNA.
THAT'S WHY I SAVED YOU.
THE SHADOW COUNCIL'S WORK IS TOO IMPORTANT.
THESE "SECRET" AVENGERS OF ROGERS' NEED TO BE WATCHED...
...AND IF NECESSARY... TAKEN DOWN.
NEXT:
KUNG FU!

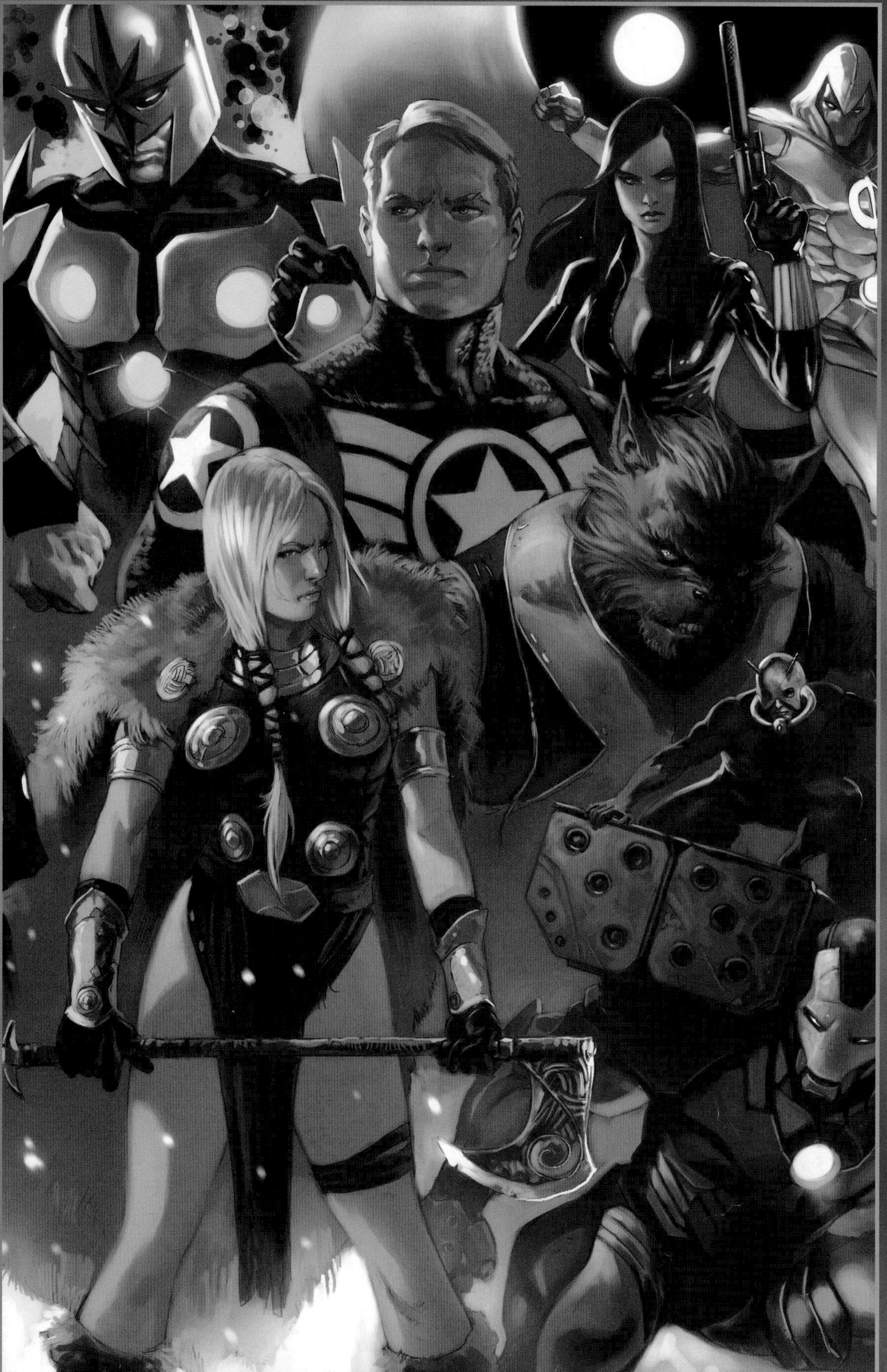

#1 VARIANT BY MARKO DJURDJEVIC

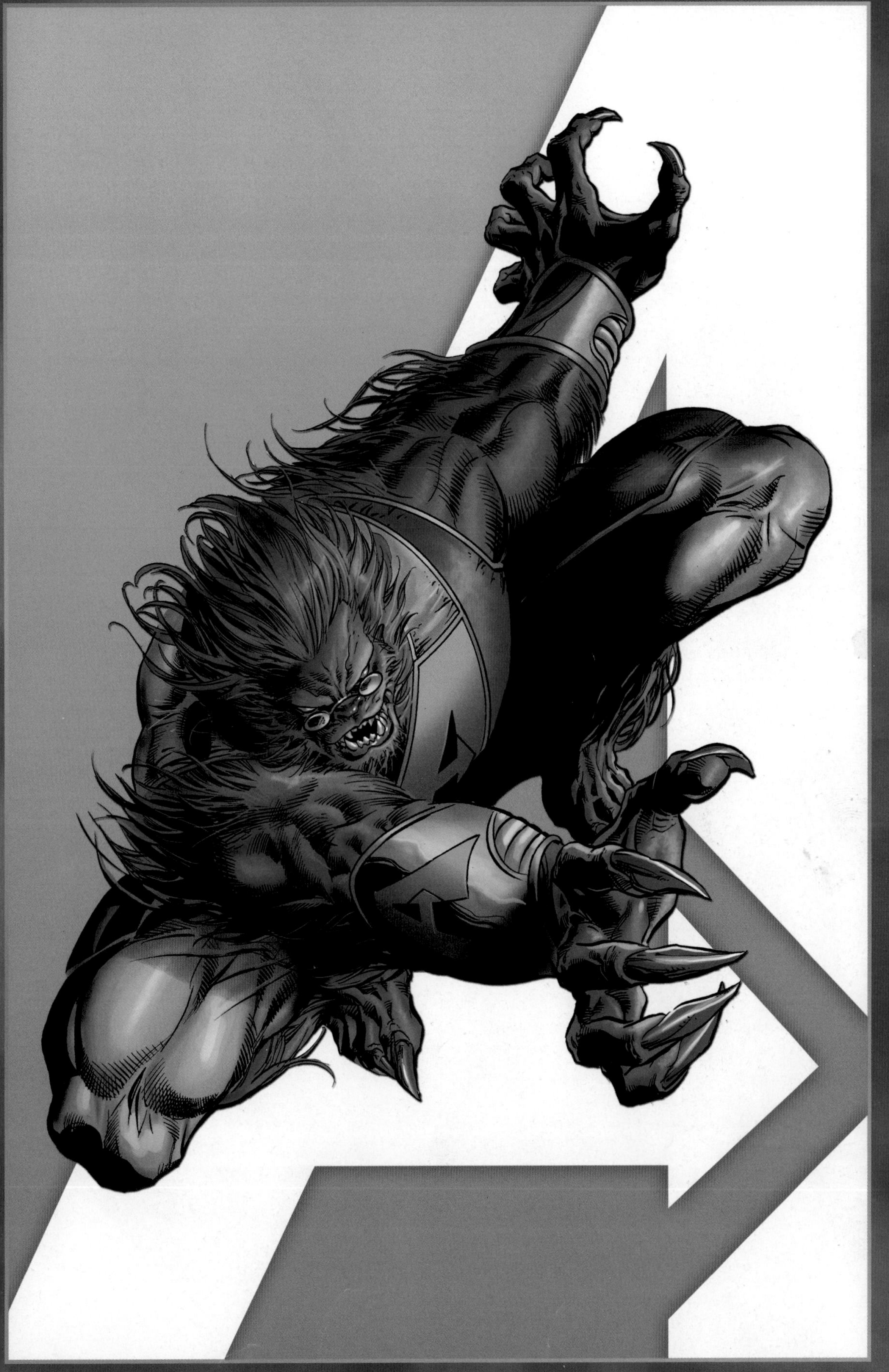

**#1 VARIANT BY MIKE DEODATO & RAIN BEREDO**

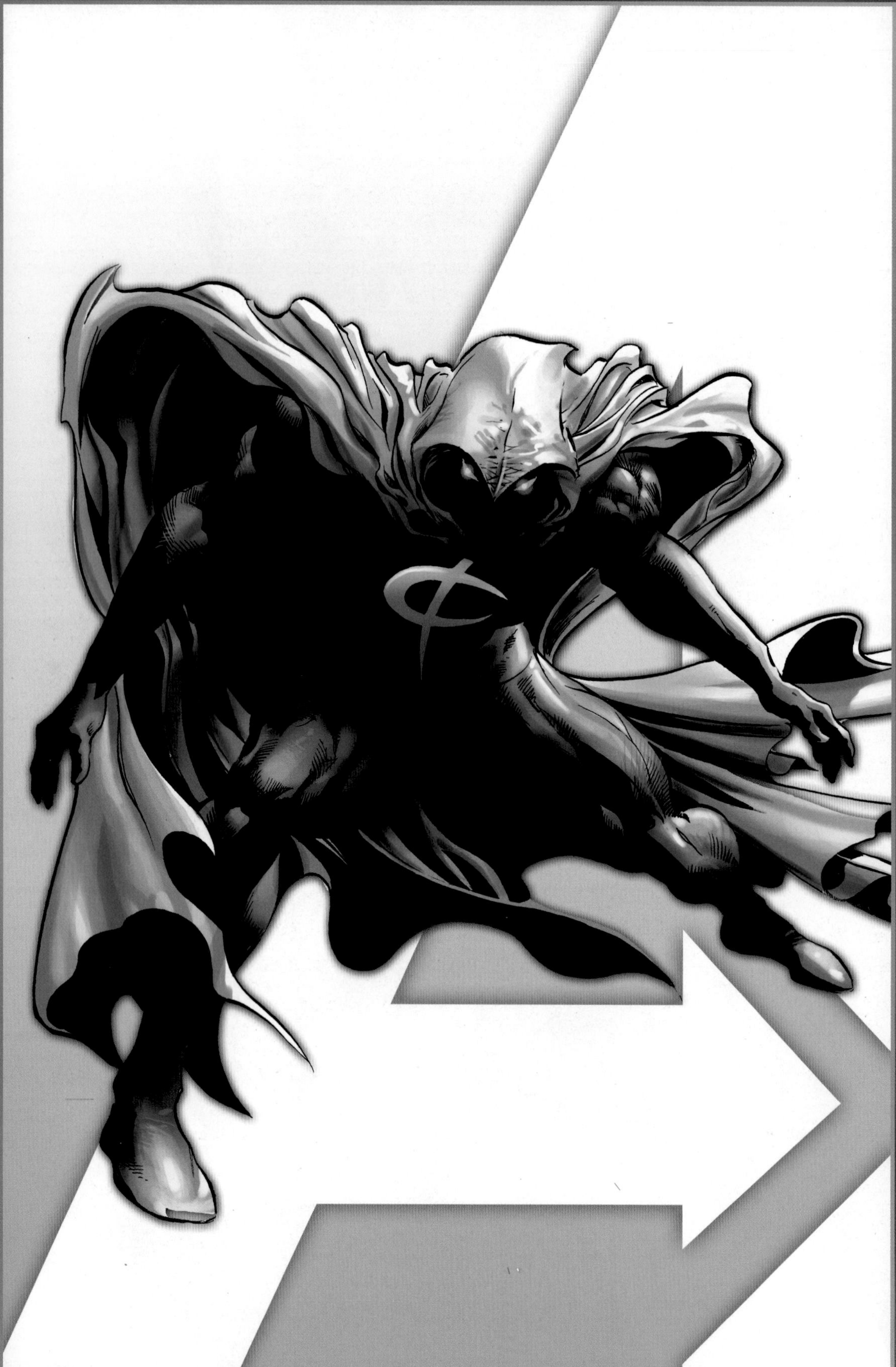

#2 VARIANT BY MIKE DEODATO & RAIN BEREDO

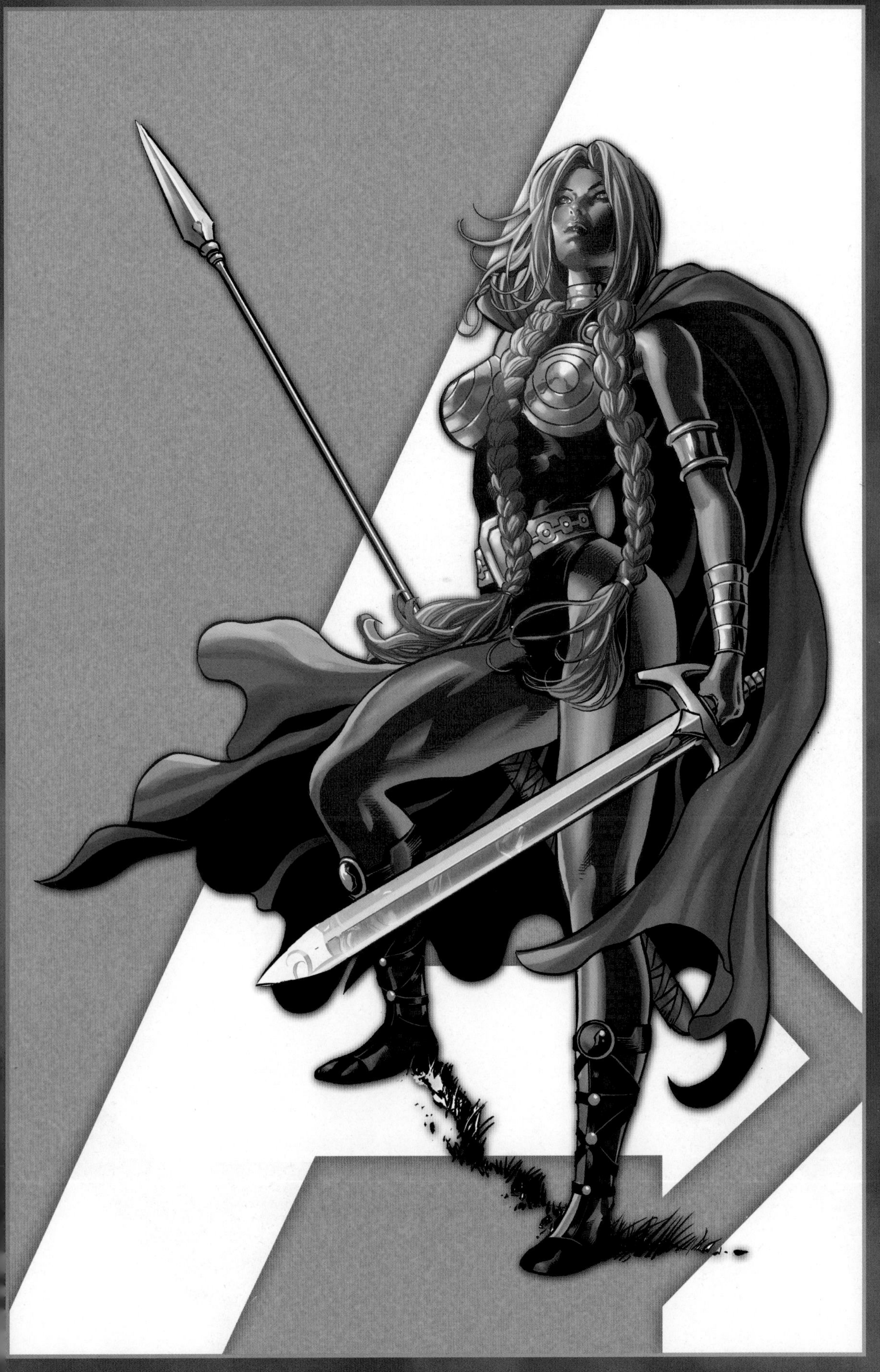

#3 VARIANT BY MIKE DEODATO & RAIN BEREDO

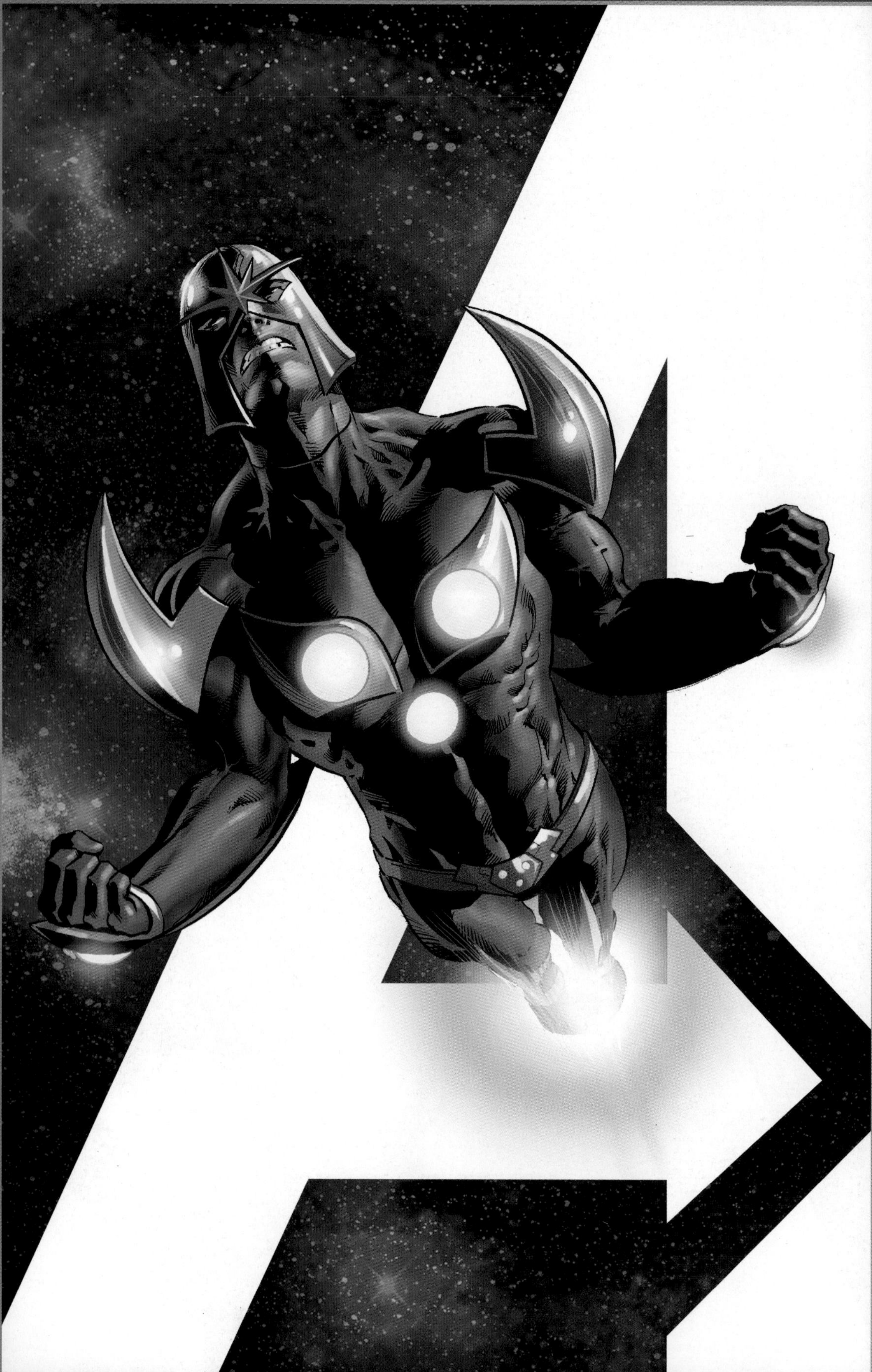

**#4 VARIANT BY MIKE DEODATO & RAIN BEREDO**

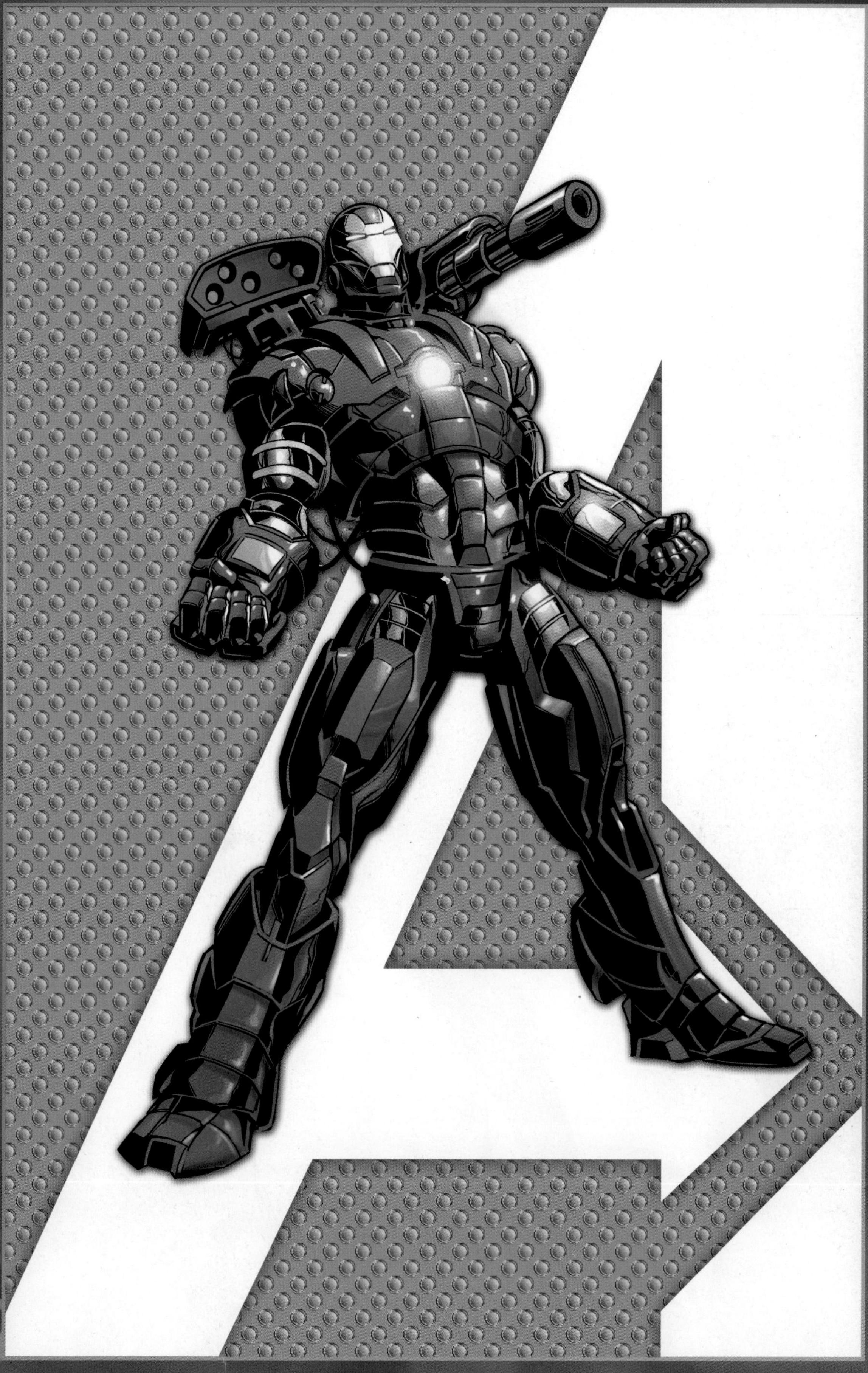

#5 VARIANT BY MIKE DEODATO & RAIN BEREDO

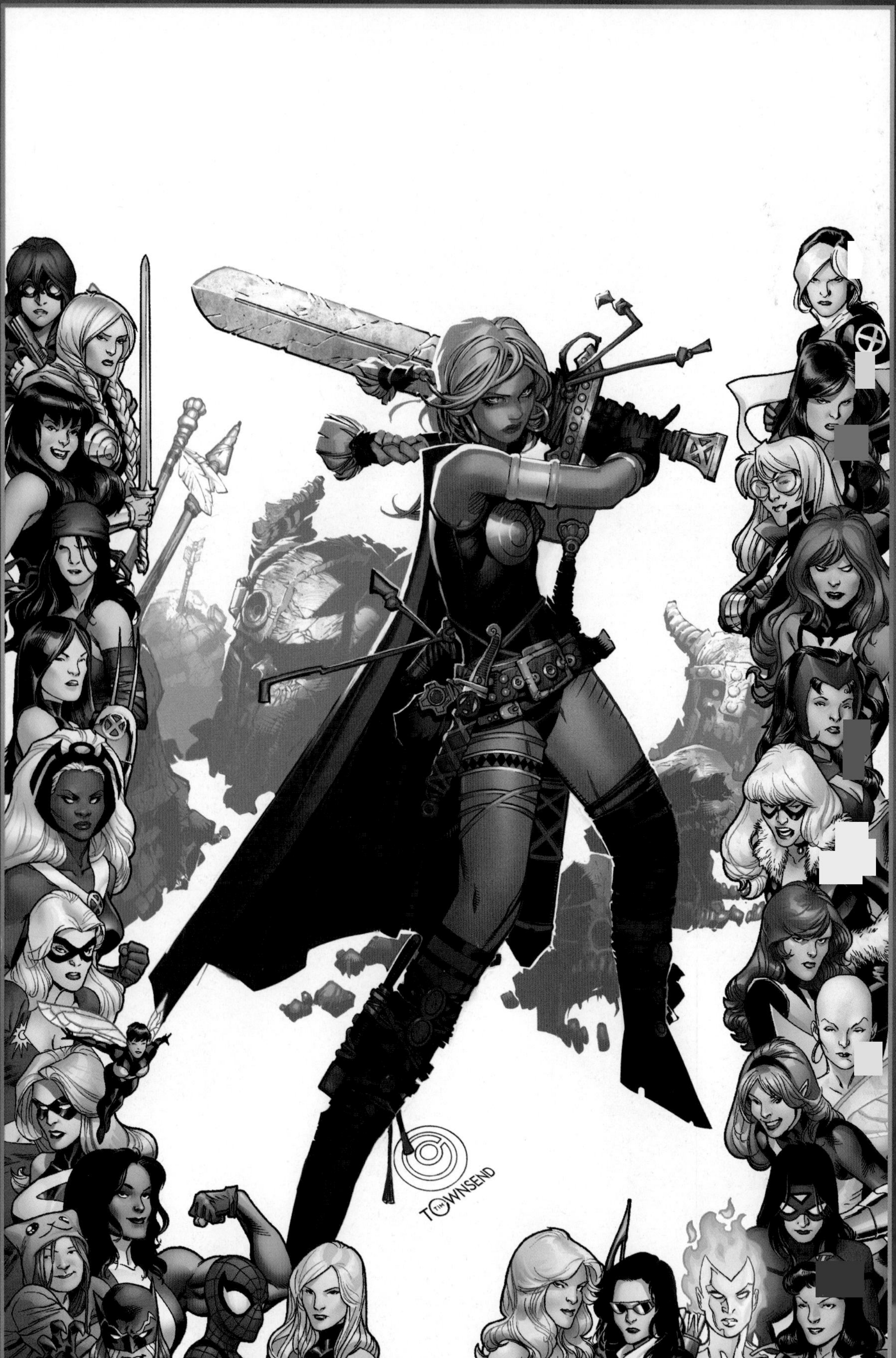
TIM TOWNSEND

#3 WOMEN OF MARVEL FRAME VARIANT
BY CHRIS BACHALO & TIM TOWNSEND